Postcolonial Hauntologies

Expanding Frontiers: Interdisciplinary Approaches
to Studies of Women, Gender, and Sexuality

SERIES EDITORS:
Karen J. Leong
Andrea Smith

Postcolonial Hauntologies

African Women's Discourses of the Female Body

Ayo A. Coly

University of Nebraska Press | Lincoln

© 2019 by the Board of Regents of the University of Nebraska

Parts of chapters 1, 2, and 3 were previously published in "Carmen Goes Postcolonial, Carmen Goes Queer: Thinking the Postcolonial as Queer," *Culture, Theory, and Critique* 56, no. 3 (2015); "Un/Clothing African Womanhood: Colonial Statements and Postcolonial Discourses of the African Female Body," *Journal of Contemporary African Studies* 33, no. 1 (2015): 12–26; and "A Pedagogy of the Black Female Body: Angèle Essamba's Black Female Nudes," *Third Text* 24, no. 6 (2010): 653–64.

All rights reserved. The University of Nebraska Press is part of a land-grant institution with campuses and programs on the past, present, and future homelands of the Pawnee, Ponca, Otoe-Missouria, Omaha, Dakota, Lakota, Kaw, Cheyenne, and Arapaho Peoples, as well as those of the relocated Ho-Chunk, Sac and Fox, and Iowa Peoples. ∞

First Nebraska paperback printing: 2024

Library of Congress Cataloging-in-Publication Data
Names: Coly, Ayo A., author. Title: Postcolonial hauntologies: African women's discourses of the female body / Ayo A. Coly. Description: Lincoln: University of Nebraska Press, 2019. | Series: Expanding frontiers: interdisciplinary approaches to studies of women, gender, and sexuality
Identifiers: LCCN 2018048743
ISBN 9781496211897 (hardback)
ISBN 9781496238887 (paperback)
ISBN 9781496214874 (epub)
ISBN 9781496214881 (mobi)
ISBN 9781496214898 (pdf)
Subjects: LCSH: Body image in women—Africa. | Postcolonialism—Africa. | Women—Africa. | Imagery (Psychology)—Africa. | BISAC: SOCIAL SCIENCE / Women's Studies. | LITERARY CRITICISM / African. | SOCIAL SCIENCE / Media Studies.
Classification: LCC HQ1220.A35 C65 2019 | DDC 305.4096—dc23 LC record available at https://lccn.loc.gov/2018048743

Set in Fournier MT Pro by Mikala R. Kolander.
Designed by L. Auten.

A James Christian Laurent Schmidt
        Tes retours et questions m'ont aidée à peaufiner mes idées

Contents

List of Illustrations ix
Acknowledgments xi

Introduction 1

1. The African Female Body: From Colonial Inscription to Postcolonial Conscription 9

2. Haunted Silences: African Feminist Criticism and the Specter of Sarah Baartman 49

3. Spectral Female Sexualities: The Politics of Sexual Pleasure in Women's Literatures 87

4. Subversive and Pedagogical Hauntologies: The Unclothed Female Body in Visual and Performance Arts 133

5. Laying Specters to Rest? On Bringing Sarah Baartman Home 183

Conclusion 207

Notes 213
References 215
Index 231

Illustrations

1. Charifou Fils, *Femme malgache civilisée*, c. 1900 26
2. Unknown photographer, *Zulu Maidens, the Difference*, c.1900 27
3. Amin with miniskirt-clad women, 1972. .41
4. Jeff Attaway, *African Renaissance Monument*, 2011 42
5. Zanele Muholi, *Beloved V*, 2005. 132
6. Grace Ndiritu, *Still Life: Lying Down Textiles*, 2007 143
7. Zanele Muholi, *Reclining Figure*, 2006. 145
8. Angèle Essamba, *Noirs*, 2001 145
9. Zanele Muholi, *Flesh I*, 2005 147
10. Angèle Essamba, *Noirs*, 2001 152
11. Grace Ndiritu, *Still Life: White Textiles*, 2005–7 161
12. Valerie Oka, *En sa présence*, 2015. 167
13. Julie Djikey, *Ozonisation*, 2013. 174
14. Wangechi Mutu, *The Ark Collection*, 2006. 179
15. Wangechi Mutu, *The Ark Collection*, 2006. 180
16. Breeze Yoko, *Ode to Sarah Baartman*, 2015 204

Acknowledgments

The ideas for this book took shape while teaching two of my favorite classes at Dartmouth College: Gender Identities and Politics in Africa and Masterpieces of Literatures from Africa. I would like to thank my students for their critical engagements with the main arguments presented in this book. My gratitude also goes to my colleagues Naaborko Sackeyfio-Lenoch and Sam Moodie for their unfailing support and friendship, Michelle Warren for her guidance and mentorship, and Kate Conley and Barbara Thompson for encouraging me to incorporate visual arts in my work.

I am particularly indebted to all the artists who have allowed me to reproduce their works in my book. Special thanks to Christraud Geary for offering generous access to her archives of colonial photography. Sincere thanks also go to my editors and anonymous readers at the University of Nebraska Press.

Postcolonial Hauntologies

Introduction

I begin with a solo performance. The dancer is Nelisiwe Xaba from South Africa. The locale is the Musée du Quai Branly in Paris. The title of the performance is *Sakhoẓi Says Non to the Venus*. Sakhozi refers to former French president Nicolas Sarkozy, a champion of anti-immigration laws mostly geared toward keeping African bodies out of France. Venus is Sarah Baartman, the South African woman who was exhibited as a freak show attraction in London and then Paris in the nineteenth century. Upon her death Baartman was dissected, and her remains were housed at the Musée de l'Homme, a museum of anthropology and ethnography in Paris. When the Musée du Quai Branly opened in 2006, the ethnographical collections of the Musée de l'Homme were moved to the new museum. The body of Sarah Baartman never made it to the Musée du Quai Branly because France had returned her remains to South Africa in 2002, following years of litigations between the two nations. In other words, the same nation that was so invested in purging itself of African bodies, to the point of paying African immigrants six thousand euros to return to their countries of origin, was holding on fiercely to another African body.

In June 2008 Nelisiwe Xaba, another South African female body, made it to the Musée du Quai Branly. The Musée had invited her as part of a performance series titled *Le corps en mouvement* (The body in movement), which featured body arts and practices from various non-Western cultures. For her performance Xaba dons a fishnet bodysuit and an apron. On the apron is printed the three-month visa Xaba was granted just to come perform at the Musée du Quai Branly. The apron relates to the "hottentot apron," the colonial terminology for the elongated labia minora of some Khoisan women. By symbolically stamping her French visa on the "hottentot apron," Xaba overlays her own story as a twenty-first-century African woman only allowed in Sarkozy's France because she is an exotic and sexualized black female body with Sarah Baartman's itinerary from South Africa to France. Baartman's presence in France was on account of her sexualized body. And like Baartman, Xaba's destination in France is the objectifying space of the museum.

What interests me in Nelisiwe Xaba's dance performance is her act of conjuring the specter of Sarah Baartman into the timescape of the living postcolonial present and into the bodies of contemporary African women. The spectral presence of Sarah Baartman acts out Jacques Derrida's notion of hauntology, which he describes in *Specters of Marx* (1994) as the condition of a present haunted by specters, resulting in a "non-contemporaneity with itself of the living present" (14). In Xaba's performance, hauntology signifies the afterlife, in the postcolonial present and on postcolonial African female bodies, of colonial discourses of the grotesque and hypersexual African female body. Hence African female bodies are haunted by the past but also the possibility of a return of the past in the future. Per Avery Gordon, whose work on spectrality alongside Derrida's organizes this book, "to be haunted is to be tied to social and historical effects" precisely because haunting is about "endings that are not over" (1997, 139). This is indeed the gist of Nelisiwe Xaba's dance performance at the Musée du Quai Branly. Likewise, *Postcolonial Hauntologies* tells of such hauntologies or nonclosures that texture the postcolonial present and African contemporaneities, in the form of the hold of the colonial past on postcolonial discourses of the African female body.

I start this book with Nelisiwe Xaba because her performance delivers a pointed interpretation of the notion of "The Body in Movement," the theme for the performance series commissioned by the Musée du Quai Branly. More specifically, Xaba's chosen response to the thematic prompt evinces my claim in this book that colonial discourses compulsively ghost postcolonial African discursive engagements with the female body. That a prompt about "the body in movement" is fodder for a metanarrative of the African body that harks back to colonialism speaks to my claim. To be sure, Xaba's performance is by no means a stretch from the theme inasmuch as her composition highlights the racialized and gendered structures that regulate the movements of African bodies. One could argue that in the context of racial politics of immigration in France, a performance piece like *Sakhozi Says Non to the Venus* was of necessity. Still, what piques my interest is that *Sakhozi Says Non to the Venus* rehearses an approach to the female body that recurs in the literatures, visual and performance texts, and critical feminist scholarship by African women. In this body of discourses the female body is often fodder for a conversation with colonial discourses of the grotesque and hypersexual African female body. Of particular note is the silence about the sexual female body in these works, including the very vibrant field of African feminist criticism (Arnfred 2004, Veit-Wild and Naguschewski 2005, Ampofo and Arnfred 2009, Tamale 2011). As I argue in chapter 2, the absence of the sexual female body in African women's discourses of the female body needs to be read in conjunction with the leitmotif of Sarah Baartman and the defensiveness around contemporary Western discussions of African female bodies in these same discourses. *Sakhozi Says Non to the Venus* thus outlines my concern in this book that many contemporary postcolonial African discourses surrounding the African female body bind themselves, again compulsively, into conversations with colonial discourses.

In *Postcolonial Hauntologies* I diagnose a postcolonial African angst about the female body. I then proceed to demonstrate how colonial discourses of the African female body haunt postcolonial African discourses and subsequently frame the tentative engagements of African women with the sexual female body. I argue that the colonial history of un/clothing black African women and inscribing grotesquerie and sexual aberration on the black African female body has inflected postcolonial African discourses surrounding womanhood. The following questions ensue: What narratives of the body are available to African women? How do African women lay claim to a body so heavily marked and under ideological siege? Can African women's discourses claim sexuoerotic agency for the female body? I address these questions by examining critical, literary, visual, and performance texts by women from different parts of Africa. These texts foreground the African female body and, taken together, illuminate a range of responses to what I identify as a postcolonial African hauntology around the female body.

The discursive trajectory of the African female body as a rhetorical element of colonial and then postcolonial discourses sets the theoretical backdrop for my analysis of the modalities of postcolonial African women's discourses of the body. In outline, my supporting argument for this book makes two propositions. First, colonial discourses of clothing worked in tandem with the sexual grammar of the colonial encounter and the colonial inscription of sexual deviance on the black female body to single out the African female body in ways that subsequently offered it for grab as a rhetorical element of colonial discourses about Africa. Second, the colonial rhetorical deployment of the African female body to signify Africa led to an African angst over the female body, sealing the fate of the African female body as a rhetorical element of postcolonial African discourses and haunting current African engagements with the female body. This rhetorical African female body, coproduced by colonial and postcolonial discourses, subsequently informs a postcolonial disciplinary apparatus and socio-ideological compass that regulate the conditions and modalities of producing discourse about the African female body, including what can (not) be said about the African female body and who can (not) speak about the African female body. I accordingly formulate the military metaphor of discursive conscription to conceptualize how the African female body is held discursively hostage by this colonially induced postcolonial African angst over the female body.

This is what haunting is about, writes Avery Gordon, "a story about what happens when we admit the ghost—that special instance of the merging of the visible and the invisible, the dead and the living, the past and the present—into the making of worldly relations and into the making of our accounts of the world" (1997, 24). Hauntology accordingly pairs the colonial hypervisibility and postcolonial invisibility of the African female body to reveal the lingering colonial interlocutors of some postcolonial discourses and imaginaries. Hauntology pairs colonial noise and postcolonial silence, colonial voyeurism and postcolonial detachment, colonial pornotropism and postcolonial prudishness, colonial exposure and postcolonial concealment. But I hasten to say that hauntology needs not be the debilitating condition that these pairings outline. After all, in Nelisiwe Xaba's performance hauntology makes for an enabling point of view on the discourses that govern the movement of bodies. Hauntology endows with a critical vision that brings to legibility some disguised repetitions and workings of oppression. Inasmuch as hauntology ferments new visions, imaginaries, and possibilities, the works by African women examined in this book are also about the types of narratives and narrations of the African female body that a postcolonial hauntology both disables and enables.

Chapter 1, "The African Female Body: From Colonial Inscription to Postcolonial Conscription," lays out the theoretical framework of my study and explains the relevance of Derrida's notion of hauntology and Avery Gordon's theorization of spectrality to the study of postcolonial African discourses of the female body. The chapter establishes how the African female body came to be a key rhetorical element of colonial and then postcolonial discourses about Africa and a site of postcolonial African hauntology. The chapter proceeds to consider the postcolonial African culture of scholarly and artistic silence around the sexual female body alongside debates and legislations about female dress codes in postcolonial Africa, most notably the prompt attention that post-independent African nations paid to female dress in the 1960s and 1970s, the 2008 anti-nudity bill in Nigeria that mostly targeted women, and the 2008 controversy over the partially unclothed woman in the Monument de la Renaissance Africaine in Senegal. By reading together the austere codes for studying and representing the female body and the strict dress codes for women, the chapter further grounds the notions of a postcolonial hauntology and a postcolonial African conscription of the female body. The two notions frame my analysis of African women's discourses of the sexual female body in the subsequent chapters.

Chapter 2, "Haunted Silences: African Feminist Criticism and the Specter of Sarah Baartman," queries and reads the silences of African feminist criticism on the sexual female body in conjunction with the leitmotif of Sarah Baartman in this field. The African feminist symbolic resurrection of Sarah Baartman in critiques of Western discourses on female circumcision and the 2009 Caster Semenya episode manifest a postcolonial hauntology that, following Jacques Derrida's and Avery Gordon's affirming theorization of a critical hauntology, seeks guidance from specters in order to read the present. At the same time, African feminist thought is yet to engage in militant sexual politics or draw theoretical inspiration and epistemological insights from vernacular expressions of African female sexuoerotic agency. The chapter accordingly argues that the postcolonial hauntology at the core of African feminist criticism falls short of the type of transformative hauntology that Derrida and Gordon advocate. In the last part of the chapter I analyze *Karmen Geï* (2001), a controversial film by Senegalese director Joseph Gaï Ramaka, for its feminist teachings about the sociopolitical potential of female sexuoerotic agency in postcolonial African contexts. *Karmen Geï* draws from indigenous African expressions of the sexual female body to model some future directions of a fully emancipated and emancipatory African feminist criticism.

Chapter 3, "Spectral Female Sexualities: The Politics of Sexual Pleasure in Women's Literatures," brings together literary texts that foreground the sexual female body. The texts are by women from different parts of the continent and different waves of African women's writing. My analysis of this corpus reveals an intergenerational narrative gesture of spectralizing the sexual female body as well as incisive but often elusive politics of sexual pleasure, including in texts where the sexual female body is at its boldest. The chapter starts by mapping the timid expressions of the sexual female body and sexual pleasure in the texts of Buchi Emecheta and Ama Ata Aidoo. I subsequently pinpoint more assertive expressions of the sexual female body and revolutionary politics of sexual pleasure in novels by Ken Bugul, Calixthe Beyala, Yvonne Vera, Léonora Miano, Chimamanda Adichie, Lola Shoneyan, and Sefi Atta. The chapter concludes with more revolutionary and nonnormative expressions of the sexual female body by novelists Calixthe Beyala and Frieda Ekotto and photographer Zanele Muholi.

Chapter 4, "Subversive and Pedagogical Hauntologies: The Unclothed Female Body in Visual and Performance Arts," brings together female African visual and performance artists who are pushing the envelope with regard to the representation of the African female body. Nathalie Mba Bikoro (Gabon), Julie Djikey (DRC), Angèle Etoundi Essamba (Cameroon), Wangechi Mutu (Kenya), Zanele Muholi (South Africa), Grace Ndiritu (Kenya), Valérie Oka (Côte d'Ivoire), Tracey Rose (South Africa), and Bernie Searle (South Africa) are female African artists who work against the grain of the postcolonial African representational economy of the female body and dare represent denuded African female bodies. Following Gordon's argument that to be haunted means to develop a critical awareness of a "something-to-be-done" (1997, 6) and Derrida's advocacy of a critical openness toward specters, I analyze how the selected artists appropriate hauntology as an enabling and emancipatory epistemology of the African female body. The artists develop subversive and pedagogical hauntologies of the African female body that strive to make space for the nude African female body as an artistic and aesthetic endeavor.

Chapter 5, "Laying Specters to Rest? On Bringing Sarah Baartman Home," takes its cue from the 2002 return of Sarah Baartman to the custody of South Africa and, by extension, to all communities that claim filiation to Baartman. The chapter brings together literary, visual, and performance texts that converse and disagree around the work of mourning Baartman and laying her specter to rest. The difference between Derrida's notion of mourning as work (2001) and the traditional Freudian understanding of mourning grounds my analysis, as I ask: What is at stake in mourning Sarah Baartman one way or the other? What is at stake in continuing to extend hospitality to the specter of Baartman, especially when she has been laid to rest at home? How does the homecoming of Sarah Baartman converse with the hauntologies examined throughout this book? What type of labor is the reclaimed body of Baartman doing, and on whose behalf? The chapter examines the works of South African poet Diana Ferrus, South African novelist Zoe Wicomb, South African performance artists Nelisiwe Xaba and Tracy Rose, South African visual artists Breeze Yoko and Senzeni Marasela, Gabonese novelist Sandrine Bessora, and Guadeloupean performance artist Chantal Loial. In light of her embrace by African and Afro-diasporic discourses to index the colonial violations of African female bodies, it seems appropriate to devote the last chapter of this book to the homecoming of Sarah Baartman.

1

The African Female Body

FROM COLONIAL INSCRIPTION TO
POSTCOLONIAL CONSCRIPTION

In 2009 controversy erupted in the West African nation of Senegal over an official state monument. The so-called Monument de la Renaissance Africaine (fig. 4) depicts a couple and their male baby in various stages of undress. The public outrage converged on the partially unclothed female body while the significantly more exposed male body remained a non-issue. The high visibility of the Renaissance woman versus the invisibility of her male counterpart evinces the sexual politics behind the visibility and visuality of the body in postcolonial Africa. Some relatively recent examples on the continent substantiate the heightened and vulnerable visibility of African female bodies. In 2008 the government of Uganda called for a miniskirt ban. The ban followed a dress code for women at the University of Makerere, the country's main university. The same year, the Nigerian Senate considered a nudity bill against improperly dressed women. These types of postcolonial African preoccupations with the female body lend themselves most immediately to a feminist reading. They indeed convene the predictable and sometimes pathologizing interpretive grid of African tensions between tradition and modernity, globalization and postcolonial African patriarchal anxieties, or again African societal uneasiness with the growing socioeconomic autonomy of women. The routine public floggings of insufficiently covered women, nowadays a characteristic of the socio-visual iconography and daily theatricality of many postcolonial African cities, certainly support this feminist line of analysis. So do the marches and online protest campaigns by young African women in 2013–15 against this dress-policing culture. Hashtag campaigns such as #SavetheMiniSkirt, #StripMeNot, #MyDressMyChoice in 2014 and protest banners such as "My body, my money, my closet, my rules" during a February 2014 demonstration in Kampala all point fingers at a threatened and insecure patriarchy.[1]

Having said this, this chapter argues for an alternative if not counterintuitive interpretation that strays away from gender as an analytical entry point to these postcolonial African preoccupations with the female body. I have found it more insightful to consider these investments in having African women properly clothed alongside the following concurrences: the absence of the sexual female body in postcolonial Africanist scholarship, including in African gender studies and feminist thought; the scarce and elusive occurrences of the sexual female body in postcolonial African arts and literary texts; the postcolonial African touchiness about Western discussions of African female bodies, from the sore topic of female circumcision to representations of the African female body by non-African artists and the 2009 gender testing of South African runner Caster Semenya by the International Olympic Committee. How do we think together the strict dress codes for women and the austere codes for representing the female body? How do we conceptualize the two parallel sets of codes as interrelated gestures of clothing African womanhood and enactments of a postcolonial discursive conscription of the African female body? What theoretical insights can we gain from such an analytical juxtaposition?

In this chapter I articulate a nongender-centric interpretive framework that teases out the latent colonial interlocutors of postcolonial African discourses of the female body, attends to the way the African female body encodes the coloniality of discursive categories and conventions, and explains how colonial discourses of the African female body came to haunt postcolonial African discourses. In making a case for the discursive trajectory of the African female body from colonial inscription to postcolonial conscription, I am mostly interested in teasing out the African female body as a colonially inherited narrative convention and a rhetorical element in discourses about Africa. Inarguably the scholarship of Ifi Amadiume

(1987), Oyeronke Oyewumi (1997, 2015), and Maria Lugones (2007, 2010) on the "coloniality of gender" (Lugones 2010) offers an important frame of analysis for colonial and postcolonial discourses of the African female body. But in thinking about postcolonial African discourses of the female body in terms of the coloniality of discursive conventions, I have a specific endeavor to attend to the semiotic character of the figure of woman in these discourses. My approach also identifies the African female body as an archive for the study of colonial and postcolonial discourses. This chapter accordingly maps the production of the African female body as a privileged rhetorical element of both colonial and postcolonial discourses about Africa. The chapter draws theoretical underpinnings for my core argument that the colonial statement of the grotesque and hypersexual African female body haunts postcolonial African discourses.

Specters of Colonialism: The Coming into Being of Hauntologies
In theorizing the female body as passage and not destination, instrument and not target, I am repurposing two seminal readings of the figure of the native woman in the discourses of colonialism and anticolonial nationalism. Frantz Fanon's "Algeria Unveiled" (1965) and Lata Mani's "Contentious Traditions: The Debate on Sati in Colonial India" (1987) are useful in different and related ways. A conjoined reading of the two texts helps illustrate the peripherality of gender in some postcolonial discourses of the female body. Mani's demonstration that tradition, and not women, was at stake in the debates on sati (widow immolation) in colonial India exemplifies the type of nongender-centric approach to discourses of the female body that I am pursuing. Mani goes looking for women in the debates on sati and does not find them. Instead, she finds that colonial and anticolonial narratives seize the native woman as a billboard for statements about cultural values, modernity, tradition, and progress. It is this absent presence of women, their invisible visibility, in discourses that invoke women that this chapter seeks to elucidate.

Next consider Frantz Fanon's reading of the function of the Algerian female body in the battle over the veil in colonial Algeria. Feminist critiques of Fanon have questioned his fetishistic approach to the Algerian female body and his metonymic association of the Algerian woman with the veil and Algeria. Tracy Denean Sharpley-Whiting (1997) has taken these feminist critiques to task for engaging in wholesale dismissals of Fanon. Her point that feminist criticism can gain insights from new engagements with Fanon guides my own recuperation of Fanon. Recuperating the Fanon of "Algeria Unveiled" for the purpose of my argument about the conscription of the African female body by postcolonial African discourses, I am struck by the persistent failure of feminist critiques of "Algeria Unveiled" to note that at the onset of his essay Fanon goes to great length to indicate that the essay concerns itself with the way colonialism determines the form and content of anticolonial resistance. Fanon writes that "on the level of the individuals the colonial strategy of destructuring Algerian society very quickly came to assign a prominent place to the Algerian woman. The colonialist's relentlessness, his methods of struggle were bound to give rise to reactionary forms of behavior on the part of the colonized.... We here recognize one of the laws of the psychology of colonization. In an initial phase, it is the actions, the plans of the occupier that determine the centers of resistance around which a people's will to survive becomes organized" (1965, 46–47). In other words, colonialism sets the terms of the debate by cornering anticolonial nationalists into the reactionary position of respondents to colonial discourses. Fanon's much-critiqued notion of an "unveiled Algeria" magnifies the coloniality of the Algerian woman, including the metonymic association of the Algerian woman with Algeria.

The first segment of "Algeria Unveiled," often overlooked by critiques, serves my theorization of the un/clothed black African female body. The segment describes the coming into being of the un/veiled Algerian woman as a discursive gesture, traced by colonial discourses and inevitably confirmed by the discourses of anticolonial nationalism. Fanon teaches how colonialism interpellates resistance into its frameworks and compels anticolonial nationalist discourses to sustain the narrative grammar of colonialism. Fanon resonates in Edward Said's observation that the discourses of anticolonial nationalism end up borrowing the binary logic and categories of thought of colonial discourses because the former are "fatally limited" by their antagonist position vis-à-vis colonial discourses (Said 1988, 14). Mani's conclusion that women were not subjects, nor were they objects, in the debates on sati retrospectively lends analytical support to Fanon by spelling out the understated thesis in Fanon that the debate about the veiled Algerian woman was not about Algerian women. Concurrently Fanon helps elucidate that the absent presence of the native woman in colonial and anticolonial discourses obeys the discursive conventions introduced by colonialism and sustained by the discourses of anticolonial nationalism. While Fanon's argument pertained specifically to the moment of anticolonial nationalism, Fanon nonetheless helps us understand how the colonial continues to live on in the timescape of the postcolonial. Indeed, my proposition in this book that the African female body in postcolonial African discourses is a rhetorical category inherited from colonial discourses extends the insights of Fanon into the postcolonial.

Reading Fanon by way of Jacques Derrida's proposition in *Specters of Marx* (1994) that the specter or the past is an obligatory inheritance, the colonial rhetorical category is a colonial inheritance that postcolonial discourses could arguably not refuse. According to Derrida, even the most reactionary of discourses are no more than "interpretations of the structure of inheritance" (1994, 68), and "a radicalization is always indebted to the very thing it radicalizes" (116). This obligatory inheritance allows the colonial to spectralize itself in the postcolonial and then live on as haunting presence in the postcolonial. In that regard the postcolonial is what Derrida calls a "hauntology," meaning a timescape where the living present plays host to a nonliving present. In my reading of the fraught postcolonial African engagements with the female body, the African female body is at once a colonial hauntology, by virtue of being saturated by colonial discourses to the point of blurring into ghostliness, and a vector and anchor of postcolonial hauntology, by virtue of being a site where colonial specters traverse into and impinge on the living postcolonial present.

In *Specters of Marx* the ghost of Hamlet's father and the enduring legacies of Karl Marx despite the fall of the Iron Curtain in 1989 are fodder for the notion of "hauntology," which describes the spectral presence of the past and future in the present and the ensuing "non-contemporaneity with itself of the living present" (Derrida 1994, xviii). The specter is both the past that haunts the present and the probable future to come that also haunts the present. Derrida pursues here his logic of deconstruction. He reprises his notion of the trace, the residual debris of absent signifiers, that always sabotages movements of negation and forces deconstruction to sustain the very structure that it is unraveling. In *Specters of Marx* Derrida refigures the trace as a specter that systemically inscribes past and absent enunciations into new utterances. Derrida enjoins us not to exorcise specters but rather to pursue hauntology, which consists in extending hospitality to specters and learning to live with specters in order to learn from them.

Fanon's model of hauntology importantly amends Derrida's in that both the oppositional relationship between the colonial and the anticolonial and the prospective situation of rupture from the colonial that the postcolonial strives to be invest a different meaning, resonance, and function to colonial specters. From a Fanonian perspective, hauntology spells the condemnation of the antagonist postcolonial subject to always return to the colonial scene, to always speak from and to the colonial scene, and to define herself or himself against, through, and thus from the colonial scene. Likewise, Valentin Mudimbe (1988) and Achille Mbembe (2001) have noted postcolonial African discourses' inevitable acknowledgment of colonial discourses about Africa. Mudimbe explains that the elsewhereness of Africa's gnosis always-already ghosts postcolonial African discursive acts. And in Mbembe's oft-cited words, "There in all its closed glory, is the prior discourse against which any comment by an African about Africa is deployed. There is the language that every comment by an African about Africa must endlessly eradicate, validate, or ignore, often to his/her cost, the ordeal whose erratic fulfillment many Africans have spent their lives trying to prevent" (2001, 5). Hauntology, as a chronic inability to break away from the colonial scene or think oneself outside of the colonial, becomes here a mechanism that repeatedly chains postcolonial subjectivities back to the colonial scene. The rhetorical category of the female body in postcolonial African discourses is a colonial scene, hence my earlier argument that the African female body in postcolonial African discourses is at once a colonial hauntology and a vector and anchor of postcolonial hauntology.

Hauntology is a tragedy. To be haunted by colonial specters means to be forced to relive the violence of colonialism. Hauntology prolongs the trauma of colonialism. In a postcolonial context hauntology is also a manifestation of the lingering violence of colonialism, the subjection of formerly colonized communities to new forms of colonialism and the apprehensive alertness of these communities to future forms of colonialism. Avery Gordon explains that to be haunted in this manner means to exist in "an animated state in which a repressed or unresolved social violence is making itself known, sometimes very directly, sometimes more obliquely" (1997, 16). Like Derrida, Gordon advocates a politics of living with and learning from specters. But hers is a socially activist hauntology that seeks to be attentive to the insidious operations of hegemony. Among these operations is the propensity of hegemony to haunt by distilling fear, mass produce socially invisible or spectral others, and camouflage itself so that it can work undetected.

In *Ghostly Matters* (1997), Gordon builds on Derrida's universalist and generalist definition of spectrality to provide a context-attentive theorization of hauntology that counterpoints Derrida's tentatively myopic theorization of hauntology. Derrida theorizes hauntology from the specters of figures of authority such as Marx and King Hamlet. He mentions, but only to gloss over, the ghosts of victims of systems of oppression and the spectrality of socially invisible figures. For her part Gordon focuses on transatlantic slavery and political state terrorism in Latin America. In so doing she is able to attend to haunting as an individual and community's lived experience of unacknowledged or supposedly past systems of oppression such as state terrorism, racial capitalism, and slavery. Haunting here, as in the postcolonial contexts I describe, constitutes a "sociopolitical-psychological state" that manifests a "repressed or unresolved social violence" and calls attention toward a "something-to-be-done" (Gordon 1997,

16). This "something-to-be-done" ranges from social activism to political action and "re-narrativization" (3). As a site of postcolonial hauntology the African female body becomes a site of this "something-to-be-done" and a site of re-narrativization. As a site the female body, and eventually the postcolonial woman, becomes a ghostly figure. One already finds this reading of the native woman as a ghostly presence in Lata Mani's reading of the absent presence of women in the battle over the sati in colonial India and in Fanon's analysis of the subsuming of the Algerian woman under the veil.

To return to the attempts to police women's dress detailed at the beginning of this chapter, I am not proposing that they do not speak of patriarchal and masculinist anxieties. I am however suggesting that gender-centric analyses, by falling into the feminist logic of the always-already policed female body in patria, are likely to miss the nongender stakes of these preoccupations with women's dress. Such approaches also overinflate postcolonial African patriarchal and masculinist anxieties. Yet patriarchal anxieties are hardly the core organizing principle of these preoccupations. Instead I argue that these preoccupations predate patriarchal anxieties. Patriarchal anxieties have caught up with and grafted themselves onto a preexisting postcolonial African preoccupation with the female body. The organizing principle of these preoccupations is what I describe as a postcolonial African angst over the female body, which threads through and together the policing of women's dress and the unspoken culture of scholarly and artistic silence about the sexual African female body. Both forms of engagement with the female body enact a gesture of clothing the female body in response to its unclothing by colonial discourses. Both forms of engagement with the female body sustain the rhetorical deployment of the African female body in colonial discourses about Africa. Finally, both forms of engagements with the female body are haunted by colonial discourses of the African female body. As a result, these postcolonial engagements produce the female body as a timescape in which the postcolonial present is bound in conversation with the colonial past, the past overwhelms the present, and, following Derrida, the living postcolonial present becomes noncontemporaneous with itself. Concurrently these postcolonial engagements that live in apprehension of the colonial statement of the grotesque and hypersexual African female body saturate the African female body with a postcolonial angst about the colonial. These engagements subsequently live in apprehension of the African female body. The African female body comes to represent a colonial hauntology by being made to play host to postcolonial anxieties about both the colonial statement of the African female body and the potential afterlife of the colonial statement in the living postcolonial present.

*The Unclothed African Female Body
as a Colonial Discursive Gesture*

In *Blank Darkness* (1985), Christopher Miller notes the unstable signification of Africa as monstrous and noble in a European colonial discourse "at odds with itself" (5). Homi Bhabha (1983) has contended that we should disregard the existence of mutually contradictory stereotypes in the colonial regime of representation. Instead Bhabha favors the more productive critical task of attending to the "process of subjectification achieved through the production of stereotypes" (1983, 18). Bhabha prefers to focus on the similar epistemic and ideological labor performed by the negative and positive stereotype, which then allows both stereotypes to belong to and work for the same regime of representation.[2] While I note with Miller the heterogeneous European representations of the African female body as ugly and beautiful or wild and demure, I am interested in how these disparate representations make the same discursive gesture and similarly subject the represented African female bodies to a rhetoric of differentiation and pathologization. Both sets of representations inscribe Africa in an economy of otherness via the African female body. In fact, Meghan Vaughan's *Curing their Ills: Colonial Power and African Illness* (1991) and Timothy Burke's *Lifebuoy Men, Lux Women: Commodification, Consumption, and Cleanliness in Modern Zimbabwe* (1996) have urged scholars of colonialism in Africa to consider the African body as an epistemological site for the study of the operations and discourses of colonialism. Both studies show the production of modern African bodies through colonial discourses of cleanliness and hygiene, in the case of Burke, and wellness and health, in the case of Vaughn. For my part, I focus on how colonial discourses of nakedness inscribed the African body, the female body in particular, by unclothing it and sexualizing its invented nakedness. But my gender-specific focus on the female body as the prime site of colonial operations and discourses services a different argument than Burke's and Vaughn's. My interest lies in the instrumentalization and instrumentality of the African female body through its metonymic signification as Africa in colonial discourses. This history makes the African female body a prime archive for the study of colonial discourses.

Studies of colonial discourses about Africa have generally not been forthcoming about the centrality of the African female body in these discourses, namely the ways in which the colonial encounter unfolded on the denuded and sexualized African female body. Valentin Y. Mudimbe's *The Invention of Africa* (1988) and *The Idea of Africa* (1994) are unquestionably the most comprehensive and authoritative studies of colonial discourses about Africa.[3] Yet the two volumes display hermeneutical blindness when it comes to the trope of the African female body in the studied colonial discourses, specifically the metonymic correspondence between Africa and the female body. This oversight is even more intriguing when one considers the strong presence of the female body in the vast corpus that the two volumes examine. For instance, in *The Idea of Africa* Mudimbe analyzes the construction of Africa in Martin de Vos's *Allegory of Africa* (sixteenth century) and Paul Gaugin's *Offerings of Gratitude* (c. 1891–93). In the two paintings, the African female body takes center stage in ways that warrant further analysis than Mudimbe does. De Vos's *Allegory of Africa* conspicuously represents Africa as a naked woman seated on a crocodile, an image whose consistent presence on seventeenth- and eighteenth-century Dutch maps of Africa Mudimbe declines to mine. A similar indifference to the female body recurs when Mudimbe attends to the production of the "savage other" in the texts of Herodotus, Siculus, Strabo, and Pliny but declines to comment on the way the female body signifies the otherness of the savage or the savagery of the other in the examined European classical texts. The oversized native female bodies of Gauguin and de Vos are visual equivalents of the narrative prominence of the native female body in the above-mentioned classical texts. In the corpus assembled by Mudimbe, the native female body assaults the male gaze because the presence of native women in spaces outside the home jars with the Greco-Roman politeia's construction of a feminine inside and masculine outside. Even as Mudimbe quickly notes that the rule of women in foreign lands is at odds with the Greco-Roman definition of civilization (1988, 90), he ultimately chooses to read in the examined texts a correlation between geographical remoteness and savagery. He downplays the equally if not more pronounced correlation between savagery and the place of the female body. By treating the images of women in these texts as mere subthemes in the Greco-Roman discourse of savagery, Mudimbe misses the interlocked discourses of gender difference and savagery. He precisely misses how the out-of-place hence deviant native female body structures the discourse of savagery. In other words, the enterprises of representing the foreign female body and the foreign place do not just happen to inhabit the same narrative space; they entertain a relationship of epistemological and discursive contingency.

I am basically faulting Mudimbe with giving very minimal analytical weight to the African female body in European texts about Africa. This fault manifests in his failure to first establish that the African female body was a trope, and then probe the ideological underpinnings of the trope. Following Anne McClintock, the troping of the African female body in colonial discourses stems from a European tradition of "porno-tropics" and "gendered erotics of knowledge" that feminized and eroticized foreign spaces but also displaced sexual aberration and excess onto foreign women, particularly African women (1995, 22–23). Yet I find the Freudian approach adopted by McClintock to be somewhat limiting as it occludes the structural function of the African female body in the construction of European imperial identities and agendas. The African female body was implicated by and in the structures of colonialism. Anne Laura Stoler, in *Race and the Education of Desire* (1995), has critically engaged and recuperated Foucault in a way that helps me illuminate the reciprocal overdetermination of the African female body and European colonialism. Stoler argues that Foucault's theorization of nineteenth-century European sexuality bypassed the colonial factor, and she proceeds to pinpoint the articulation between the sexual and imperial histories of Europe. A critical analysis of the trope of the African female body in European colonial texts benefits from Stoler's argument that colonial discourses of racial difference shadowed nineteenth-century European discourses of sexuality by working to clarify, fuse, and consolidate the categories of Europeanness and whiteness. The new categories then served to "map . . . the moral parameters of European nations" (Stoler 1995, 7). In their function as libidinal outlets, the pornotropics served the ultimate function of purging and defining the European body by creating a taxonomy of bodies and mapping a pathologized geography of difference. For the purposes of my argument about the instrumentalization of the African female body by colonial discourses, it is Stoler who ultimately facilitates the argument that the African female body was a foundational and structural element of the co-invention of Europe and its others. The pornotropics and the African female body served the function of exiling and safely confining the immorality of "perverse" sexuality outside the frontiers of Europe. The moral parameters of Europeanness that colonial discourses charted through the inscription of deviance on the African female body formed claims about moral superiority and authority. In turn, these claims became moral arguments for colonization. The deviant African female body in colonial discourses became a privileged space of enunciation of European moral superiority and leadership.

The African female body became an effective space of enunciation by virtue of being constituted by colonial discourses as a timescape where Europe could safely watch its potential past history, see how far it had progressed, and guard itself against the possibility of a regression to that potential past. In the European colonial psyche the African female body embodied at once what we could have been, what we will not have allowed ourselves to be, and what we could still be. The temporal tenses of the past conditional, the future perfect, and the future conditional that traverse the African female body show how the female body aided the colonial mapping of time and space onto each other. In addition, the juxtaposed projection of past and future temporalities onto the African female body and the displacement of the body from present temporalities participate in what McClintock describes as the colonial invention of the African female body as "anachronistic space" (1995, 42).

Following Michel Foucault on the rules of formation and circulation of statements, the anachronistic African female is the constitutive effect of a colonial statement. As described by Foucault, the statement is never "said once and for all . . . the statement, as it emerges in its materiality, appears with a status, enters various networks and various fields of use, is subjected to transferences or modifications, is integrated into operations and strategies in which its identity is maintained or effaced. Thus the statement circulates, is used, disappears, allows or prevents the realization of a desire, serves or resists various interests, participates in challenge and struggle, and becomes a theme of appropriation or rivalry" (1972, 105). In the European texts examined by Mudimbe (1988, 1994), "unclothed Africa" is a nascent colonial statement, as shown in the iconography of Africa as a naked and socially overbearing woman. The colonial statement, which uses the African female body to displace Africa to anachronistic space, imposes a discursive frame around Africa and sets up the conditions of possibility for ways of seeing, knowing, and doing Africa in both colonial and postcolonial times.

It's not the point of this book to provide a counterhistory to the colonial narrative of an unclothed Africa since the book concerns itself with hegemonic colonial discourses of the African female body. Scholars of dress and cloth in Africa have debunked the colonial narrative by documenting the existence of precolonial African traditions of handwoven cotton garments and elaborate dress, all of which the colonial statement of the unclothed African female body disregards.[4] The African female body constructed by colonial discourses is also the result of a discursive gesture of erasing the heterogeneity of African cultures when it comes to clothing and dress. After all, hegemonic discourses oversimplify, overgeneralize, and flatten in order to construct a target for their operations.

Gender and specifically the female body were structuring themes of colonial discourses, as McClintock (1995) has noted. But the African female body entered the colonial visual orbit in unique ways. First, the sociospatial location of African women beyond the home and in spheres of sociopolitical authority (Amadiume 1987; Oyewumi 1997) deviated from eighteenth- and nineteenth-century European norms of proper womanhood and civilized society. Oyeronke Oyewumi has argued in *The Invention of Women* (1997) that gender and the out-of-place African female body were prime targets of reform for European colonialism. The sociopolitical presence of women in the Yoruba society studied by Oyewumi rendered Yoruba female bodies excessive and hypervisible to the European colonial gaze. This excess explains why Joseph Conrad's *Heart of Darkness* (1899) foregrounds the African female body, Kurtz's wild mistress, at the expense of the shadowy African male figures. In the European encounter with Africans, the African female body catches and drives the European gaze. The African female body enters the European visual orbit in a way the African male body does not.

Second, some African female bodies became naked when subjected to European constructions and connotations of dress and nakedness (Beidelman 1968; Comaroff 1996; Allman 2004b; Bastian 2005; Masquelier 2005; Levine 2008). In her comparative analysis of the colonial iconography of foreign spaces, McClintock observes, "India, for one, was seldom imagined as a virgin land, while the iconography of the harem was not part of Southern African colonial erotics. North African, Middle Eastern and Asian women were, all too often, trammeled by the iconography of the veil, while African women were subjected to the civilizing mission of cotton and soap. In other words, Arab women were to be 'civilized' by being undressed (unveiled), while sub-Saharan women were to be civilized by being dressed (in clean, white, British cotton)" (1995, 31). A hierarchization of spaces and bodies, based on European norms of female occupation of space and body coverage, organizes this colonial system of signification. The colonial representation of Asia encodes the evidence of civilization that the colonial gaze read onto the covered and confined bodies of Asian women. The nakedness of Africa, despite the existence of cultures and traditions of full female body coverage in some precolonial African kingdoms, versus the sumptuous clothing of Asia in colonial iconography (Loomba 1998, 152) reflects how the socio-spatial location and perceived nakedness of African female bodies function as semantic correlates and grant coherence to the colonial iconography of the African woman. If the socio-spatial location of the African female body signified disorder and lack of civilization, its sexualized nakedness meant immorality and confirmed the first signification. The African female body made possible the correlation between morality and civilization. As a visual referent, the unclothed African female body of colonial discourses offered itself as semiotic evidence and confirmation of barbarous Africa. As a colonial statement, the constructed unclothed African female body became a conceptual metaphor for the ontologies of lack that colonialism attached to the continent. Lack cleared an anchor space for the civilizing mission and a magnet for European discourses of deviance, abnormality, perversion, and underdevelopment.

Ifi Amadiume offers an anecdote that speaks to the sociocultural constructions of dressed and naked bodies. Amadiume recounts asking to take a photograph of her female informant, the prominent priestess of the Land of Nnobi. The priestess postponed it to a later day, informing her that she was naked, although Amadiume could see that the priestess was fully dressed in a blouse and wrapper. On the appointed day, Amadiume recounts, the priestess "came out posing topless, radiating confidence, pride and dignity through her poise. I needed to quickly make sense of our differing understandings of the meaning of nakedness, plainness, and being dressed" (2008, 55). The priestess's body was decorated with scarification markings and various painting designs that reflected her status in society. She was clothed in conformity with the norms of Nnobi society.

Notions of dress are culture specific. In colonial times European notions of dress and sexualized readings of nakedness were an inadequate grid for reading some African bodies. The relocation of these African bodies from an African to a European semantic context resulted in a mistranslation and signification of African bodies as naked and lascivious. I read this mistranslation as a gesture of unclothing in that the process of contextual and semantic displacement of African bodies stripped the bodies naked and made them lacking in clothing. The extensive colonial photographical archive probably offers the most compelling documentation of the encounter between the culturally incompetent European gaze and the African female body. The commonplace acceptance of photography as "evidence" (Sontag 1977) and the resultant function of photography as an instrument of colonial discourses (Geary 2003) offer a prime site to study the engineering, circulation, and effects of colonial statements. The strong presence of the African female body in the colonial visual archive aligns with the metonymic construction of Africa and the African female body. Of importance is the pervasive representation of naked and bare-breasted African women in colonial photography and ethnography, leading Johannes Fabian to call the latter discipline a "provider of soft pornography" (2000, 236). Suffice it to cite George Basden's ethnographic studies of the Ibos of Northern Nigeria in the 1920s and 1930s and the work of French photographer François-Edmond Fortier (1862–1928). The subsequent circulation of these representations of African women in the form of postcards magnifies the colonial composition of unclothed and naked Africa as a statement that will live on as a colonial hauntology of the African female body. Picasso's appropriation of a 1906 Fortier postcard for his 1907 *Demoiselles d'Avignon* provides an instance of the circulation of statements as not descriptive, but prescriptive and inscriptive utterances. Picasso's conceptual translation of the topless African women in the 1906 postcard into prostitutes illustrates the colonial inscription of immorality, perverse sexuality, and deviant womanhood onto the African female body. *Demoiselles d'Avignon* translates ways of seeing and knowing the African female body in colonial times.

The circulation of unclothed Africa and the evolution of the statement into a hegemonic regime of truth about Africa speaks precisely to the

Foucauldian injunction to focus on the statement, not as a descriptive utterance but a discursive event; not for what is says but what it does (Foucault 1972). Of importance, then, is the life of the unclothed African female body as a rhetorical element of colonial discourses about Africa. The unclothed African female body aligns with the "unclean" African body (Burke 1996) and the "unwell" African body (Vaughan 1991) in constructing a body in need of intervention and legitimizing the colonization of African bodies. The seminal colonial gesture of unclothing, through the imposition of European notions of dress, made possible the subsequent colonial gesture of clothing. Both gestures seized the African female body to denote Africa's proximity with civilization, morality, and normalcy. The rhetorical dichotomization of unclothed Africa and clothed Europe, similar to the dichotomized juxtaposition of the fully clothed and demure Intended with the seminaked wild African mistress in Joseph Conrad's *Heart of Darkness* (1899) served the colonial civilizing mission whereby clothing the African female body became a justificatory metaphor for the colonial project of reforming Africans. Clothing quickly delineated different regimes of African bodies and created a hierarchy of African bodies: clothed-civilized-religious Africans versus unclothed-uncivilized-heathen Africans. Eric Savarese has similarly documented how colonial discourses evaluated the progress of colonization on the clothed African female body (2000, 43). Consider the caption *Femme malgache civilisée* (Civilized Malagasy woman) in the first colonial postcard (fig. 1) and the rhetorical juxtaposition of the fully clothed and the seminaked in the second one (fig. 2), with the inscription *Zulu Maidens, the Difference*.

How (Not) to Represent African Women:
The Postcolonial Afterlife of a Colonial Statement
The colonial statement of naked Africa finds an afterlife in postcolonial African discourses. Returning to Fanon (1965) on anticolonial resistance, the colonial statement of unclothed Africa, more precisely the colonial rhetorical deployment of the African female body, imposes the African female body as a narrative modality of postcolonial African discourses.

1. Charifou Fils, Madagascar, *Femme malgache civilisée*, c. 1900, collotype, postcard. Courtesy of Christraud Geary.

2. Unknown photographer, *Zulu Maidens, the Difference*, c.1900, silver gelatin print, postcard. Courtesy of Christraud Geary.

The colonial statement paved the trajectory of the African female body from colonial inscription to postcolonial conscription. I approach the gesture of postcolonial conscription as a manifestation of hauntology, meaning a postcolonial African present haunted by colonial specters. If Derrida writes that the specter is an obligatory inheritance that the receiver can nonetheless "sort out" (1994, 18) and "restructure" (67), the gesture of postcolonial conscription then participates in what Derrida insists is the "task" of inheritance (67) and Avery Gordon (1997) calls a "re-narrativization."

Postcolonial Africanist scholarship and arts have generally adopted a very conservative approach to the female body, which manifests in the desexualization of the female body. The shift in the treatment of the female body from classical to contemporary African arts is noteworthy in that respect. While the African classical tradition featured the denuded female body, the tendency in contemporary arts is to cover it up. Ikem Stanley Okoye has noted that the female sculptures of Nigerian female sculptor Sokari Douglas Camp, unlike her male sculptures, are typically disembodied (1988, 28–29). Nathalie Etoké also observes an avoidance of the female body in African literary studies (2006, 41–44). While Etoké suggests that the field has a conservative approach toward the female body, the fact is that African writers themselves have not written about the female body in a way that warrants critical attention. In other words, very few African authors have given literary scholars something to write about.[5] A special issue of the journal *Matatu* titled *Body, Sexuality, and Gender* has its guest editors address this void and underscore that "it is only recently that a new generation of African women writers have dared to touch on the 'unsafe issue' regarding the woman in her femaleness and her corporeality" (Veit-Wild and Naguschewski 2005, xii–xiii). The backlash against Calixthe Beyala, one of the "daring" African women writers, illustrates the charged politics of representation surrounding the African female body. Charges of pornographic and colonialist representation of African women for the benefit of Western readerships recur in studies of the novels of Beyala.[6]

This touchiness about the female body comes alive again in some African responses to Western attention to African female bodies. When the Olympic Committee raised questions about the sex of South African runner Caster Semenya in 2009, African critics, including the South African government, immediately invoked the degrading experience of Sarah Baartman. African feminist scholarship paradigmatically compares Western engagements with African female circumcision to the Western exhibition of Sarah Baartman. Such a symbolic resurrection of Baartman recurs in African and Afro-diasporic feminist discourses, including literary texts, visual arts, performance arts, and critical thought.

The treatment of the female body in postcolonial African scholarship, letters, and arts illuminates a postcolonial disciplinary apparatus and socio-ideological compass that regulate the conditions and modalities of producing discourse about the African female body, including what can (not) be said about the African female body and who can (not) speak about the African female body. This is what I call the postcolonial discursive conscription of the African female body. Consider, for instance, the trenchant critique by art historians Okwui Enwezor (1997) and Olu Oguibe (1997) of white South African female artists for what the two art historians deemed a pornographic appropriation of the African female body. Probably as noteworthy as their critique were the rebutting responses, mostly from white art critics and artists. The rebuttals showed a lack of historical perspective and sensitivity on the question of racial representation. Jeremy Cronin called Enwezor a "vigilant sentinel," a "gatekeeper," and a "global bouncer" who condemned white women artists for "daring to portray black women" (1999, 95–100). Most telling is how Carol Becker related the subsequent debate between the white female artists and the two art historians:

> Then a heated debate between Enwezor, Oguibe, and several women artists . . . ensued. I was somewhat shocked to hear these sophisticated, diasporic Nigerian men insisting that if white women were to use images of their sisters' naked bodies in their work without the consent of these black women, Enwezor and Oguibe would want to

"strangle" the white women artists, even if the intent of their work was to expose sexism, pornography, or colonial violence. The paternalism in such statements was astounding and the scorn for white feminists, painfully obvious. Accusations were flying and everyone was waiting for the black South African women present to take the lead; but when they did not, African-American women and diasporic women from other parts of Africa, now living in New York, spoke up in favor of the positions taken up by Enwezor and Oguibe. But no black South African woman ever spoke. (1998, 97)

I must address the assumptions and disingenuous misconstructions in Becker's statement. Foremost is her misconstruction of the silence of South African women as detachment, which paves the way for Becker's suggestion that the controversy is a false debate created by non-African Africans. On the solidarity of the black women in attendance with Oguibe and Enwezor and not their white sisters, Becker is impervious to the fact that the women rallied around Enwezor and Oguibe not out of racial solidarity but in defense of the black female body. But again Becker, like Cronin and the white female artists she is defending, is totally impervious to the charged history of the black female body. My point here is about the histories of degradation, humiliation, pain, and dehumanization that are embedded in and continue to enframe the black female body. In the face of African and Afro-diasporic defensiveness about the black female body, we need to account for what Beverly Guy-Sheftall (2002) calls the unique "body dramas" of women of African descent. The lack of sensitivity displayed by the white female artists and their defendants, more specifically their sense of artistic entitlement to the black female body, brings home Guy-Shetfall's point that "there is nothing sacred about Black women's bodies, in other words, they are not off-limits, untouchable, or unseeable" (2002, 18).

The accusations of "gatekeeping" leveled at Oguibe and Enwezor complement my formulation of the military metaphor of discursive conscription to frame postcolonial African discourses of the female body. The metaphor aims to conceptualize how a colonially induced postcolonial angst over the female body holds the African female body hostage. The notion of postcolonial conscription is not unlike Darby English's (2007) notion of "black representational space." English describes the politics of representation that police black artistic engagements with black bodies. The postcolonial conscription of the African female body dictates the discursive culture of silence about the sexual African female body. The postcolonial silences and defensiveness surrounding the African female body enact a gesture of covering/clothing the African female body, in response to its uncovering/unclothing by colonial discourses. This is where I see a merger with the preoccupation with female dress codes detailed at the beginning of the chapter and analyzed later in this chapter. The desexualization of the African female body in postcolonial African scholarship and in arts and literatures and the preoccupation with female dress codes are both gestures of clothing the African female body. The same postcolonial angst over the African female body threads together the two gestures. In applying the rather stern metaphor of military conscription to both gestures, I specifically endeavor to conceptualize the compulsive enrollment of the African female body into postcolonial African representational politics. I am interested in bringing to the surface the existence of a restrictive and prescriptive postcolonial African regime of representation for the African female body. This is a regime that regulates how to inhabit or be an African female body as well as the conditions and modalities of producing discourse about the African female body.

I frame the postcolonial politics of representation surrounding the African female body in the broader context of the postcolonial discursive and semiotic reappropriation of Africa from colonial discourses. Most attempts to explicate the politics of representation surrounding the African female body overlook the important link between the colonial gesture of unclothing and the postcolonial gesture of clothing. The colonial inscription of sexual deviance, lack of femininity, and grotesquerie on the African female body and the postcolonial African investment in the female body form a dialogical pair. Postcolonial African engagements with the female body do not necessarily speak to existing African gender dynamics but rather to colonial discourses. The loosening of postcolonial African discourses of the female body from the exclusive theoretical grip of gender opens up a new reading of female dress codes in postcolonial Africa. The new reading that I pursue below further bears witness to the postcolonial hauntology around the female body and the postcolonial conscription of the female body.

*Clothing African Women: Dress Codes
as a Postcolonial Discursive Gesture*

The attention that early African nation-states paid to female dress throughout the 1960s and 1970s illuminates the trajectory of the African female body from colonial inscription to postcolonial conscription. Of interest is Jean Allman's (2004b) insightful analysis of the construction of the un/clothed female body as a gauge of the nation's modernity in the 1958–66 anti-nudity campaigns in Ghana. Allman documents that Mrs. Amateifio, the secretary general of the Federation of Ghana Women, lectured that female nudity jeopardized the "high respect and reputation this country has achieved among the world" (2004b, 149). Meanwhile a government official ordered all women to clothe themselves because "many visitors come to this country and some of them take photographs of the nude women which they take away to their countries to show people to the discredit of Ghana" (154). The unclothed female body undermined the modernity that the new African nation was so bent on showcasing in order to secure a place on the international stage. As a prime site where colonialism constructed Africa's backwardness and need of foreign leadership, the female body inevitably became a prime site where African nations would anxiously contest colonial constructs of Africa and assert their modernity.

Fast-forward to 2008: an anti-nudity bill went before the Nigerian senate. The Nigerian bill is of interest because it represents to date one of the rare instances on the continent where female dress went through an extensive legislative process. Attempts to regulate female dress on the continent have mostly taken the forms of anti-nudity campaigns and government miniskirt bans. The Nigerian anti-nudity bill thus offers a case study for the conscription of the female body. The Nigerian "Bill for an Act to Prohibit and

Punish Public Nudity, Sexual Intimidation and other Related Offences," also known as the "Public Nudity Bill," was sponsored by Senator Eme Ufot Ekaette. The bill went through two senate readings (October 17, 2007, and February 6, 2008) and a well-attended public hearing (July 9, 2008). In July 2009 the Senate dropped the bill on the grounds that the bill was discriminatory toward women, attempted to legislate morality, and failed to consider the cultural diversity of Nigeria with regard to dress codes. Although the bill was withdrawn, it is noteworthy that it made it through two senate readings and received strong support from the senators. The dismissal of the bill occurred amid its severe critique by the United Nations and a staunch reprimand of Nigeria at the 2009 United Nations General Assembly. It is fair to speculate that the bill would have made it through were it not for the pressure of the General Assembly of the United Nations and the United Nations Committee for the Elimination of Discrimination Against Women. One of the Nigerian officials with whom I spoke, under the cover of anonymity, confided that the Senate had scheduled the bill for a third reading but then dropped it from the schedule without explanation. "The bill was killed," my informant said.

Gender matters are definitely at the crux of the bill, and the bill is clearly discriminatory toward women. For instance, during the second senate reading of the bill sixteen of the twenty-one senators in attendance spoke in favor of a dress code for women, with some senators blaming the high incidence of rape crimes in Nigeria on female dress (Nigeria Senate 2008a). Yet I am reluctant to privilege gender as the entry point and analytical lens for reading the bill. Gender does not constitute an exhaustive interpretive framework and does not allow us to ask the best questions of postcolonial African preoccupations with the female body. Recovering the African female body in postcolonial African discourses, not as gender effect but colonial effect, entails pursuing what Gaurav Desai calls "a reading for rhetoric rather than a reading for sense" (2001, 5). It means being attentive to both the obliqueness of gender, even when gender is positioned as the immediate referent, and the presence of the colonial factor, even when there is no reason to look for such a presence.

This consists in engaging in sideline reading, meaning a reading that strays from what the text foregrounds, to dig into its discursive underpinnings and tease out its "ghostly matters," to borrow from Avery Gordon, who advocates this mode of reading. This is also the mode of reading that allows Derrida to tease out the "spectrology" of Marx's texts, meaning the specters that haunted Marx (Derrida 1994, 132).

Consider how gender, although of relevance here, takes a back seat when one reads the Nigerian anti-nudity bill, not from its textual core, but from the preface that Senator Ekaette read to the Senate: "In my desperation to find a redress to this moral decadence, I was forced to examine the laws of various advanced democracies of the world and other highly religious nations. The laws of the United States of America, Great Britain, Canada, Saudi Arabia, Iran, Israel, Germany, India, China, and so on. They were all looked into. It was surprising to note that all these countries have laws prohibiting and punishing public nudity or lewdness. For example, there exist in the law of the various countries statutes which prohibit lewdness and public nudity viz." (Nigeria Senate 2008a, 2123).

Bibi Bakare-Yusuf has noted that Senator Ekaette is blind to the distinction between the different endeavors of secular democracies (Great Britain, United States, Germany) and theocratic nations (Saudi Arabia, Iran) in putting such legislations into place (2011, 120). Yet the amalgam observed by Bakare-Yusuf is hardly peculiar when one considers the interplay between modernity and religion in colonial encounters in Africa. Religion was one of the idioms of colonial modernity, hence the collapse of the secular and religious dimensions in the colonial project and in many postcolonial African projects. In colonial terms, and as reflected in the "three c's of Christianity, civilization, and clothing" (Rovine 2008, 191), the modern and civilized body is a religious (Christianized) body. The Nigerian anti-nudity bill derives from a colonial framework that has fused religion, civilization, and modernity to uphold the discourse of the dirty, naked, immoral, and heathen African body.

In their function as referential anchors for the Nigerian gesture of clothing, the semiotic categories of "advanced democracies" and "highly religious nations," which subsequently reappear in different guises in the proceedings of the bill's reading at the Nigerian Senate, disclose how the temporality of colonial modernity haunts postcolonial time. Simon Gikandi has argued that "postcolonial temporality, exists in an uneasy, dialectical relation with the politics of modern time and historicism" in that "postcolonialism is a condition that must be contained both within and beyond the causality of colonial modernity" (2001, 641). The semiotic politics ingrained in the Nigerian gesture suggest that we delve further into the postcolonial subversion of and compliance with modernity to investigate how postcolonial "contra-modernity" (Bhabha 2004) formally narrates itself and the extent to which that narration repudiates the semiotics of colonial modernity. If we go back to Fanon (1965), Mbembe (2001), and Mudimbe (1998), the discursive mechanisms set by colonialism and the subsequent tenacity of colonial statements often derail such semiotic autonomy. In positioning the Nigerian female body as a sign of the nation's contemporariness and qualification for representation by the categories of "highly religious nations" and "advanced democracies," the Nigerian anti-nudity bill reprises exactly the rhetorical semiotics of colonial discourses of modernity.

Even more troubling is the language of the bill. At the public hearing for the bill most speakers followed the language of the bill in using nudity and indecent dressing interchangeably. Some speakers nonetheless highlighted the ambiguous definition of nudity in the proposed bill by pointing to the difference between nudity and indecent dressing (Nigeria Senate 2008b). Senator Uche Chukwumerije was the first to point out that the bill lacked conceptual clarity about the notion of nakedness:

> I have one problem with this bill. I read through the whole bill and did not find anywhere where the word naked is defined. . . . By nakedness, are we referring to the stark madman or woman in the street, picking things in the dust bin? It did not say so. The nearest it came to defining it is on page 2, paragraph 2. By implication, it says: *Recently, we have received reports of arrests and harassment of females*

and males on account of indecent dressing by security agencies. I want to take the above implication to mean that if this is the sponsor's definition of nakedness, the least I can say is that many of us may not agree with this definition. If we remember the recent incidence of the arrest she is alluding to, then the arrest was not even made by security agencies. Most of the arrest[s] . . . are through mob action and . . . against ladies wearing jeans; they were not naked in the street. (Nigeria Senate 2008b, 2126)

The representative of Nigeria's Center for Democracy and Development lectured about the cultural significance of nakedness as a mechanism of protest for Nigerian women. She contended that "if you pass this bill, you will also be robbing women of their last resort when they do protest. I want to remind you of Aba Women Riot, the Bayelsa Women Riot" (Nigeria Senate 2008b, 55). Bibi Bakare-Yusuf has argued that the senator "conveniently misunderstands" that public nudity laws in so-called advanced democracies are concerned not with dress codes but with the lewd exhibition of genitalia (2011, 120–21). In fact, the synonymous use of nakedness and indecent dressing in the bill is a carryover from colonial discourses of clothing, namely the colonial imposition of Western constructions of dress and nakedness on African bodies (Beidelman 1968; Comaroff 1996; Allman 2004b; Bastian 2005; Masquelier 2005; Levine 2008). By defining inappropriately covered bodies as naked, the bill adopts the colonial lexicon of African bodies. Bakare-Yusuf highlights what she sees as contradictions. On the one hand, she writes, the senator upholds the moral conservatism of Nigerian culture against a Western-influenced culture of indecent dressing. On the other hand, by making an exception to nudity during Nigerian cultural events, the bill recognizes so-called indecent dressing to be an abiding feature of Nigerian culture. Hence for Bakare-Yusuf, the real culprit and target here are not Western-induced immorality but nonmodern Nigerian cultures and corporeal practices. Bakare-Yusuf argues, "If certain forms of nakedness or state of undress were an abiding feature of Nigerian festivals and tradition, why then would the bill propose a waiver in that area? The obvious underlying point here is that the senator is well aware that to this day and outside of the large cities partial nudity is commonplace in Nigeria, as is attire that exposes the body in ways that contravene the definitions of the proposed bill. What the text of the bill unwittingly reveals is a repressed indigeneity" (2011, 121). I would like to venture that the contradictions identified by Bakare-Yusuf stem not as much from a "repressed indigeneity" as from the bill's latent conversation with colonial modernity. The contradictions speak to the lingering colonial interlocutors of some postcolonial discourses. A close reading reveals the underground counternarrative of African bodies that the bill crafts in response to colonial modernity's narrative of African bodies. "Repressed indigeneity" is a collateral result of this discursive exercise.

The bill is very invested in overwriting and rewriting African nudity to reposition African bodies alongside Western bodies. The alignment of Abrahamic and so-called African religions early in the bill participates in that endeavor to assert coevalness between Africa and the West: "We are a people under the Almighty; we should therefore live under His laws, commandments, injunctions and statues [*sic*]. We are Christians, Muslims or traditionalists, all subject to the laws of the Almighty. All our religions forbid public lewdness, public nudity or public nakedness. All of us are on the side of the Almighty" (Nigeria Senate 2008a, 2122). The bill's subsequent exemption of nudity for "sports, festivals, theatre/stage acting and swimming exercises" feigns blindness to the widespread and commonplace seminudity noted by Bakare-Yusuf. The bill chooses instead to relocate African seminudity to "festivals," read ritual performances and ceremonies. The bill produces shared conventions and norms of body coverage between the West and Africa in order to assert the contemporariness of African bodies. The narrative of African bodies that the bill strives to impose evidences the hold of colonial modernity and colonial discourses of clothing on the Nigerian anti-nudity bill. The postcolonial bill thus operates in the semiosphere of colonial modernity and from the site of the colonial hauntology of the African female body.

However, to slightly complicate Bakare-Yusuf's point with Bhabha's (2004) notion of contra-modernity evoked earlier, the bill both acquiesces to and contests colonial modernity, mimicking as it were the discourses and frameworks of colonial modernity only to unravel them. By recurrently foregrounding the moral conservatism of Nigerian society and the corrosion of Nigerian cultures by Western influences, the bill crafts a counternarrative of African and Western bodies that reverses the colonial hierarchy of bodies. And this is where the bill ultimately turns the narrative of colonial modernity on its head and redefines nakedness, even as the bill is concurrently abiding to colonial discourses of modernity and nakedness by feigning ignorance of the banality of partial nudity outside of urban centers in Nigeria. The bill's non-acknowledgment of "other" Nigerian bodies, which I have earlier linked to the bill's endeavor to assert the contemporariness of African bodies, conversely acknowledges these other bodies as not naked since these bodies are not targeted by the bill. In the bill, nakedness does not stem from the lack of clothing or the wearing of traditional attire that leaves part of the body bare. Nakedness stems from the adoption of items of Western clothing deemed indecent, as in the proposed Ugandan bill where miniskirts and tight pants signify indecency.

This is where I link up the proposed bills in Nigeria and Uganda with the 1960s–1970s decency campaigns throughout post-independent Africa. These early campaigns against indecent clothing, while speaking to masculine and patriarchal anxieties about changing gender dynamics (Mazrui 1968; Wipper 1972; Hansen 2004; Ivaska 2004), partake nonetheless in the postcolonial angst over the female body. The campaigns also deployed the female body rhetorically, following inherited colonial discursive dynamics. While these early postcolonial discourses of the female body firmly lodged themselves in the colonial narrative of the clothed versus unclothed body, they concurrently manipulated that same narrative from within, rearranged the colonial hierarchization of bodies, and produced a new hierarchy that placed African bodies on top. This is a case of the inheritor "restructuring" their obligatory inheritance (Derrida 1994, 67). Campaigns against articles of Western female clothing deemed indecent articulated negative commentaries on the semiotics of the clothed Western female body and, by extension, the moral backwardness of Western societies. Audrey Wipper, in her study of these campaigns as they unfolded in East and Central Africa in the mid-1960s and early 1970s, writes that "the mini-skirt provided an opportunity, par excellence, to lash out at the moral turpitude of western nations that produced it and whose women were the first to wear it" (1972, 332). This postcolonial counternarrative positioned African female bodies on higher moral grounds and produced a new hierarchy of bodies that demoted European bodies and promoted African bodies. In this new narrative of bodies European bodies are unclothed and deviant bodies whereas African bodies are clothed and yield higher moral ground. A sign at the airport of Malawi reads, "In Malawi it is traditional for women not to appear in public in dresses that expose any part of the leg above the knee ... also restrictions for women are shorts and trousers worn in public. Thoughtful and courteous visitors will respect our local customs and avoid any possibility of embarrassment by conforming with our conventions on female attire" (quoted in Child 1974, 12). Of course, the addressees of this sign are Western visitors to Malawi.

When Jean and John Comaroff place clothing at the center of a "long conversation" between colonized and colonizer (1997, 22), the two scholars are attending to the structures and conventions of discourse put in place and then entrenched by colonialism, but with the participation of the colonized. The ways the Tswanas studied by the Comaroffs participated in and contributed to the conversation, even reframing it at times by adopting and then adapting European clothing, models the promiscuous intimacy between the colonial and the postcolonial that I see reflected in African engagements with colonial discourses of nakedness. What I mean by this, and in a pointed effort to fend off the notion that the African in European garb is a docile colonial subject, is that the colonized is always already postcolonial. The colonized subject converses with colonial discourses from the very onset of the colonial encounter. Such a conversation eventually creates an afterlife for the colonial statement as postcolonial subjects "manipulate, use, transform, exchange, combine, decompose, and recompose, and possibly destroy" the statement (Foucault 1972, 105), with an endeavor to force a caesura into the colonial statement that Africa is naked. The Comaroffs' approach allows us to recuperate the subversive nature of these engagements and their postcolonial character. Africans are not passive recipients of the colonial statements, even when they adopted colonial discourses of clothing, as in the cases of early postcolonial nation-states and the anti-nudity ban in Nigeria. Africans flipped the colonial statement on its head and restructured their colonial inheritance.

The foregoing analysis illustrates how the colonial deployment of the female body as a rhetorical element sealed the similar fate of the female body in postcolonial discourses. The female body being a prime colonial discursive site where colonialism constructed Africa's backwardness and need of foreign leadership will inevitably be a prime postcolonial discursive site where African nations contest such colonial constructions and assert their modernity. Uganda under President Idi Amin Dada, probably more than any other African nation, shows the rhetorical deployment and postcolonial conscription of female dress as a site where postcolonial contra-modernity is negotiated. This function of the female body came to full light as Amin successively courted Western modernity and conservative Islam. Amin developed an almost chronic obsession with the "improper" and "imperialist" attire of Ugandan women. He enacted an ever lengthening and almost hilarious series of bans against miniskirts, skirts that did not precisely hit the knee line, skirts that did not completely cover the knee line, hot pants, wigs, and cosmetics, always adding to the list to the point where Ugandan women finally came up with a style of dress called "leave me alone Amin." Alicia Catharine Decker (2007) has observed that the sartorial policing of Ugandan women started once Amin severed his relationship with Israel in 1972 and started courting Arab nations. Amin's fashion dictates constantly conscripted the Ugandan female body for his new geopolitical endeavors. Amin was eager to project the image of a Muslim nation, although Muslims were a minority in Uganda. Before his dalliance with the Muslim world, Muammar Gaddafi and King Abdallah in particular, Amin was invested in the narrative

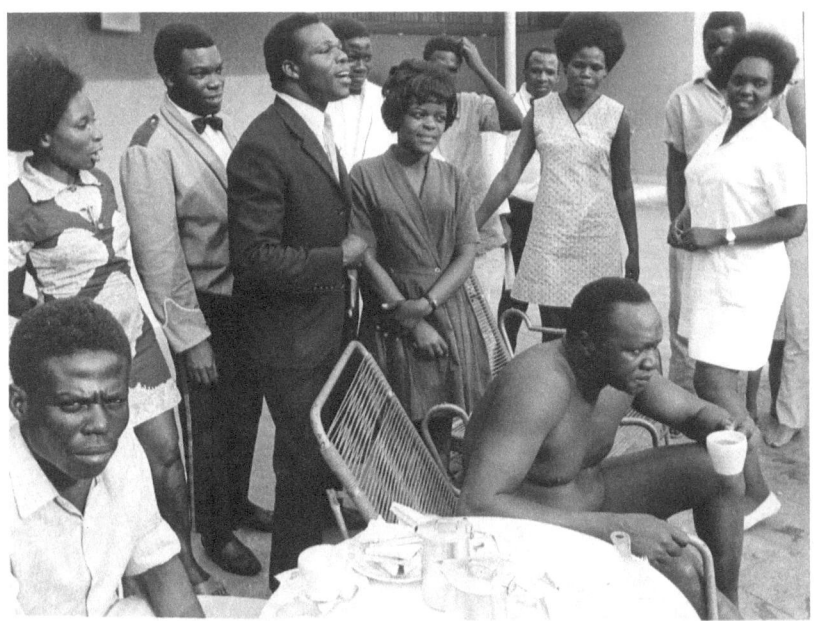

3. Amin with miniskirt-clad women, 1972. Press photo. Courtesy of Ayo A. Coly.

of Western modernity. In a 1972 picture, mini-clad Ugandan women surround Amin (fig. 3), just months before he would start courting the Muslim world then ban minis. Decker (2007, 130) also documents an official photograph of Amin posing with mini-clad women in 1972.

The poses of Amin with the mini-clad Ugandan women find a parallel in the controversial African Renaissance monument in Senegal (fig. 4) The idiosyncratic gesture of unclothing the female body in the monument is best unpacked by inscribing the unclothed Senegalese female body within the global circuits of cultural and ideological capital. More specifically, this gesture reflects the scramble of the postcolonial African state for validation on the global stage. The quest for global validation via the unclothed female body enacts the same postcolonial angst over the female body that informs the gesture of clothing the female body in Nigeria.

Senegalese president Abdoulaye Wade erected the Senegalese monument in 2009 to celebrate the so-called African Renaissance. The monument

4. *African Renaissance Monument - From Above*. Photo by Jeff Attaway. Provided under the terms of the creative commons public license, or CCPL. https://flic.kr/p/9t4ANy.

met nationwide public outrage when President Wade unveiled it. The unclothed female body in a country where Islam is the dominant religion by no means translates the dominant self-image of the national population. A consideration of the agenda behind the monument explains the flagrant disjunction between the monument and the Senegalese populations. President Wade, the creative designer of the monument, explained that the couple emerging from the earth signifies Africa's reemergence on the global stage, moving away from centuries of foreign domination toward autonomy and a stronger international presence (Cessou 2009). The monument is therefore not meant to be a site of common identification for the Senegalese citizenry, and the Senegalese populations are not the intended audience for the monument. Instead the monument responds to a need for increased visibility and consideration on the global stage. It aims at clearing a space on the global stage for the postcolonial nation. I propose that the gesture of unclothing the female body fits into that agenda of a monument meant not for local consumption but instead to garner positive global recognition for the postcolonial African nation-state.

African analysts of global geopolitics have noted how globalization has economically and politically dwarfed the progress of the newly formed postcolonial African nation states, maintaining these states in positions of dependency and accountability to Western power structures (Traoré 1999, 2002, 2008; Baenga 2002; Diouf 2002a, 2002b; Ki-Zerbo 2003; Sissako 2006). Postcolonial African nation-states usually enter the global stage as problems and projects: be it civil wars, health crises, poverty, or oppression of women. This type of infantilizing presence on the global stage reenacts a colonial dynamic whereby the African continent is often approached not as an interlocutor or partner but as an object of development, a project for the problem-solving skills of more advanced nations. As with colonialism, Africans under globalization are bodies to be acted upon and whose fates lie in foreign hands. As with the discourses of colonialism, the female body is routinely invoked on the global stage to signify underdevelopment and backwardness and then concurrently legitimize foreign intervention in the targeted nations. The circumcised African female body and the maternity-weighed-down African female body have become familiar rhetorical tropes in global geopolitics. They serve as justificatory frameworks for international intervention under the banner of globalization and human rights. The tropes also legitimize the political disenfranchisement of certain nation-states on the global stage.

Globalization, like colonialism, sets up the female body as an index of development and a rhetorical element. As such globalization prolongs and intensifies the colonially induced postcolonial African angst over the female body. Senegal is both an African nation and a predominantly Moslem nation. This is a nation whose public identity is shaped by two narratives with negative currency on the global stage, particularly when it comes to women's issues. I consequently argue that the Senegalese gesture of unclothing the female body is an attempt to build ideological, political, and cultural capital on the global stage in order to reposition the postcolonial nation as a legitimate actor on that stage. In light of the narratives about the gender politics of Muslim societies, unclothing the African Muslim female body converts into ideological, political, and cultural currency on the global stage.[7] If the monument, in the words of President Abdoulaye Wade, represents the new Africa, the unclothed female body serves as a rhetorical trope for that new Africa. The spectacle of the unclothed female body for the global stage performs a palatable Islam and modern Africa by projecting the image of an emancipated female body. The liberation theme is compounded by the fact that the woman is unburdened. She is carrying nothing, not even her child. Senegalese feminist Fatou Kiné Camara (2010) has argued that the nudity of the woman is not offensive; rather she takes issue with the fact that the man, and not the woman, gets to carry the child. But this decision to have the man carry the child shows again how gender is a careful rhetorical strategy. The image of the woman without the baby is purposefully against the grain of the global cliché of the African woman with a child and a load on her head. That image, which in various African arts was a celebration of maternity and motherhood, has been resignified by the discourses of modernity, development, and Western feminisms. The image of the African mother with child now signifies subjugation and illiteracy. The trope has become the visual accompaniment for global discussions of the state of African womanhood.

    At the same time, a close reading of the monument unravels its narrative of modern African womanhood and confirms the rhetorical function of the unclothed female body. It is a rhetorical accessory of modern African masculinity. The unclothed and unburdened female body speaks to and showcases an emancipated African manhood. The gesture of carrying the baby is carefully chosen to project a man who liberates his mate from the burden of motherhood and wifehood. In other words, the nation, read postcolonial men, has liberated its women. Men take credit for the liberation of women. But that gesture of liberation falls short as the father carries the baby as a prize and achievement, in sum a symbol of masculine virility. The position of the three figures also undermines the projected message of women's liberation and emancipated manhood. The man has a central place in the visual narrative. He leads the action and is the exclusive head of his modern Western-style nuclear household. Of relevance here is Oyeronke Oyewumi's (1997) argument that colonialism forced onto African societies the Western construction of wifehood as both an all-encompassing identity for married women and a relationship of subordination to a husband. While the woman in the monument appears liberated and unburdened, she cannot self-realize. In the modern Senegalese family, an emulation of the Western nuclear model, she becomes an appendage of her husband.

Of course, gender matters. My analysis could not sidestep gender after all. But the point is not as much that gender matters but how gender matters. Gender is not necessarily foundational to postcolonial African preoccupations with the female body but often enters these preoccupations sideways. The convergence between postcolonial African discourses of the female body from divergent sites supports the argument of a postcolonial African angst over the female body. While this argument helps loosen African preoccupations with the female body from the exclusive theoretical grip of gender, a gender-related caveat is nonetheless in order. African women and feminists certainly have immediate stakes in the postcolonial recovery of the African female body from colonial discourses. The protective silences about the sexual female body in African feminist thought and African women's literatures and arts participate in that postcolonial recovery effort. If, per Avery Gordon, haunting positively creates a "something-to-be-done," meaning "something different from before, seems like it must be done" (1997, 16), the protective silences in African women's discourses are indeed doing something different from before.

But haunting also "produces its own insights and blindness," pursues Gordon (1997, 22). The angst-filled relocation of the African female body from colonial inscription to postcolonial conscription presents potential pitfalls for African women because of the broader patriarchal environment that hosts this postcolonial recovery project. The vulnerability of the female body in patriarchal contexts, namely the patriarchal control of women through the repression of the sexual female body, dictates feminist vigilance. The postcolonial protective gesture of covering and desexualizing the African female body runs alongside the patriarchal war on the sexual female body and patriarchal anxieties about changing gender roles and norms. The patriarchal hierarchy of bodies in the Senegalese monument and the correlation between women's dress and rape in the Nigerian anti-nudity bill illustrate the potential for a patriarchal hijacking of the postcolonial protective gesture of covering and desexualizing the African female body. The postcolonial gesture then releases the female body into the custody of patriarchal discourses. My uneasiness with the postcolonial African feminist gesture sounds off Bibi Bakare-Yusuf's compelling warning to African feminist discourses:

> Positioning women as weak or damaged subjects gives renewed legitimacy to patriarchally motivated discourses of control and protection. What this does is to set artificial limits on how we talk about women's sexual agency in experiential, political, social and symbolic terms. It thereby circumscribes the production of meaning and the development of alternative narratives that attempt to portray and articulate female lived experience—today and in years to come. But most debilitating of all, we lose our capacity to resist and change our situation, and to imagine new horizons of possibilities around sexual safety, choice, autonomy, and pleasure. (2013, 28–41)

In the subsequent chapters of this book, I approach African women's discourses of the female body through the prism of these two intersecting ideologies, namely the postcolonial recovery effort and the patriarchal agenda. How do African women's discourses work within, with, outside, and against the intersection of these ideologies? Are African women's discourses able to claim custody of the female body? What does such custody mean and entail? What types of affiliations and disaffiliations, complicities and disavowals, resistances and compromises accompany African women's discursive engagements with the female body? The underlying question pertains to the possibility of uninhibited and self-emancipatory African women's discourses of the female body when hauntology has already claimed custody of the female body. If specters pertain to hegemonic processes of exclusions and inclusions, agendas of renarrativizations are also systems of counterrepresentations that aim to create what Gordon calls a "countermemory" (1997, 22). But how do processes of renarrativizations engage in acts of spectralization by instating categories of representability and nonrepresentability? Fanon's (1965) argument about the limitations of counterhegemonic discourses by their inheritance of hegemonic discursive codes tells of such imposed silences, presences, and absences. Yet Derrida, who pursues an optimistic hauntology, reassures us that an inheritance can be sorted out and restructured.

In answering these questions in the next chapters, I revisit Derrida's and Gordon's argument about the possibility of a critical hauntology, meaning a consciousness-raising and activist hauntology that fosters a conscientious awareness of past injustice and a militant turn to the present. Are the engagements of African women with the female body along the lines of a critical hauntology? Does such a critical hauntology subsequently emancipate African women's discourses of the female body from colonial specters?

2
Haunted Silences

AFRICAN FEMINIST CRITICISM AND
THE SPECTER OF SARAH BAARTMAN

Why is the sexual female body barely a presence in African feminist criticism? Under what discursive circumstances does the sexual female body eventually appear? What conceptual vocabularies have African feminist critics developed for the sexual female body? Through these and similar questions, this chapter addresses the silences of African feminist criticism on the sexual female body, assesses the emergent process of breaking these silences, and analyzes the spectral presence of Sarah Baartman in African feminist criticism. The reclamation of the African female body from colonial and neocolonial discourses is a prime agenda of African feminist criticism. But such reclamation entails an advocacy of the sexual female body as opposed to the very tentative engagement with the sexual female body that pervades African feminist criticism. In this chapter I read the timid engagements with the female body in African feminist criticism in conjunction with the leitmotif of Sarah Baartman in the field. The chapter argues that at the core of African feminist criticism lies a potentially crippling hauntology that falls short of the type of transformative hauntology that Derrida (1994) and Avery Gordon (1997) theorize. In the last part of the chapter, I analyze *Karmen Geï* (2001), a controversial film by Senegalese director Joseph Gaï Ramaka, for its feminist teachings about the sociopolitical potential of female sexuoerotic agency in postcolonial African contexts. *Karmen Geï* draws from indigenous African expressions of the sexual female body in order to model future directions of a fully emancipated and emancipatory African feminist criticism.

Colonial Noise and the Silences of African Feminist Criticism

Signe Arnfred (2004, 2009) correctly singles out leading African feminist scholars Ifi Amadiume and Oyeronke Oyewumi for ignoring female sexuality. The sexual female body is also a glaring absence from major anthologies of African feminist criticism, including *Sisterhood, Feminisms, and Power* (1998), *African Women and Feminism* (2004), *African Gender Studies: A Reader* (2005), and *Gender Epistemologies in Africa* (2011). In their introduction to *African Feminist Politics of Knowledge: Tensions, Challenges, Possibilities* (2009), coeditors Akosua Adomako Ampofo and Signe Arnfred point out the absence of female sexuality in African feminist criticism, but the edited volume nonetheless glosses over sexuality. Their neglect of sexuality seems all the more purposeful that the two editors explain that "many African feminists do not see the need to privilege sexual pleasure. They see issues of protection from HIV infection and abuse as very important and, from a historical perspective, they see silences around sexuality as legitimate" (Ampofo and Arnfred 2009, 17). Arnfred also previously edited a volume on African sexualities (2004). By not integrating sexuality in this new project, Arnfred positions sexuality as a special category or isolated arena of gender work. As I argue later in this chapter, there is much to be gained, epistemologically and politically, by making the exploration of female sexuality an important component of any African feminist project.

In response to my concern with the absence of the sexual female body in African feminist criticism, a respondent to a presentation I gave at a conference contended that such an absence is barely glaring. After all, she pursued, even Western feminists have shied away from the female body until the past twenty years. It is correct that Western feminist critics have barely disposed of the gendered Cartesian dualism that has pervaded Western systems of thought. The dualism had led feminists to keep the body at bay and uphold the ideal of disembodied subjecthood. It was only in the late 1980s that Elizabeth Grosz (1987, 1994, 1995), Alison Jaggar and Susan Bordo (1989), Susan Suleiman (1986), and Janet Wolff (1990), among other Western feminist critics, launched the female body on its remarkable scholarly course. The Cartesian dualism was not only gendered; it also underpinned bio-racist discourses in the eighteenth and nineteenth centuries. The racial subtext of the Cartesian logic means that African feminist thought probably has a more contentious relationship to the body than Western feminist thought. African feminists have to be cognizant of both race and gender. But in my review of African feminist thought, Cartesian dualism is hardly, if at all, an interlocutor of African feminist thought. It may be the case that the somatophobia that, according to Grosz (1987), underlies Western thought systems appears absent from African ones. According to Oyeronke Oyewumi (1997), the reduced importance of visuality in some indigenous African epistemologies means that the body is not the basis for categorization, identification, and eventual stigmatization in these African thought systems.

Where Western feminisms have been concerned with "the body either as something to be rejected in the pursuit of intellectual equality according to a masculinist standard, or as something to be reclaimed as the very essence of the female" (Price and Shildrick 1999, 2–4), African feminisms have rather been concerned with reclaiming the African female body from colonialist discourses. The history of the black African female body is unlike that of the white female body. African feminisms have been invested in restoring the moral and aesthetic dignity of the African female body that colonial discourses of the lascivious and grotesque African female body compromised. At issue here are not embodiment and corporeality as such but the colonialist regimes of representation of the African female body. In contrast, the debate in Western feminisms focuses on the fact and act of representing in itself, and not the content or modalities of representation. Unlike in Western feminisms the absence of the female body in African feminist thought is not a consequence of the Cartesian dualism.

Many scholars identify patriarchy as the inevitable culprit behind the silences of African feminist on the sexual female body. In what is probably the most forceful critique of these silences, Patricia McFadden (2003) argues that African feminisms operate in a patriarchal habitus that socializes women "to conceal what they know about their bodies, to express shame about their bodies, to apologise for their bodies, and to lose touch with what Alice Walker has called 'the secret of joy.'" However, McFadden's argument leans quite heavily on the notion of a universal female subordination popularized by Western feminist thought. The response of McFadden is indeed straight from the textbooks of Western feminist thought, whose trademark lines she uses to frame African feminist silences on the sexual female body. Yet African feminist scholars have consistently challenged such a universalization of patriarchy and female subordination. Scholars such as Ifi Amaduime (1987, 1997), Oyeronke Oyewumi (1997, 2015), and Nkiru Nzegwu (2012) have cautioned against reading Western gender norms and constructions into African contexts. In the latter contexts gender takes different forms and is not always an organizing principle, and sex has different and sometimes nongendered social consequences. Once we take into account these cautions, we cannot draw a straightforward causal link between patriarchy and the silences of African feminists on the sexual female body. McFadden's patriarchy argument is too hasty of an explanation for these silences. Her deployment of patriarchy is precisely what Judith Butler had in mind when she cautioned that the "very notion of patriarchy has threatened to become a universalizing concept that overrides or reduces distinct articulations of gender asymmetry in different cultural contexts. As feminism has sought to become integrally related to struggles against racialist and colonialist oppression, it has become increasingly important to resist the colonizing epistemological strategy that would subordinate different configurations of domination under the rubric of a transcultural notion of patriarchy" (1993, 46). When McFadden deploys patriarchy as a universalized explicative framework, patriarchy becomes a colonizing epistemology that is blind to the specificities of the discursive terrain that African feminisms navigate. By privileging patriarchy, McFadden can only misread the silences of African feminist thought as evidence of a feminism at the infancy stage, barely able to stand up to patriarchy and probably in need of tutelage. But multiple discourses traverse African gender politics and consequently African feminist thought. Patriarchy is just one of those discourses. McFadden overlooks the role of colonial discourses and neocolonial discourses in turning the sexual African female body into a charged topic for African feminist scholars and then shaping the decried African feminist silences. In her response to McFadden, Charmaine Pereira (2003) correctly asks, "Why should these silences simply be condemned, given the historical conditions of imperial expansion and racist fascination with the hypersexuality projected onto Africans by Europeans?" She pursues that "we need to understand what the silences are about, what noises are filling those silences, and how to transform those silences into more appropriate responses." Like Pereira, Signe Arnfred, along with the contributors to her edited volume *Re-thinking Sexualities in Africa* (2004), has considered the colonial link. Arnfred explains that she chose to title her own chapter "African Sexuality/ Sexuality in Africa: Tales and Silences" because of the abundance of "tales" about African sexualities and her suspicion that "there might be an inner connection between this type of tales and one type of silence: the general absence of sexuality as an issue in African feminists' writings" (59).

This is not to say that patriarchy does not factor into the silences of African feminist criticism. But patriarchy is not the sole interlocutor of these silences. My approach insists that African feminisms are not always respondents to patriarchy, and their resistances are not always against patriarchy. Jane Bennett's reading of the women's self-circumcision episode in mid-1950s Kenya further illustrates my argument. Bennett takes her cue from the Kenyan girls who circumcised themselves when the council of male elders in Meru cooperated with the colonial administration and banned clitoridectomy in 1956. Bennett argues that this episode of the anticolonial activism of African women teaches that "it is not possible to read women's resistances in African contexts as ever monoaxial—as a strike against patriarchy alone or a strike against military rule alone" because African women's resistance in the twentieth century "has always been embedded in local and regional stories of the resistances of the continent itself against colonial and neo-colonial economic and political policies, ideologies and systems" (2011, 90).

Delving further into the silences noted but not really explored by scholars of African feminist thought, I argue that there is an immediate connection between these silences and colonial discourses of the African female body. I further take my cue from Pereira in order to analyze the natures of these silences and what is being done to fill them. In specifying earlier that these silences have interlocutors, I aim to convey that these silences are a form of speech and enunciators of discourse. Sylvia Tamale lists silence among the concepts that "carry specific social meanings steeped in Western ideology and traditions" (2011, 3) and contends that "though in the dominant Western tradition voice is valorised and silence constructed as a total blank, in many African cultures silence can be as powerful and as empowering as speech" (13). Trinh T. Minh-ha also states that "within the context of women's speech silence has many faces" because "silence is commonly set in opposition with speech as a will not to say or a will to unsay and as a language of its own has barely been explored" (1989, 372–73). Minh-ha pursues that "silence as a refusal to partake in the story does sometimes provide us with a means to gain a hearing. It is a voice, a mode of uttering, and a response in its own right" (83). As a pointed refusal to aliment and center the colonial narrative of the African female body, African feminist silences "unsay," to borrow from Minh-ha (1989), the sexualized African female body. By keeping silent on the sexual female body, the work of leading African feminist scholars such as Ifi Amadiume and Oyeronke Oyewumi, whom Arnfred singles out for the conspicuous absence of sexuality in their work, starts a new discursive thread about the African female body. Their silences thereby perform a reclamation of the female body from colonial discourses and, as Avery Gordon would have it, work on a "re-narrativization" of African womanhood.

The distinction Irène D'Almeida makes between being silent and being silenced, in her examination of francophone African women's writings, is useful for assessing the effectiveness of African feminist silences. D'Almeida cautions against conflating silence as a "strategic ploy," in which case silence is "eloquent" and self-imposed, with a "coercive" silence that we must destroy because it conveys emptiness (1994, 3). What is at stake in the silences of African feminisms on the sexual female body then? As shown in the preceding chapter, colonial discourses of the African female body trouble postcolonial discourses. In postcolonial Africanist scholarship, the African female body is shrouded in an academic culture of enforced silence on the sexual female body. The African female body moves from colonial hypersexualization to postcolonial desexualization. The notion of a self-imposed African feminist silence is thus not totally exact. Silence in this context is an imposition from colonial discourses and substantiates the hold of the latter discourses on postcolonial discourses. We are back here to the limitations of postcolonial counterdiscourses, as outlined by Fanon (1965) and Said (1988). While performing a re-narrativization of African womanhood, the silences of African feminist criticism nonetheless evince an acceptance "as is" of the colonial inheritance and not the emancipatory restructuring of the inheritance that Derrida envisions.

Specters of Sarah Baartman

A pattern that scholars are yet to tease out is the leitmotif of Sarah Baartman in African feminist thought. Baartman is a routine and now predictable response to Western engagements with African female bodies. Baartman has served to articulate responses to Western critiques of female circumcision, the gender testing of South African Olympic runner Caster Semenya in 2009, and Western development initiatives geared toward African women. The conceptual repurposing of the story of Sarah Baartman is not unique to African feminist criticism. The fate of the body of Sarah Baartman has Afro-diasporic resonances, and visual artists and feminist critics from the African diaspora have mostly spearheaded the repurposing of Sarah Baartman. But Zine Magubane has critiqued such "theoretical fetishization of Baartman" on the ground that Baartman, a Khoikhoi woman, may not have been considered black in the context of the nineteenth century (2001, 818). Magubane also contends that the curiosity surrounding the anatomy of Baartman was hardly unique because Irish male skulls and women with excessive hair were also medical curiosities in the nineteenth century.

Despite Magubane's argument that Baartman was not a black racial representative at the time of her exhibition, there are nineteenth-century references to the Hottentot Venus as a black woman. William Makepeace Thackeray's novel *Vanity Fair* (1847) refers to a black woman as a Hottentot Venus. Against Magubane's claim that Europeans viewed Baartman as a Khoikhoi rather than an African, her captors exhibited Baartman as an African woman and made her to signify Africa. Africa is a major operative signifier in the poster for her Piccadilly exhibition in 1811. The hook was clearly her African origins. The notion of the "interior of Africa" on the poster capitalized on eighteenth- and nineteenth-century European imaginations of Africa as the "dark continent" in order to signify the absolute and authentic otherness/blackness of Sarah Baartman. In sum, Magubane is arguably right that the perceived peculiarity of the anatomy of Baartman, more so than her race or African origins, spurred her exhibition. It is, however, important to note that the anatomical peculiarity of Baartman came to service unfolding nineteenth-century European discourses about Africa.

So, what does it matter, as Magubane contends, that Baartman was not the only Khoikhoi or South African woman to be exhibited in such a way? Sarah Baartman was the most known of these exhibited women, and as such African and black feminisms appropriated her as an emblem and a metonym for all other unnamed exhibited bodies. Metonymy, as a form of strategic essentialism, brings these unnamed bodies and submerged histories to visibility. While I heed Magubane's argument about the potential sloppiness of the Sarah Baartman metaphor, I am not willing to let go of Baartman that easily. From a postcolonial African feminist standpoint the story of Baartman is useful in decoding, transcoding, naming, and genealogizing attitudes toward African female bodies. It is noteworthy that the itinerary of Sarah Baartman preceded and premodeled the colonial photographic voyeurism of African women in the first half of the nineteenth century (Coly 2008). In the end Sarah Baartman matters and is useful for what she allows African and black feminist critics to see, understand, and articulate about black female bodies. Baartman is important for the narratives that she allows us to tease out and deconstruct and for the epistemological and political vigilance that she affords us. Jennifer Nash similarly argues that the mobilization of Sarah Baartman "as an analytic point of departure has enabled black feminisms to offer a 'real' theory of the public nature of black women's bodies, a theory rooted in the practice of Baartman's exhibition" (2008, 57). Nash may as well have been describing the way African feminist thought has put Baartman to use.

Sarah Baartman has offered African feminist critics a theoretical handle to tease out the colonialist ideologies and voyeuristic agendas woven into some contemporary Western engagements with African female bodies. Baartman makes routine appearances in the female circumcision debate where African feminists often equate Western attention to female circumcision with colonial voyeurism.[1] Obioma Nnaemeka, a leading figure in African feminist thought, edited *Female Circumcision and the Politics of Knowledge: African Women in Imperialist Discourses* (2005), in which the different contributors read Western discourses on female circumcision against the background of the colonial history of the African female body. In her introductory chapter Nnaemeka sets the tone by evoking the story of Sarah Baartman, writing that "western fascination with African women's body parts and sexuality has a long history.... In the nineteenth century, the problem was the African woman's buttocks. The current debate is about another body part—the vagina" (2005, 34–35). Baartman resurfaces again, following the subjection of South African Olympic athlete Caster Semenya to gender testing in 2009. All the essays by Africanist scholars on the controversy invoke Baartman.[2] Carina Ray's essay, in particular, frames from the start Semenya as a modern Baartman. The essay opens with a re-narration of the story of Sarah Baartman and proceeds to state, "Fast-forward nearly 200 years and the genitals of another young South African woman, runner Caster Semenya, have once again become target of Western scientists' prodding and poking" (Ray 2009).

These constant retellings of the story of Sarah Baartman in African feminist criticism participate in the type of ethical memory at the core of the critical hauntologies of Derrida and Gordon. Derrida writes about hauntology as a "politics of memory, of inheritance and of generations" (1994, xix). For Gordon, hauntology offers an opportunity to "put . . .

life back where only a vague memory or a bare trace was visible [and] repair representational mistakes" in order to create a "countermemory, for the future" (1997, 22). The fixation of African feminist critics on the colonial statement thus extends reparative justice to the African female bodies flattened by the colonial statement. The constant engagement with the colonial statement brings these bodies out from under the colonial statement. Concurrently, the specter of Sarah Baartman functions as a memorial placeholder for the damaging encounter between the African female body and the European colonial gaze. The omnipresence of Baartman is also a function of her embrace by African feminist critics as a figure of clarification, which Gordon and Derrida offer as further reason not to exorcise but embrace the ghost. For "following the ghosts is about making a contact that changes you and refashions the social relations in which you are located," writes Gordon (1997, 22). African feminist thought has embraced the specter of Baartman to clarify contemporary discourses of the African female body and contest the continuing overdetermination of the African female body as a signifier of absolute otherness. Here Baartman, as a colonial hauntology, enables critical vigilance or what V. Y. Mudimbe (1988) calls "epistemological vigilance." Reading Western discourses on female circumcision and the Western scrutiny of Caster Semenya from the colonial hauntology of the African female body makes legible the reiteration of the colonial objectification of African bodies. In the end one may argue that the specter of Baartman or the hypersexualized African female body is useful for what it allows African feminist critics to see, understand, articulate, and critique about past and present narrativizations of the African female body.

Having said this, the silences of African feminist criticism about the sexual female body, which I argue later are counterrevolutionary, veer African feminist criticism from a critical hauntology and more toward the hauntology of antagonism described in Fanon's "Algeria Unveiled" (1965) and aptly invoked in Edward Said's statement that anticolonial nationalist discourses are "fatally limited" by their antagonist position vis-à-vis colonial discourses (1988, 14). Certainly the silences, as a reclaimative gesture of clothing the African female body and a site for new narratives for the African female body, illuminate a critical consciousness of a "something-to-be-done" (Gordon 1997, 16). The new narratives of the African female body are attempts to do something to colonial discourses. However, the avoidance of the sexual female body in these new narratives strongly suggests that colonial discourses still have the upper hand, since this hauntology of vigilance remains one of antagonism after failing to emancipate itself from the colonial scene. In that respect the specter of Sarah Baartman, as deployed in African feminist criticism, falls short of being the ferment for revolutionary epistemologies and future possibilities that Derrida and Gordon envision. Derrida's affirmative and slightly utopian theorization of spectrality endows the specter with ethico-political potential because the specter can spur critical and civic discourses when reimagined as a messianic structure. Derrida recommends that we allow the specter to haunt us a both "revenant" and "arrivant." In Gordon's less utopian hauntology, the specter should bear witness to the past but also move us beyond the past by helping us map out possibilities and emancipatory futures.

The African feminist epistemological vigilance fostered by the specter of Baartman has installed an epistemological guardrail around the African female body. The desexualization of the African female body in African feminist thought and the touchiness about Western engagements with African female bodies show how Sarah Baartman has become a disciplinary apparatus and socio-ideological compass that regulate the conditions and modalities of producing discourse about the African female body, including what can (not) be said about the African female body and who can (not) speak about the African female body. I have already documented in chapter 1 the explosive debate in the wake of the representation of the African female body by white South African female artists. What I am hinting at here is the inhibiting effect of the specter of Sarah Baartman. The thematic privileging of motherhood, reproductive health, and sexual violence in African feminist scholarship shows how the specter has instituted scholarly cultures of censorship and self-censorship around the African female body.

This inhibition may explain why, in their rebuttals of Western engagements with female circumcision, African feminist critics rarely use the sexual enhancement aspect of female circumcision as a counterargument. They opt instead to focus on exposing the racism of Western feminisms and memorializing Sarah Baartman through the exhibited circumcised African woman. African feminist scholarship hardly addresses those cases where female circumcision functions to enhance and not curtail a woman's sexual pleasure. A few scholarly voices have documented the alternative function of female circumcision, but due to the monopoly of the topic of female circumcision by the Baartman angle these voices are barely audible. For instance, Nkiru Nzegwu contends that what is often labeled female genital mutilation is in fact better read as a way of "sculpting the erotic body" (2011, 261–63). Brigitte Bagnol and Esmeralda Mariano (2011) make a similar argument about the stretching of the labia in Mozambique.

The colonial hauntology of the African female body has cornered African feminist criticism into a feminism of rebuttal when it comes to the female body. This is a reactive and defensive feminism, not in opposition to local patriarchies, but in opposition to Western feminisms. Achille Mbembe's polemical "African Modes of Self-Writing" (2002) is relevant to my discussion of the limitations in African feminist criticism. Like Derrida, Mbembe advocates future-oriented turns to the past. Mbembe is concerned that the specters of colonialism, slavery, and apartheid have driven Africanist thought into a dead-end of neurotic and cultic metanarratives of African victimhood. Mbembe is adamant that such an ethos of victimization breeds a "conspirational reading of history" and a "logic of suspicion" that stalls African critical thought and intellectual practice (2002, 12). Like many critics of Mbembe, I fault his theory of an African victim mentality with trivializing the violence of colonialism, slavery, and apartheid. Mbembe dismisses the brutal legacies of these histories in the daily lives of contemporary Africans and also neglects the neocolonial subjection of Africans to Western powers. It is in light of these colonial legacies and continuities that I have been prefacing my critiques of African feminist thought with the acknowledgment that African feminisms exist in a discursive context where colonial and neocolonial discourses still overdetermine the African female body.

I am not sold on Mbembe's African victimhood theory and would rather approach the African "conspirational reading of history" and "logic of suspicion" as epistemological vigilance. Still, I share Mbembe's conclusion that African modes of living with the specters of colonialism potentially cripple African intellectual discourses. In deploying Sarah Baartman as an argumentative trope, African feminist criticism is treading a very fine line between epistemological vigilance and the African logic of conspiracy and suspicion decried by Mbembe. My notion of an epistemological guardrail around the African female body shares in Mbembe's fear that African thought may be driving itself into a dead end. Mbembe specifically reverberates through my own concerns that the hauntology of the African female body may foreclose new African feminist discursive imaginaries and conceptual creativities.

A Jacketed Feminism? Mothernormativity, Marriagenormativity, and the Pitfalls of Hauntology

It is not that the sexual female body is totally absent from African feminist thought. But when one goes looking for the sexual female body in African feminist thought, one finds that the biomedical approach predominates. The overall privileging of reproductive health, procreative sexuality, and sexual violence performs a desexualization of the African female body. The thematics of sexual violence and female circumcision in African feminist thought reverses the colonial trope of the sexually promiscuous and lascivious black African female body. The focus on a desexualized sexuality negates the sexual African female body at the very moment it is being enunciated. In this reactive African feminist script of the African female body, African women don't enjoy sex. African women endure sex, and sex is something done to them. Through these representational choices and politics of representation, African feminist scholarship has installed a counterhegemonic regime of representation for the African female body, albeit one that refuses to claim sexual agency for the African female body.

The prominence of the trope of motherhood in African feminist thought (Bakare-Yusuf 2003) coheres with the postcolonial desexualization of the African female body. The trope appears to perform a discursive labor of dignification of African womanhood. Motherhood becomes a rhetorical trope of African female cultural distinction and moral superiority that disputes the colonial trope of the black Venus. In its insistence on the tropes of motherhood and desexualized African womanhood, African feminist thought resembles the so-called African American feminism of respectability.[3] As a result of the history of the black female body, both African and Afro-diasporic feminisms share the same silences around the sexual female body and gravitate toward the figure of Sarah Baartman. The African American feminism of respectability finds a conceptual counterpart in the notion of "jacketed feminism" formulated by African feminist scholars Jane Bennett and Charmaine Pereira (2013) to describe how African feminist scholars negotiate notions of respectability and credibility by shying away from the sexual female body. African feminist scholars are jacketed women by virtue of their position as educated hence good and respectable women. The jacket of respectability is a "straightjacket" that curtails engagements with topics deemed improper by one's community (Bennett and Pereira 2013). Accordingly, the role of the jacketed African feminist scholar is to cover up the African female body, in the wake of its uncovering by colonial and neocolonial discourses.

The pitfalls to these politics of respectability invested onto African feminists are obvious. The African feminist repression of the sexual female body and promotion of motherhood as the paradigm of African womanhood lend a hand to the heteropatriarchal policing of women's sexuality. Bibi Bakare-Yusuf (2003) and Sylvia Tamale (2006) have critiqued the trope of motherhood in African feminist scholarship for its patriarchal underpinnings, with Tamale arguing that the conflation of motherhood and womanhood feeds an African feminist culture of "mothernormativity" and "marriagenormativity" (2006, 40). Both mothernormativity and marriagenormativity constitute antifeminist ideologies that police women's sexuality by regulating when, where, how, and why women can have sex. Basile Ndjio has also explained that the reactionary and anticolonial sexuality politics of African nationalisms and the nationalist endeavor to create "an exclusive African sexual identity" have meant that many African postcolonial states tie sexuality to respectable citizenship (2013, 120). The 1994 International Conference on Population and Development, which initiated the notion of sexuality as a right, was a case in point. Several African states resisted the application of the language of rights and choice to sexuality on the grounds that such a framework would negate religious guidelines about gender, sex and family (Klugman 2000). With mother-normativity and marriagenormativity at its core, African feminist thought may enter into a dangerous liaison with nationalist discourses of the female body. The African feminist repression of the sexual female body walks a thin line with the gender and sexual politics of nationalism, namely the nationalist conscription of the female body to signify the cultural values of the nation and the nationalist privileging of desexualized motherhood as both virtuous womanhood and proper female citizenship.[4]

By self-censoring around sexuality, African feminisms set themselves up for hijacking by postcolonial patriarchal agendas. An essay by African feminist critic Obioma Nnaemeka on "nego-feminism" does little to assuage my uneasiness about the alliances between African feminist discourses and patriarchal agendas. Nnaemeka coined the term "nego-feminism" to describe how African feminisms successfully challenge patriarchies through "negotiation, accommodation, and compromise" and how they proceed by "defining and modulating their feminist struggle in deference to cultural and local imperatives" (2004, 380). The cautious engagements of African feminists with the sexual female body may then well describe nego-feminism. Nego-feminism conflicts with Sylvia Tamale (2006) and Patricia McFadden's (2003) call for a more sexually radical African feminism. Given that the scripts of postcolonial African citizenship, as described by Ndjio (2013), prescribe male sexual agency and supremacy versus female sexual passivity, what is then at stake for African nego-feminisms when they choose to negotiate and compromise with patriarchy? One wonders whether female sexual expression and the sexual female body do not end up being sacrificed in this alliance? Ndjio correctly argues that African women who are in charge of their sexual desires and pleasure "put at risk the foundation of post-colonial power" by "contesting the supremacy of the male phallus" (2013, 136).

It is precisely the supremacy of the phallus that makes the sexual female body an important political project for African feminists. The sexuoerotic passivity of women sustains patriarchal governmentalities. Following Achille Mbembe's (2001) theorization of the centrality of the phallus in postcolonial African governmentalities, the claiming of African female sexual pleasure is per force a political feminist project as Ndjio argues. Ndjio's argument about the potential sociopolitical repercussions of female sexuoerotic agency supports Sylvia Tamale and Patricia McFadden's call for a nonconciliatory Africa feminism against the nego-feminism of Nnaemeka. It is important to note that while these affirmations of the sexual female body by Ndjio, Tamale, and McFadden echo Carole Vance's (1982) eponymous feminist advocacy of female sexual pleasure, the three scholars go beyond Vance to provide a political framework to her pleasure-for-the-sake-of-pleasure approach. Consider how Vance concludes her essay on sexual pleasure:

> Above all, feminism must be a movement that speaks to sexuality, that does not forfeit the field to reactionary groups who are more than willing to speak. We cannot be cowardly, pretending that feminism is not sexually radical. Being a sex radical at this time, as at most, is less a matter of what you do and more a matter of what you are willing to think, entertain, and question.... Feminism must put forward a politics that resists deprivation and supports pleasure. It must understand pleasure as life-affirming, empowering, desirous of human connection and the future, and not fear it as destructive, enfeebling, or corrupt.... It is not enough to move away women from danger and oppression; it is necessary to move towards something: towards pleasure, agency, self-definition. Feminism must increase women's pleasure and joy, not just decrease our misery. (1982, 23–24)

Although one can tease out from this excerpt Vance's understanding of the political potential of female pleasure, Ndjio, McFadden, and Tamale envision a more steadfast articulation between female sexual pleasure and sociopolitical change. Despite a lack of political tenor, Vance reinforces my point about the limitations of silence as a strategy or form of speech. When feminist voices keep silent, however justified these silences may be, reactionary voices misappropriate and fill these silences.

It is a political imperative for African feminist discourses to speak the sexual female body. Speaking the sexual female body means learning to live otherwise with the specter of Sarah Baartman and the hauntology of the African female body. The theoretical takeaway from Mbembe's (2002) critique of African intellectual discourses is that a failure to engage properly with the inheritance dooms the inheritor to become a victim of the past. The inhibitions of African feminist discourses about the sexual body and the sociopolitical consequences of these inhibitions are a case in point. The response of Paul Zeleza to Mbembe's essay confirms to me the urgency for African feminist critics to place sexuoerotic agency at the core of their research agendas. Zeleza dismisses Mbembe's recommendation that African thinkers open their research agendas to topics beyond colonialism and underdevelopment. Zeleza contends that the "pressing issues of the time" for African scholars are decided for them by their lived realities of material poverty, political tyranny, and underdevelopment. According to Zeleza, African scholars are justifiably more "preoccupied with questions of development and democracy than about gazing at sexuality that seems to titillate the intellectual imaginations of some of our colleagues in postmodern societies" (2003, 392). Sexuality does not make it into Zeleza's list of legitimate African scholarly preoccupations. Zeleza's dismissal of sexuality draws a "respectable" research agenda for African feminisms. His dismissal of sexuality as an unworthy African scholarly endeavor also overlooks the entanglements of sexuality with what he deems to be "pressing issues of the time." Sexuality is inevitably a site where questions of development and democracy pose and resolve themselves.

Mbembe himself, while favoring sexuality as a site for insightful theoretical discourse, shows a disconcerting inability to imagine the African female sexual body. Throughout his scholarship, Mbembe theorizes colonization through the metaphor of the castrated African male subject. This allows him, in *On the Postcolony* (2001), to read the African postcolony through the phallus and in a way that makes no room for female subjects. How would a consideration of female sexuoerotic agency have complicated Mbembe's analysis of postcolonial African governmentalities and opened up possibilities for political transformations?

Lessons from Karmen Gei

The last part of this chapter addresses this question by putting into conversation *Karmen Gei* (2001) by Senegalese director Joseph Gai Ramaka and Mbembe's *On the Postcolony* (2001). Of interest is how in *Karmen Gei*, female sexuoerotic agency interrupts, by way of queering, the phallic economy of the postcolony and sets the ground for a new ethico-political system. As a queer feminist rewriting of *On the Postcolony*, Ramaka's *Karmen Gei* models the possible theoretical breakthroughs and direction toward livable futures of an uninhibited African feminist engagement with the female body. Most importantly, indigenous Senegalese mechanisms of female sexuoerotic agency facilitate the feminist queering of the phallic economy of the postcolonial nation.

Karmen Gei is the first African adaptation of Bizet's opera. The film garnered attention for its indulgent sexuoerotic rhetoric and its reinvention of Bizet's "excessively heterosexual femme fatale" (Powrie 2004, 287) as a nonheteronormative outlaw and political dissident. Apart from Ramaka's reinvention of Carmen, the plot remains generally faithful to Bizet's *Carmen*. In *Carmen*, set in nineteenth-century Seville, gypsy factory worker Carmen seduces Corporal Don Jose but then switches her affections to the dashing toreador Escamillio. Driven by jealous rage, Don Jose kills Carmen. In Ramaka's adaptation, Karmen is freed from prison after she seduces and beds her female warden. She proceeds to crash the wedding ceremony of Corporal Lamine Diop, lures him away, and recruits him into her smuggling ring. Lamine and the warden sink into madness and self-destruct after they are rejected by Karmen. The warden commits suicide, and Lamine murders Karmen. By placing a female-gendered subject at the scene of postcolonial possibilities, action, and happenings, the film shows an attention to gender that has generally been lacking in the master texts of postcolonial theory. In Mbembe's *On the Postcolony*, ruler and ruled are flagrantly male-gendered. Mbembe's abundant recourse to metaphors of emasculation, penetration, and virility to describe power and his overall fixation on phallic agency displace women from the postcolonial scene.

The opening scene of *Karmen Geï* is set in the yard of a woman's prison. The scene features a sabar, a sexually suggestive Senegalese dance performance, during which Karmen successfully seduces her female warden. I start with and dwell on this scene because it effectively operates a mise en place of female sexuoerotic agency in what Mbembe has described as the phallic sociopolitical architecture of the postcolony. Additionally the sabar dance, which grounds the film in the sociocultural context of Senegal, establishes the existence of indigenous mechanisms of female sexuoerotic agency that can counterbalance the hegemony of the phallus. In the opening shot, the camera gradually uncovers a space that is segmented and regulated yet materializes into a Deleuzean smooth space when Karmen seduces the warden, reorganizes space, and rewrites the power dynamics between ruler and ruled. The jubilant dancing of Karmen in this first shot gives way to a reverse shot of the warden; then the last frame reveals the historical House of Slaves on Senegal's Gorée Island. In other words, the sexual dance is taking place in a woman's prison, itself housed in a former slave dungeon. This imbrication of spaces and temporalities, further underscored by the fusion of the jazz score and the African drums throughout the film, invokes most immediately a Foucauldian heterotopia and heterochrony. But the simultaneous enunciations and dissolutions of power effected by Karmen's dance create a Deleuzean smooth space.

The new spatial assemblage drawn by Karmen theoretically correlates the convivial logic of power and carnivalesque practice of space in Mbembe's postcolony. Mbembe describes the postcolony as a theatrical meta-parody where all disciplinary norms and signifying practices are eventually fair game for poaching, including relations of power whose "convivial logic" effects a systemic breakdown of binaries and a porosity of categories. It is this porosity of boundaries and unsustainability of categories in the postcolony that account for the thread of improper and transgressive sexual intimacies in *Karmen Geï*, from nonheteronormative affects to illicit and disruptive intimacies between ruler and ruled. If the conviviality between ruler and ruled in Mbembe's postcolony allows the ruled to discover and act out the simulacra of power and hollowness of master signifiers, turning official signs and images inside out so to speak, the film translates this demythologization as a process of feminist queering that interferes with the postcolony's phallic economy of representation, signification, and subjectivation. The slave-dungeon-turned-postcolonial-prison encodes this postcolonial phallic economy while the sabar dance translates the resistive indigenous female sexuoerotic agency.

A representation of postcolonial governmentality, or what Mbembe calls the postcolonial commandement, the carceral structure lays out the correspondence between the technologies of discipline and subjectivation of the postcolonial state and such machineries of corporeal subjugation as slavery and colonialism. The women's prison is named after Koumba Kastell, a Senegalese female spirit known to seduce men and women. The geographical placement of the prison in the phallic structure of the castle, all complete with canons and always represented through long vertical shots, allegorizes the strict policing of the female body and sexuality in the heteropatriarchal postcolony. If this mise en abyme of space appears overdrawn, it is because the film leverages representational space to set up the over-the-top staging and performance of power in the postcolony. The narrowing concentric spatial frames that encircle and close in on the female bodies in the opening scene evince the tight-proof grids of biopower and the ensuing pervasiveness of disciplinary power in the postcolony. Subsequently, the way power in the postcolony always makes itself seen and known, hence is always on view and on stage, enacts the commandement's over-the-top display of an omnipotent, absolute, and virile power.

Mbembe explains that the spectacle orchestrated by the commandement institutes the absolute power of the commandement and the complete docility of the subjected (2001, 111).

The ability of female bodies to move provocatively in such a tightly patrolled space indicates a failure to protect master signifiers and moor subject positions and identities. Throughout the film, Karmen and her cohort of female prisoners are able to take on and down the agents of the commandement. Successively the warden, the guards, the corporal, and the police force are literally and figuratively stripped of their rigid khaki uniforms in a way that short-circuits the phallic economy of the postcolony. The warden falls for Karmen and then commits suicide when jilted. The armed guards on top of the prison tower fail to stop Karmen's takeover of the warden and fail again to prevent her disruption of an elite wedding ceremony. Karmen lures away a police corporal and recruits him into her smuggling ring. Karmen's mother verbally takes down a police unit that raids her clandestine bar. The hollowness of power in the postcolony thus revealed is further encoded in the recurring song lyrics in the film: "The eagle soars through the sky. Ramatou, the little bird, flies under his wings."

The technique of the reverse shot allows the filmmaker to show Karmen outperforming and thus demythologizing the commandement, with the movement from material to representational space exposing the simulacrum of phallic power. The environment and power structures that encircle yet fail to regulate Karmen's performance are gradually revealed to the viewer. As they appear on the screen, the phallic symbols of power encoded in representational space are simultaneously affirmed and negated, then ultimately mocked when the female inmates take over the courtyard during the sabar dance. For instance, by the time we realize the phallic structure of the slave house, complete with armed guards on top, Karmen's seduction of the warden is well underway. That Karmen is able to undertake such a daring enterprise under the watch of the commandement shows, following Mbembe, the "disparity between the images that the state projected of itself and society, and the way people played with, and manipulated, these images—and people did so not just well away from officialdom, out of earshot or sight of power, but also within the arenas where they were publicly gathered to confirm state legitimacy" (2001, 105). This constant poaching of meaning and interference with hegemonic regimes of signification, very much like the image of the little bird poaching into the eagle's space, is feminist queering at work in the postcolony, as part of the practices of everyday life.

The possibility of the homoerotic sabar dance in the heteropatriarchal structure, like the image of the little bird poaching into dominant space, points to a repertoire of tactics that the dominated use to clear for themselves spaces of corporeal and affective autonomy. I am using tactics here to encompass both Michel de Certeau's (1984) notion of tactics as the "art of the weak" and the Deleuzean "lines of flight" (Deleuze 1987). Tactics opportunistically seize line of flights, meaning opportunities inadvertently generated by the system, to move things around and mess (with) the system. Tactics are accordingly able to queer the system through lines of flights generated by the system. The simulacrum of power and the convivial and ludic relationship between ruler and ruled in Mbembe's postcolony constantly generates "avenues of escape from the commandement" that allow the postcolonized subject to "travesty the metaphors meant to glorify state power," "interpret and reinterpret" officialdom and "feed further significance back into the system," "glue back together their fragmented identities," or again "unpack," "disenchant," and "gently repack" officialdom (Mbembe 2001, 105, 105–6, 108, 111, 129). The antistructural female sabar dance that replaces the structured operatic score of Bizet when Carmen goes postcolonial is such a line of flight, organic to the Senegalese context and effecting the inevitable feminist and queer translation of *Carmen*. The Senegalese sabar dance is a socially authorized timescape and modality of female expression, hence its symbolic occurrence in the controlled and bounded environment of the prison yard. As performed by Senegalese women, the dance is the ultimate expression and theatrical performance of erotic autonomy. It is a space of sexual and homosexual theatricality because in the space of the sabar an endless scripting and unscripting of sexualities occur, erotic allegiances are constantly in flux, and it is not unusual that the audience find themselves hailed into and rescripted by the performance. The successful seduction of the khaki-clad and stiff female warden by Karmen in the course of the dance is a case in point. The seduction is an enactment of the propensity of the postcolonized to "drain officialdom of meaning" (Mbembe 2001, 129) and a correlate to Peter Brooker's explanation that to queer is "to estrange or defamiliarize identities, texts and attitudes which are taken for granted or assumed to have fixed meaning" (1999, 182).

Through dance, a playful practice of space, Karmen reorganizes and takes over space in order to open up a timescape of resignification. As she flirts with the warden, messing with the latter's desire when she dances toward her and then gives a lap dance, the camera zooms in on Karmen's feet as they vigorously work the sandy ground of the prison courtyard. The inconspicuous yet subversive labor of Karmen's feet on that striated territory signifies the way tactics slyly redraw space and cartographies of power by stretching the opportunities opened by lines of flight to their limits. Karmen is simultaneously playing with and playing the commandement, in a way made possible by the commandement itself. Mbembe has argued that "by dancing publicly for the benefit of power, the 'postcolonized subject' is providing his or her loyalty, and by compromising with the corrupting control that state power tends to exercise at all levels of everyday life, the subject is reaffirming that this power is incontestable—precisely the better to play with it and modify it when possible" (2001, 129). With Karmen intensifying her seduction, the stiff body of the seated warden loosens until she gives in and lets Karmen lure her out of her authoritative seat of power into the sexually provocative dance. The authoritative representative of the postcolonial commandement moves from stiff spectator and overseer of the dance to a significantly loosened up dancing body as she is hailed into the dancing circle and joined by all the female inmates. The phallic economy is short-circuited. A new feminist and queer cartography erupts when all the female inmates join Karmen and the warden on the dance floor.

This coming together of the bodies of ruled and ruler fleshes out the convivial logic of relations of power in the postcolony, as drawn by Mbembe.

It is such a logic whereby the commandement invites its subjects to play with and for it, "requisition[ing]" postcolonized bodies to the stage to co-perform and ultimately co-author the grand spectacle of the postcolonial commandement, that offers the ruled an opportunity to play the commandement by outperforming and beating the commandement at its own game (Mbembe 2001, 114). The incarcerated dancing female bodies flood the screen, take over the courtyard, and surround the warden. As is often the case in sabar dances, the bodies draw closer and merge into a messy and tangled corporeality of desire and affect that signifies a spontaneous rescripting of sexualities, spaces, and power relations, a "queer assemblage" Jasbir Puar (2007) would say. Puar means "the unexpected, the unplanned irruptions, the lines of flight, the denaturalization of expectation through the juxtaposition of the seemingly unrelated, working to undo the naturalized sexual scripts of terror that become taken-for-granted knowledge formations" (2007, xv).

The film inscribes the dislocation of meaning on the phallus. Karmen's lesbian cooptation of the female warden and feminist queering of space under the watch of the armed guards unravel the phallus. Before she intensifies her seduction of the warden and delivers the coup de grace, Karmen casts a quick glance upward to the guards on top of the building as if to seize up and taunt the commandement. The shot also establishes the phallus to be Karmen's target and destination. When the warden succumbs to her seduction, Karmen winks knowingly at the other female inmates. The women run over to join Karmen in the sabar dance and complete the takeover of the symbol of heteropatriarchal power. Being unable to enforce order and regulate meaning and the circulation of signifiers, as shown by the chaotic and improper jumble of the bodies of the inmates and the warden, means that the phallus is disabled and brought down by being exposed as simulacrum. The phallus is queered. The inmates' celebratory taunting amid the efforts of the guards to restore order convey as much. After the piercing shrill of a whistle cuts through the voices and the guards are shown forcing the inmates back into their cells, the camera cuts to the canons on top of the prison tower, then back to the now locked-up inmates mocking the guards and the warden with obscene gestures, their pelvises thrust forward to mimic domineering sexual penetration. The tripartite sequencing (unruly bodies, canons, unruly bodies) is particularly effective in rendering the short-circuiting of the phallic economy and the simulacrum of power in the postcolony, meaning that "the fetish, seen for the sham it is, is made to lose its might and becomes a mere artifact" (Mbembe 2001, 108). While celebrating in their cells, the inmates chant "she [Karmen]'s got her, it worked," followed by a traditional Wolof song: "*Asa lo, Asabombe, Mu dem ni, Asabombe, Mu dem ne*" (Where does it go? / Wherever you like. / It goes here. / Wherever you like. / It goes there). Babacar M'Baye writes that the word *asaaloo* accompanies the act of "throw[ing] (something desirable) up in the air or away so that someone in a group can get it, while the term asabombe is the response that the audience offers to the person who gives away things." For M'Baye, "Asaaloo perfectly conveys Karmen's major role in Ramaka's film, which is to arbitrarily distribute pleasure, feeling, and movement even when this generosity ends up having tragic consequences on her life" (2011, 120). The bits and pieces of wardrobe that Karmen tosses around for grab during the celebration symbolize the spoils of war and enact the demythologization of the commandement. The commandement has been shredded into pieces, and its demythologization is complete, as its bits and parts are being eaten up by its subjected. Such demythologization is akin to the "theopagy" that, Mbembe writes, we routinely find in the postcolony when citizens "dismember" and "devour" the "gods that African autocrats aspire to be" (2001, 112).

It is this in-built process of constant interrogation and tearing apart of signifiers, a result of the conviviality between rulers and ruled and the simulacrum at the heart of postcolonial power relations, that subsequently authorizes the undoing of various identity scripts, including sexual scripts. Most importantly, the process endows female sexuoerotic agency with sociopolitical potential. M'Baye is right to call Karmen a distributor of "pleasure, feeling and movement" (2011, 120). But building on Deleuze and Guattari's notion that every assemblage is foremost a "social assemblage of desire" (1986, 82), I argue rather that Karmen's sabar dance reroutes flows of desire in the postcolony in order to redistribute affective agency. The theatrical mode and convivial logic of the postcolony make affect a modus operandi of postcolonial relations of power. Karmen fiddles the postcolonial assemblage when she cunningly manipulates affect to move bodies around, displace and emplace bodies, make and unmake corporealities. In short, she insidiously choreographs bodies against the grain of normative and phallic arrangements. The queer assemblage of bodies, following Karmen's dance in the opening scene, magnifies the affective response she is able to invoke.

A subsequent scene shows how the convivial and affective mode of the postcolonial favors an indigenous feminist queer praxis like the sabar. After she escapes from prison, Karmen crashes the elite wedding ceremony of Corporal Lamine Diop and the daughter of a high-ranking government official. From nowhere, Karmen interrupts the ceremony during a ritual recital of praises for the wedding party, and she starts entertaining the assembly of dignitaries with a sabar dance. The queer workings of affect ensue, enabled by the convivial moment, itself authorized by the postcolonial system. Karmen proceeds to affect the assemblage of bodies in a way that mobilizes and recruits them into a new and dissident corporeality. Her suggestive dancing lures the proper bride into a dance-off that queers the unfolding heteronormative moment. As Karmen's dance becomes increasingly suggestive, the coy body of the proper young bride fills with sexuoerotic tension and loosens in composure. Going back and forth between the vain attempts of the police uniform–clad groom to keep his bride seated and Karmen's performance, the camera sets up the scene as a convivial dance-off between the commandement and its postcolonial subject. The bride is thrust out of the phallic economy of the postcolony when she joins Karmen on the dance floor, and the two female bodies come together in a homoerotic sabar dance-off that undercuts the heterosexual wedding. Thrusting her loins forward, Karmen symbolically penetrates the young bride before the husband gets to consummate the wedding. In fact, the police officer–husband never consummates the wedding, as he is seduced away by Karmen and later becomes her conspirator in a smuggling operation. In the Sedgwick triangle, the exchange of one woman between two powerful men allows them to express homosocial desire, in a trope prevalent throughout English and American literature and film (Sedgwick 1985). The film offers a different scenario: a female-male-female triangle sabotages the phallic economy of exchange and queers the postcolonial national family romance.

Sheila Petty has underscored the division of space in this scene, with the juxtaposed shots of the seated bridal party and a dancing Karmen "align[ing] Karmen with the masses against the rigid hierarchy of the dignitaries" (2009, 105). But this spatial division does not go unchallenged. In the course of her dance performance, Karmen is able to displace the bride but also the audience of dignitaries. Of political consequence is the ability of Karmen to affect the wedding guests, getting them to both applaud when she launches onto a critique of the postcolonial regime and cheer when she throws the bride on the ground. The camera shows the spontaneous emergence of a dissident corporeality and a new body politic when the bodies open up and converge toward the rebellious body of Karmen. Such political affect dovetails Amit Rai's point that "affective confusion allows for new affects, and thus new politics, to emerge" (quoted in Puar 2007, 208). Affective confusion is indeed what sabar dances generate while they also showcase female sexuoerotic agency.

The wedding vignette in *Karmen Geï*, which is the moment when the film establishes Karmen as a political dissident, powerfully brings home Mbembe's argument throughout *On the Postcolony* that the theatrical mode and convivial logic of the postcolony unwittingly open up multiple spaces and enactments of citizenship. In turn, this multiplicity calls for alternative theorizations of governance, civic engagement, and political participation. The film renders these alternative models intelligible by uncovering Karmen as a political dissident during the wedding ceremony. A soon as she takes center stage during her dance, Karmen harangues the elite assembly: "You've swallowed up the country but it will stick in your throat." The film frames the unfolding interruption and feminist queering of the heteronormative ceremony as a civic engagement and political intervention that aim to alter the course of the postcolonial state by preempting its reproduction. Karmen is also laying out a political agenda for the citizenry of the postcolony, urging citizens to become strangleholds for the commandement. Queering acts out that agenda. Through the incessant feminist and queer praxis of Karmen, the film illuminates the dynamic existence and workings of both feminist citizenship and political participation in the autocratic and despotic postcolony. Feminist queering embodies the way Karmen as a postcolonial female citizen engages the postcolonial state by debilitating its agents and interfering with the law. Queer feminist citizenship works by creating blockages and short circuits, in short, by setting up the commandement for failure.

But Karmen dies, as does the female warden. Corporal Lamine Diop sinks into madness. Both the corporal and the warden are destroyed by Karmen, who, in turn, is murdered by the corporal. In other words, the whole system is wiped out, both ruler and ruled are debilitated in a denouement that appears to implement Mbembe's thesis about the nil sociopolitical impact of such acts of sabotage as Karmen's. Mbembe has argued that while the intimacy between ruler and ruled in the postcolony may allow the postcolonized to play and demythologize the commandement, this entanglement also results in a "mutual zombification" of ruler and ruled where each robs the other of vitality and both are left impotent (2001, 104). Several scenes in the film articulate that impasse in the postcolony in the form of a dead end, an impossibility to move forward as if the filmic narrative itself was undermining or unraveling the queerness that it was upholding. A firm restoration of order always succeeds the moments of queer feminist disorder in the film. The parenthetical anatomy of queerness in the film resembles what Mbembe describes as "potholes of indiscipline on which the commandement may stub its toe" (2001, 111). The futility of the subversive actions of Karmen is perhaps best suggested when Karmen has visions of death represented in rows of women in whiteface. "I see death, only death," she tells Samba, her male confident, to which the latter responds: "You dig, dig and are surprised to find what you buried."

These resonances notwithstanding, Mbembe and Ramaka actually part company when it comes to the possibilities of resistance and political transformation in the postcolony. The theorist and the filmmaker part company in ways that illuminate why the manifest queer pathways in Mbembe's analysis are forestalled and why the queer is the harbinger of postcolonial futurities in *Karmen Geï*. Mbembe's conceptualization of the postcolony as a deathscape is dooming, for it sets up a framework of negative nihilism. The numerous respondents to *On the Postcolony* have argued that Mbembe's framework cannot accommodate transformative political action and futurity for the postcolony. Jeremy Weate (2003) has demonstrated that Mbembe's theoretical investment in the impossibility of resistance in the postcolony forecloses on the many possibilities for sociopolitical agency and transformative action opened up by the convivial, ludic, and baroque practices in the postcolony. Weate argues that Mbembe's privileging of textuality and theoretical dismissal of the postcolonized body, gender, grassroots actions, and everyday life practices, all of which *Karmen Geï* focuses on, stunt his analysis of power and resistance in the postcolony. Following Weate, I argue that Mbembe's postcolony is doomed because Mbembe fails to pick up on the rather strong queer dynamics that his analysis excavates. By foreclosing on queer analysis, Mbembe is able to write the postcolony off. The argument may be made that *On the Postcolony* does not take up the queer as a lifeline because Mbembe is, in Weate's words, a "thinker of death not birth" (2003, 39). As such, Mbembe binds himself to nihilistic frameworks and methodologies that imagine the postcolony as a deathtrap. In contrast, Ramaka envisions a futurescape. Ramaka's enabling approach of the postcolony commands an affirmative reading of death and allows the film to eventually subvert the Mbembe-like denouement of "mutual zombification" that its plot constructs.

If Mbembe's postcolony is characterized and ossified by an economy of death, Ramaka has a deep investment in the potentiality and possibility for newness, in tracking movements toward what Deleuze calls "people to come" (1989, 174), in the Fanonian labor of corrosion against death and toward newness that death performs (Fanon 1961). For queerness is "anticipatory," write Lauren Berlant and Michael Warner (1995, 344), a bearer of "potentiality or concrete possibility for another world," according to José Esteban Muñoz (2009, 1). Karmen's consistent sabotage of spaces in the film is a refusal to be engulfed by the economy of death allegorized by the slave-dungeon-turned-postcolonial-prison from which she successfully escapes. Karmen's refusal to settle, which then unsettles the postcolony, shows the postcolony to be passage and not destination. The death of the commandement (the warden and Corporal Lamine Diop) and the postcolonial subject (Karmen), as a culminating event or outcome of the restlessness and recklessness of Karmen, calls into being futures in which the postcolony is post.

I have just referenced Fanon (1961), whom Mbembe has acknowledged as being his interlocutor in *On the Postcolony*. Due to the pronounced masculinism and heteronormative biases of Fanon, it is counterintuitive to carry his ideas into queer theory, to mobilize him against Mbembe's queer incapacities and for Ramaka's queer and feminist proclivities. Fanon's native is queer, unbeknownst to Fanon, who relates that the settler says that the native is "the corrosive element, destroying all that comes near him ... the deforming element, disfiguring all that has to do with beauty or morality" (1961, 41). Karmen the saboteur and Mbembe's postcolonized subject play (with) the system and short-circuit the constitution of a normative grammar in order to impose spontaneous grammars. Likewise, the Fanonian native resists the regimes of the normal. Death as a denouement of such subversive gestures is, according to Fanon, not failure or an indication of the futility of resistance. Fanonian death is not terminal. A disposal of both the colonizer and the colonized, death is event. Death is an intended denouement of anticolonial struggles because it explodes the economy of death and ushers in newness. Fanon, throughout his chapter on violence in *The Wretched of the Earth* (1961), guides his readers toward the conclusion that "decolonization is quite simply the replacing of a certain species of men by another species of men" (1961, 35). Reading Fanon today, against the backdrop of queer theory, Fanon's injunction to violence, his program of "complete disorder," and "creation of new men" (Fanon 1961, 36), was a call for a queering of the self, an unthinking of received categories and scripts of identities. Decolonization for Fanon was a labor of unraveling and unbecoming—in short, a program of queering. Revisiting Fanon today, especially his writings on anticolonial resistance, we find "fore-echoes" of the Deleuzean "people to come" and the investment of queer theory in futurities. The inability of Mbembe to follow through with Fanon on resistance, death, and becoming, as well as Mbembe's unsteady theoretical commitment to the Deleuzean framework of *On the Postcolony*, say as much about Mbembe's inability to embrace an anticipatory or promissory orientation—in short, his inability to do/go queer.

Back to *Karmen Geï*. Fanon's assertion of death as the birthing of a new subject enables my affirmative reading of the annihilation of both ruler and ruled in *Karmen Geï*. Karmen is Fanon's (queer) native. The Fanonian intertext is further supported by the alignment, throughout the film, of Karmen the queer feminist saboteur with celebrated Senegalese anticolonial heroines. In placing Karmen in this lineage of historical freedom fighters who have sacrificed their lives for decolonial futures, the film is able to recover Karmen's tactics and ludic acts as resistance where Mbembe fails to recognize agency and resistance. The use of orality in *Karmen Geï* further participates in this recovery of indigenous resistance and foregrounds the anticipatory and promissory denouement of postcolonial resistance. The foremothers of Karmen are immortalized in the praise songs that the chorus sings in the film. These songs drive Karmen throughout the film. When Karmen dies, she is also immortalized in a praise song. The spirit of feminist queerness therefore lives on, orally passed on from generation to generation. In fact, Koumba Kastell, repeatedly identified throughout the film as Karmen's ancestor and whom Karmen herself invokes whenever she confronts the commandement, is the protector of the island of Gorée and a (queer) Senegalese spirit known for seducing away men and women. By drawing on that rich indigenous repertoire of oral narratives, dance, and fluid sexualities, *Karmen Geï* anchors the queer in the postcolonial and brings home Weate's point that Mbembe's focus on "the writerly sphere of academic, juridical and overtly political texts, not on the street or the ghetto or within the practices of everyday life," skews his analysis of the possibility of resistance and agency in the postcolony (2003, 11). In *Karmen Geï* the site of the clandestine bar, owned by Karmen's mother, is a locus of queer feminist resistance and agency. It is in this bar that the chorus first invokes the heroines of anticolonial resistance as Karmen's mother confronts and drives away a pack of policemen. The clandestine bar, the native ground and habitus of Karmen, represents the vernacular loci and enunciations of feminist and queer resistance in the postcolony.

What makes *Karmen Geï* a production of theoretical interest to African feminisms is the film's affirming enunciation of the sexual female body and visionary articulation of the emancipatory potential of female sexuoerotic agency. Of interest is also the ability of the filmmaker to draw theoretical inspiration and epistemological insights from African vernacular expressions of female sexuoerotic agency. The film's exploration of the sociopolitical potentials of female sexuoerotic agency finds validation in the Sexual Pleasure Project initiated in Nigeria by the Centre for Reproductive Health and Rights. According to Dorothy Aken'Ova, who reviewed the project, the aim was to coach women "to negotiate safer sexual relationships, make choices that are right for them, to be assertive and to demand and negotiate for their needs and desires, including for much-tabooed sexual pleasure" (2013, 89). Aken'Ova relates that at the conclusion of the project the participants not only excelled at "negotiating orgasms," but they also felt entitled to rights "not directly related to sexual reproductive health and rights, such as further education, acquisition of literary skills and jobs" (2013, 89).

The evidence from the Sexual Pleasure Project and the insights from *Karmen Geï* prove that much is at stake in the African feminist neglect of the sexual female body. The sexual female body is an essential anchor for the type of militant politics of female sexuality that can set into motion postpatriarchal futures. In hindsight, dismissive arguments such as Paul Zeleza's that sexuality is a scholarly preoccupation for Western-based African scholars who are spared the daily spectacles of poverty and political tyranny in Africa confirm the necessity of a robust African feminist engagement with the sexual female body in order to establish the importance of sexuality.

Letting Go of Specters: New Developments in African Feminist Criticism

Throughout this chapter, I have noted the very tentative African feminist engagement with the sexual female body. But I close this chapter with a second round of literature review that foregrounds the slow emergence of female sexuality as an area of African scholarly concerns. Even more noteworthy is who is writing about African female sexuality and where they are located. The modest peak is being generated not by Western-based African feminist scholars, as Zeleza would have us believe, but instead by scholars working and living on the continent. The South Africa–based journals *Feminist Africa* and *Agenda* are pioneers in the study of African sexualities and the sexual female body in particular. *Agenda* devoted a trilogy to African feminisms and sexuality in 2005, with journal editor Gil Harper explaining in her editorial to volume 63 that the trilogy "sought to ask why pain, suffering and death are often associated with African sexualities and reinstall pleasure, desire and sexuality (and indeed freedom)" (2). Jane Bennett and Charmaine Pereira's coedited *Jacketed Women: Qualitative Research Methodologies on Sexualities and Gender in Africa* (2013) came out of an African continental research seminar titled "Mapping Sexualities." The African Gender Institute at the University of Cape Town organized the seminar. The different chapters of the book attend to African women as sexual beings and speak to the risks of conducting feminist research on a taboo topic. Another coedited volume, *Human Sexuality in Africa: Beyond Reproduction* (2007), edited by Eleanor Maticka-Tyndale, Richmond Tiemoko and Paulina Makinwa-Adebusoye, also originated from a seminar on sexuality and was published by a South African press. The Africa Regional Sexuality Resource Center (ARSRC) in Lagos put together the seminar, as part of its quarterly seminars on sexuality in 2005. The center also has an online magazine entitled *Sexuality in Africa*. The edited volume *Human Sexuality in Africa* is most important for its insistence on the feminist urgency of framing African female sexuality beyond reproduction. The book's adamant disavowal of the absolutist paradigm of female-sexuality-for-reproduction resonates with my earlier critique of the motherhood paradigm in African feminist thought and my argument in favor of sexuoerotic agency. Some passages from the introduction are worth quoting at length for their militant tenor and the discursive space that this militant approach is clearing for future feminist scholarship on the African sexual female body:

> The hegemony of reproduction-oriented sexuality is nothing but the hetero-normative masculine conception of human sexuality. The emphasis on reproduction-oriented sexuality has overshadowed women's own perspective on sexuality. . . . Important to the dissociation of sexuality and reproduction is the identity and lives of female members of society. Conflating sexuality with reproduction simply confuses womanhood with motherhood. The implication of this goes beyond the confusion between the function or role and the person, to compromise women's identities and rights outside of reproductive age. Sexuality beyond reproduction is an important concept in research and in advancing a rights-based approach to sexuality and reproduction. It explicitly recognizes the importance of reproduction in human sexuality, but equally and unambiguously calls for an attention to various forms of sexual expression. (Maticka-Tyndale, Tiemoko, and Makinwa-Adebusoye 2007, 10–11)

Overall *Human Sexuality in Africa* is a great contribution, but most of the chapters in the book fall short both theoretically and conceptually in their explorations of the female sexual body. The chapters limit themselves to describing the various constraints to African women's sexual pleasure but never delve into female sexual pleasure as such.

African Sexualities: A Reader (2011), edited by Sylvia Tamale, is another landmark study. This is a well-conceived and ambitious project, with broad coverage of the continent. But the book veers into what Patricia McFadden (2003) calls "permissible sex talk" and "not owning pleasure." Only part

4 of the 9-part book discusses African sexualities in relation to desire and pleasure. And even here only two essays by Bagnol and Mariano and by Nzegwu examine sexual pleasure. The remaining nine contributions in part 4 are fictional pieces. Part 4 is placed in the middle of the book and sandwiched between permissible approaches to African sexualities such as "Mapping sexual representations and practices of identity" and "Reproduction and rights." As such, the novel approach to sexuality contained in this segment of the book ultimately gets lost. Although not published on the continent, but featuring authors based in Africa, Signe Arnfred's *Re-thinking Sexualities in Africa* (2004), an edited volume, does not foreground female pleasure and sexuoerotic agency. Here again most contributions just describe the lay of the land with regard to studying African sexualities.

The limitations outlined in my overview of all these groundbreaking studies of the African sexual female body show a discursive tentativeness and a lack of theoretical vigor in the exploration of the sexual female body. The pattern in this scholarship consists predominantly in noting the scholarly silences about African women's sexualities, describing the obstacles to conducting research on the topic, and examining the societal obstacles to an affirming female sexuality. It is significant that even though these studies are breaking new grounds, the colonial history of the African female body is a routine preface here. Some of the chapters in Tamale's *African Sexualities*, including the framing chapter by Tamale, "Researching and Theorizing Sexualities in Africa," display sensitivity to colonial discourses. In her chapter, "Representing African Sexualities," Desiree Lewis provides a detailed history of Western representations of African sexualities and explains that writing today about African sexualities "means first exploring how they have been thought about" (2011, 200). A similar prefacing occurs in Arnfred's *Re-thinking Sexualities in Africa*. The first lines of the book announce that rethinking sexualities in Africa entails "thinking beyond the conceptual structure of colonial and even post-colonial European imaginations" of African sexualities (Arnfred 2004, 7). The book is structured accordingly, with the first part, "Under Western Eyes," doing deconstructive work while the two remaining parts,

"Problems of Pleasure and Desire" and "Female Agency," attempt to look at African sexualities on their own terms.

What does it mean that feminist scholars on the continent are taking the lead on discussions of African sexualities and the sexual African female body? I go back to Desiree Lewis's and Signe Arnfred's above-mentioned statements for what they reveal about how different engagements with the specter of Sarah Baartman enable or disable specific approaches to the African female body. That the colonial history of the African female body functions as a preface in Africa-based scholarship tells of an African feminist strand that has opted to live otherwise with the specter of Baartman. By having the specter dwell in the *hors-texte* that the preface represents, the scholars takes note of the past while working to proceed forward in new directions. The specter remains relevant but is decentered and de-troped by its prefatorial placement and function. With the trap of the epistemological guardrail thus circumvented, African-based feminist scholars can start elaborating more emancipatory and creative discourses of the African sexual female body. The difference in the ways African- and Euro-American-based African feminist critics have each repurposed the colonial history of the African female body stems from their respective locations in different racial environments. African feminists based in the West evolve in a context where race is a key organizing principle and degrading narratives of black womanhood prevail. The colonial history of the black African female body, as symbolized by Sarah Baartman, has a very close resonance for black women in the West.

That it is *Karmen Gei*, a film by a male director, that models the potential theoretical breakthroughs of a robust African feminist engagement with the sexual female body speaks to the loose sociocultural regulations around male discourses. Patriarchy polices women's engagements with their sexual bodies and grants men physical and discursive entitlement to the female body. *Petit pagne* (2008), a potentially bold video production by Senegalese female visual artist Rackie Diankha Diallo, is a case in point of the patriarchal sexual politics that further constrain African women's discourses of the female body. Diallo celebrates the bethio, an erotic handmade underskirt that Senegalese women don in the bedroom. The video shows bethio-clad women dancing suggestively while a text explains to the viewer the significance of the bethio. The video is of interest for its unequivocal expression of the female sexual body. But I am also concerned that Diallo's expression of the female sexual body partakes in patriarchal pleasure politics. In the context of everyday life in Senegal, the bethio is a manifestation of vernacular sexuoerotic agency. But as depicted in this specific video, the bethio solely serves to produce the female body as a site of male sexual pleasure. The video consists of six vignettes on the significations, functions, and merits of the bethio. The first two vignettes set up the bethio within a very patriarchal framework of marriage and domesticity. They showcase the merits of the bethio by relating how the erotic undergarment helped a woman avert a potential marital strife. The remaining vignettes feature different bethio designs, and the accompanying text still speaks to male pleasure. In one vignette a man longs for the bethio-clad body of his wife while another vignette has a man affirming that he would rather see a bethio than have a beer. The video features trendy bethio designs whose names further reinforce my concerns with the pleasure politics of the bethio in Diallo's work. Names like "keuyitukeur bi" (I am getting the title of the house) and "thiabi auto bi" (I am getting keys to a car) do not speak of female pleasure. Neither do names like "beggu sucaar" (sugar) and "saf sap" (hot spice), which construct the female body as a site of male pleasure.

    The subdued sexual boldness of Diallo's video meshes with the tentative handling of sexual pleasure in the emerging body of African feminist scholarship on the sexual female body. These gender-conforming enunciations of sexual pleasure segue into my examination in the next chapter of whether fiction offers African women writers more leeway to explore the sexual female body.

3
Spectral Female Sexualities

THE POLITICS OF SEXUAL PLEASURE IN WOMEN'S LITERATURES

Rackie Diankha Diallo's (2008) gender conformist pleasure politics evoked in the previous chapter are on par with Nigerian writer Chimamanda Adichie's disconcerting assessment of the sex scenes in *The Joys of Motherhood* (1979) by Nigerian writer Buchi Emecheta. Adichie has declared in an interview that Emecheta's novel, "which is often talked about as a feminist and political text, actually is a fantastic love story and has a very good sex scene, which I quite like" (quoted in K. Jones 2014). However, the scene in question has very fraught sexual politics because the depicted sexual encounter involves marital rape and sexual punishment. An accident leaves Agbadi weak and unable to be intimate with his wife, Ona. Ona resorts to taunting him, probably in an effort to shake him up and rescue him from self-pity. Feeling emasculated, Agbadi forces himself onto his wife, stopping only when she moans until she wakes up the whole compound:

> He knew he had reduced her to longing and craving for him. He knew he had won. He wanted her completely humiliated in her burning desire. . . . Grunting like an excited animal with a helpless prey, he left her abruptly, still unsatiated, and rolled painfully to the other side of the goatskin. Having hurt her on purpose for the benefit of his people sleeping in the courtyard, he had had his satisfaction. She hated him in that moment. "All this show just for your people, Agbadi?" she whispered. Unable to help herself, she began to cry quietly. (1979, 20–21)

While Emecheta has Ona experience some sexual pleasure in this scene, I am concerned that the writer conforms to a patriarchal economy of pleasure. The husband authorizes, provides, and regulates female sexual pleasure. Ona has no sexual agency in this encounter. Her sexual body only exists in as far as it is summoned by the structures of patriarchy. This act of summoning the sexual female body, akin to a Derridean gesture of summoning the specter into and for the self-serving purposes of the living present, spells the spectrality of the sexual female body in this setting. Emecheta's novel conforms to a representational economy of the female body that spectralizes the sexual female body through conditional representability, if not through nonrepresentability. Still, this sex scene in *The Joys of Motherhood* remains bold in the context of African women's writings. If anything, Adichie's enthused response to this scene more than three decades later alerts us to the sparse and tentative presence of sexual pleasure in African women's literatures.

For the purposes of this chapter I have culled literary works that foreground the sexual female body. My analysis of the different texts reveals an intergenerational narrative gesture of spectralizing the sexual female body as well as incisive but often elusive politics of sexual pleasure, including in texts where the sexual female body is at its boldest. The chapter starts by mapping the timid expressions of the sexual female body and sexual pleasure in African women's writings and proceeds to pinpoint more assertive expressions in novels by Ken Bugul, Calixthe Beyala, Yvonne Vera, Léonora Miano, Chimamanda Adichie, Lola Shoneyan, and Sefi Atta. I then turn to more revolutionary and nonnormative expressions of the sexual female body by novelists Calixthe Beyala, Frieda Ekotto, and photographer Zanele Muholi.

Buchi Emecheta, Ama Ata Aidoo

My reservations with her reading of the sex scene in *The Joys of Motherhood* notwithstanding, Adichie is right to single out the scene for its audacious departure from the faint representations of sex in African women's literatures. One is hard pressed to find a sex scene comparable to Emecheta's among her contemporaries in African women's writings. With too few exceptions, the succeeding waves of writers have also been timid in their exploration of female sexuality. Aside from *The Joys Motherhood*, Emecheta does not engage the sexual female body in her novels. Her writing is otherwise chaste, and her female characters don't enjoy sex. In the autobiographical texts of Emecheta, sex is an inconvenience and burden for the female protagonist. Among the generational peers of Emecheta, which include Mariama Bâ, Ama Ata Aidoo, Flora Nwapa, Aminata Sow Fall, and Grace Ogot, only Ghanaian writer Ama Ata Aidoo comes close to pushing the envelope.

In her novel *Changes* (1991) Aidoo embarks Esi, her restless female protagonist, on a quest for emotional and sexual intimacy. Like the theme of Rackie Diankha Diallo's video, the storyline of *Changes* offers a perfect canvas to express the sexual female body and delve into sexual pleasure. But Aidoo's hesitation to "go there" stalls *Changes*' latent narrative of female sexual pleasure and sets up Esi for failure. Esi's failure in her quest for sexual self-actualization is a narrative consequence of the nonrepresentability of the sexual female body in the postcolonial African economy of representation of the female body. Such nonrepresentability dooms the sexual female body to spectrality or, as in the case of *Changes* and *The Joys of Motherhood*, a conditioned representability that furthers the spectrality of the sexual female body. Following suit from *The Joys of Motherhood*, the most explicit sex scene in *Changes* is an episode of marital rape. Once Esi leaves her husband for a more sexually fulfilling partner, Aidoo's narrative falls flat and almost reverts to slut-shaming Esi for her choices. Aidoo sets up false tensions between motherhood and sexual fulfillment in such a way that the narrative and also the reader ultimately chastise a now unsympathetic Esi for her irresponsibility, immaturity, selfishness, and self-absorption. The construction of Esi as a bad mother who falters in her maternal obligations subsequently frames sexual pleasure as the villain in the story and the cause of Esi's demise.

The inability of Aidoo to carry through with her narrative of sexual fulfillment is typical of the conflicted representational politics of many

African women's texts that venture into sexuality. Going back to *The Joys of Motherhood*, the novel also has a nonconformist and tentatively positive subnarrative of sexual fulfillment. Adaku, the assertive and independent co-wife of the self-sacrificing protagonist Nnu Ego, successfully reconciles motherhood and sexual fulfillment where Aidoo could not be brought to make Esi succeed. Obioma Nnaemeka (1994) reads Adaku as a positive countermodel to Nnu Ego's depersonalizing over-investment in motherhood and domesticity. However, Nnaemeka argues, Emecheta sidelines Adaku's storyline in favor of the story of self-sacrificing mother Nnu Ego. I read this act of sidelining Adaku as a narrative gesture of spectralizing the sexual female body. Emecheta writes off Adaku from the narrative as soon as the latter leaves her husband to seek fulfillment outside of the bonds of marriage. The narrative decision of the novelist reflects what Nnaemeka terms the "nervous conditions" of African women writers who constantly negotiate cultural discourses of proper African womanhood and apprehend the chastising gaze of their African (male) readers. Emecheta, like Aidoo, cannot have the back of her nonconformist character although she tentatively sides with the choices of Adaku. After all, as Nnaemeka argues, it is revealing that Nnu Ego dies a lonely death and Adaku thrives as a successful trader. I agree with Nnaemeka that Emecheta does not endorse self-sacrificing and hard-working Nnu Ego as a model, but I disagree that she positions Adaku as a model. Emecheta's inability to affirm Adaku as a model transpires in the way she first introduces Adaku to the reader as a conniving and victimizing co-wife who is after the semblance of well-being that Nnu Ego is securing for her household. Adaku cannot muster the sympathy of the reader in these circumstances. It is telling of the ambivalence of Emecheta toward Adaku's sexual assertiveness that the writer would first cite the conniving character of Adaku on her sexuality. A precarious economic situation forces the co-wives and their husband Nnaife into a one-room accommodation. The co-wives take turns sleeping on the marital bed with their husband. The first night Adaku takes her turn on the marital bed, which is the very day she joins the household, she delivers a most memorable and character-defining performance that seals the reader's response to her persona for the rest of the novel:

> She [Nnu Ego] tried to block her ears, yet could still hear Adaku's exaggerated carrying on. Nnu Ego tossed in agony and anger all night, going through in her imagination what was taking place behind the curtained bed. Not that she has to do much imagining, because even when she tried to ignore what was going on, Adaku would not let her. She giggled, she squeaked, she cried and she laughed in turn, until Nnu Ego was quite convinced that it was all for her benefit. At one point Nnu Ego sat bolt upright looking at the shadows of Nnaife and Adaku. No, she did not have to imagine what was going on; Adaku made sure she knew. (1979, 124)

The writing of Adaku's insidiousness into her sexuality frames female sexual pleasure as an indicator of depravity and shows Emecheta's conflicted characterization of her sexually liberated character. As in Aidoo's *Changes*, *The Joys of Motherhood* expresses and then immediately holds in check the sexual female body. This conditioned representability of the sexual female body, whereby the sexual female body is summoned to uphold the construction of a desexualized and virtuous African womanhood, becomes an act of exorcising the specter of the sexual female body by virtue of being a negative summon of the specter. For, as Derrida reminds us, acts of conjuring specters are also acts of summoning specters in order to exorcise them (1994, 58). In both novels, the narrative strategies of the authors rewrite the enunciated sexual female body as a hauntology that threatens the ontologies of desexualized "mothernormativity" and "marriagenormativity" (Tamale 2006, 40).

Ken Bugul, Calixthe Beyala, Yvonne Vera

The pattern of tiptoeing around and spectralizing the sexual female body carries on with the subsequent wave of African women writers. However, Ken Bugul from Senegal, Calixthe Beyala from Cameroon, and Yvonne Vera from Zimbabwe stand out for their explicit engagements of the female sexual body and female sexual pleasure. Although her texts are much less graphic than Calixthe Beyala's, Ken Bugul is particularly bold because her writings are autobiographical. In her autobiographical trilogy, which recounts her turbulent journey from Senegal to Europe and back to Senegal in quest of identity, Bugul lets her readers in on her sex life. In affirming Bugul as a sexual subject, her autobiography stands in stark contrast with the autobiographies of African women that generally focus on their lives as mothers and political figures. The suggestion of her publisher that she publish under a pen name speaks to the boldness and nonconformity of her autobiographical disclosures. The pen name also turns the author into a ghostwriter of her own autobiography.

In *Le baobab fou* (1982), the first volume, Bugul comes forth about her sexual promiscuities in Belgium, sharing such information as her out-of-wedlock pregnancy and abortion, her ménage à trois with two gay men, and her prostitution stints. Sex for Bugul in *Le baobab fou* is not about sexual pleasure. Sex serves to sort out her identity and navigate her locations as a painfully dislocated colonized subject, a young Muslim woman, and a black African woman in Europe. The next two volumes, *Cendres et braises* (1994) and *Riwan ou le chemin de sable* (1999), relate her homecoming, following her disillusion with Europe. Bugul recounts her polygamous marriage to a Muslim religious leader who keeps a harem-like household of secluded women. She becomes his twenty-ninth wife, and the two volumes are invested in persuading the reader and probably Bugul herself of the judiciousness of her choice. Bugul frames her polygamous marriage as evidence of her recovery from colonial alienation (Coly 2010, 29–30). How does this new ideological location and self-positioning of the author frame her approach to the female sexual body in the last two volumes? For certain, the two volumes are very bent on reversing and even overwriting the life of sexual libertinage that the author disclosed in *Le baobab fou*.

Riwan ou le chemin de sable is of particular interest because the volume delves in depth into Ken Bugul's relationship with her polygamous husband and addresses the sexual lives of her co-wives. While the previous two volumes engage the sexual female body through the author's sexual promiscuities, *Riwan ou le chemin de sable* addresses female sexual pleasure. This last volume of the autobiographical trilogy opposes the sexual pleasure made possible by Bugul's Senegalese culture to the sexual libertinage without sexual pleasure that the West makes available. Images of female sexual pleasure pepper the volume to ingrain female sexual pleasure and eroticism in the Senegalese cultural fabric. Bugul upholds a narrative of African female sexual pleasure that explicitly refutes Western feminists' colonialist obliviousness to the pleasured African female body and pronounced attention to the violated, mutilated and famished African female body. In this sense, while Bugul partakes in the postcolonial African rhetorical deployment of the female body to write back to colonial discourses, her project is engaging another corpus of colonial discourses of the African female body. As a result her texts foreground the sexual female body in unique ways. Many of the sexual references in *Riwan ou le chemin de sable* work to establish indigenous Senegalese cultural anchors for female sexual pleasure. Bugul describes the Senegalese cultural ritual of the xaxar, where a new bride flaunts her sexual savoir faire by performing an erotic and very sexually suggestive dance before an audience of women (1999, 202). The bethio, an underskirt worn by Senegalese women, is a recurrent motif of sexuoerotic agency in Bugul's narrative. The author explains that the bethio, whose erotic designs can be mandated by the customer or elaborated by the creator herself, fosters sexuoerotic development and agency. She shouts out that the bethio is testimony to Senegalese women's "Liberté d'expression! Tout un génie de créativité qui se développait avec ce pagne de la sensualité, du désir, de la provocation, de l'amour, de la jouissance!" (1999, 197) (Freedom of expression! This cloth of sensuality, desire, provocation, love, and sexual pleasure bore witness to an immense creativity).[1] The courtyard where the secluded co-wives hang out during the day brims with sexual and erotic energy. When describing daily life in the courtyard, Bugul regularly mentions the bethios that the wives are designing for themselves and other customers. The courtyard also hosts impromptu erotic women's dances, to the delight of the cloistered wives.

However, the harem-like situation at the center of the volume mars Bugul's affirmations of sexual pleasure. While some of the wives, including Bugul, revel in their sexual intimacy with their husband, most of the wives are sexually deprived. The husband progressively abandons older wives for younger ones. The secluded wives may engage in erotic dances in the courtyard, dance themselves into collective orgasm at night, or exert freedom of sexual expression as designers of erotic lingerie, but they clearly hold the short end of the stick in their sexual relationship with their husband. In fact, Bugul's attempt to sexually affirm the wives through their ability to be in tune with their sexual body and self-procure sexual gratification unwittingly exposes their sexual neglect by their husband. This situation of sexual deprivation pushes Rama, one the wives, to commit adultery and flee back to her parents' home. But upon her arrival, the family home mysteriously catches fire and decimates Rama and her family.

How does the author reconcile her promotion of Senegalese cultures of female sexual pleasure and her own complicity, through marriage, with this system of blatant sexual deprivation of women? She does not. And she cannot, for as I have argued in *The Pull of Postcolonial Nationhood* (2010), this polygamous marriage was the last lifeline of Ken Bugul. Bugul's imperative homecoming after her near-death experience in Europe dictates her submission to the gender ideologies of the postcolonial nation. The story of Rama's demise following her adultery, a quest for sexual satisfaction, constitutes a cautionary tale of women's sexual rebellion (Coly 2010, 25–30). The inclusion of the story of Rama sets up a boundary around the sexual female body enunciated in the text. By punishing the sexually deprived Rama for seeking sexual satisfaction outside of the marital compound, the narrative strives to sanitize and make amends for its enunciation of the sexual female body.

Avery Gordon explains that abusive systems of power control by haunting, meaning through the circulation of fear (1997, xvi). The story of Rama's ill-fated attempt at sexual self-actualization evinces the apprehensions embedded in Bugul's narrative project of enunciating the sexual female body. The fate of Rama magnifies the controlling hegemonic narrative that haunts and polices the narrative project of Bugul. In a sense, Rama represents the former self of Bugul, as described in the first two volumes of her autobiography. The disclosures of Bugul about her sexual life in the first volume lead her publisher to suggest that she adopt a pen name. Bugul chose the pen name Ken Bugul, which means "nobody wants this/him/her" in the Wolof language of Senegal, to signify her alienation from Senegal and her condition of social outcast. Like Rama, Bugul strayed away and faced a predicament of social death. The negative reception of the first volume of her autobiography in Senegal spelled both her social doom and her premature death as a budding writer. In the Wolof society, the name Ken Bugul is given to a child born to a woman whose previous children did not survive their first years. The name, which is meant to conjure away that fate, marks the child as a spectral being, hovering between the worlds of the living and the dead. By adopting that name, Ken Bugul signifies her own spectral status, a result of her social death. As a social outcast, Bugul is made to dwell in the spectral zone of invisible visibility. As a hauntology that threatens the ontology of normative Senegalese womanhood, she is subject to vigilant exorcism. The two subsequent volumes of her autobiography are attempts to remove herself from spectrality by conforming to the norms of her society. In these two texts, the autobiographical subject accordingly bears the real name of the author.

As a result of her endeavor to be reabsorbed into society, the pleasure politics of Bugul's narrative are inevitably convoluted and steeped in patriarchal sexual politics. When Bugul revels in her husband's generous lovemaking, she upholds the polygamous patriarch as the regulator and agent of female sexual pleasure. Sexual pleasure becomes a male gift to the female body, and her generous lover is no less than a benevolent patriarch:

> C'était la première fois qu'un homme m'avait fait l'amour avec tant de tendresse. Moi qui croyait que c'était les autres qui s'y connaissaient. Tout ce que j'avais connu, c'était l'amour discuté, expliqué, analysé, planifié. . . . La sensation de mon corps et de mon plaisir du moment me semblait une première. Jamais avant je n'avais senti

autant de douceur chez un homme. Et combien de fois j'avais joué au jeu de la jouissance, comme des milliers de femmes, qui, comme moi, jouaient aux femmes émancipées, aux femmes modernes. (1999, 165)

(It was the first time a man had made love to me so tenderly. I, who used to believe that only the others excelled at lovemaking. All I had known until now was a form of lovemaking that was subject to discussion, explanation, analysis and planning. . . . The sensation of my body and the pleasure I was discovering now were new experiences. I had never experienced so much tenderness with a man. Yet how many times had I played the game of orgasm, like thousands of women who, like me, played the role of the emancipated and modern woman.)

The sexual benevolence of the African husband and the sexual plenitude of the African wife clearly prop the Manichean narrative of Africa and the West that structures *Riwan ou le chemin de sable*. We are then back to the postcolonial deployment of the female body as a rhetorical trope against colonial and neocolonial discourses. Because Bugul's writing of the female body is haunted by another corpus of colonial discourses of the African female body, those of the sexually passive hence non-emancipated African female body, her narratives uphold the sexual female body in ways that run counter to the dominant postcolonial protective gesture of "clothing" the African female body. But as shown by her convoluted narrative, Bugul is also haunted by the specter of her dissent from the postcolonial norm. Her text reveals the patriarchal underpinnings of that norm.

The tight embrace of Senegal in the last volume of Bugul's autobiographical trilogy redresses her near fatal drift away from Senegal described in the first two volumes. In *Mes hommes à moi* (2008), a subsequent autobiographical novel, Bugul appears to have transcended her homecoming phase. Her new optic makes for a brutally frank take on the gender politics of sexual pleasure. Bugul relates various relationships throughout her life, including with African men, none of whom have her experience sexual pleasure because, she writes, "Ces hommes-là pensaient que pénétrer une femme avec leur sexe était l'essentiel du rapport sexuel. Le vagin pour moi, je parle pour moi, c'était pour faire les bébés. Le clitoris était pour la jouissance . . . je n'avais plus besoin d'un homme pour jouir" (2008, 174) (Those men thought that sex was limited to sexual penetration. But the vagina, at least for me, served to make babies. The clitoris served to achieve orgasm . . . I no longer needed a man to achieve orgasm). Masturbation becomes a leitmotif in the novel. As the author goes from one sexual partner to the next, she eventually decides not to settle for less than pleasure. She also ascertains that heterosexuality is not the sole source of pleasure and that sexual self-gratification serves her best. Bugul suggests that the heteropatriarchal gender politics that frame her different sexual encounters are incompatible with female sexual pleasure. This approach to female sexual pleasure resonates with Calixthe Beyala's.

Calixthe Beyala shocked the African literary scene with her graphic sex scenes, which include scenes of female sexual pleasure. In her novels Beyala has consistently asserted feminine sexual pleasure as a feminist agenda. Tanga, the protagonist of her second novel, *Tu t'appelleras Tanga* (1988), best expresses this agenda:

> Ainsi l'homme a construit son monde, fabriqué son histoire. Désormais, je saurai que faire de ma géographie. L'homme me reconnaitra à peine nommée, j'irai vers lui, je me hisserai sur un escabeau pour inscrire mon âme dans son désir. Ensuite, je pivoterai sur moi-même, je prendrai le spectacle de mes dépouilles passées, je glisserai vers elles, je soulèverai leur pagne, je frotterai leur clitoris, j'incendierai le plaisir, j'effacerai de ma vie le vol de l'oiseau noir, je lancerai mes jambes vers la frontière, alors seulement, j'accéderai aux zones confisquées du bonheur. (1988, 32–33)

> (That is how man has constructed his world, put together his history. From now on, I'll know what to do with my geography. Man will recognize me though I will hardly have been mentioned. I'll go to him, I'll hoist myself on top of a ladder to inscribe my soul in his desire. Then I'll pivot around myself. I'll take the spectacle of my

past slough, slide towards it, lift up its pagne, rub its clitoris, set fire to pleasure, erase the flight of the black bird from my life, send my legs flying in the direction of the frontier; only then will I have access to the confiscated regions of happiness. [1996b, 20])

In positioning the clitoris as the cornerstone of the new geography that she is convening, Tanga attacks the phallic economy of the postcolony.

Beyala draws on a political approach to sexual pleasure articulated most brilliantly in her first novel, *C'est le soleil qui m'a brûlée* (1987), a top feminist political novel and her best novel to date. In this novel Beyala conjoins sexual pleasure with political agency and postcolonial governmentality in a way that writes back to the phallic economy of Mbembe's postcolony analyzed in the previous chapter. Beyala achieves this conjunction by having the sexual awakening and agency of Ateba, her young female protagonist, shadow her political development (Coly 2010, 42–55). In *C'est le soleil qui m'a brûlée*, Beyala consistently pinpoints women's subordination to male sexual pleasure and the resulting spectralization of the sexual female body. She then correlates the heteropatriarchal structuring of sex to the subaltern position of women in the postcolonial nation. For Beyala, sex is a political structure. Giving or receiving sexual pleasure is a correlate and outcome of one's location in the power structure. Sexual pleasure is therefore political. Throughout the novel, scenes of heterosex reflect the subaltern positioning of women. Ateba is repeatedly forced down on her knees by her male sexual partners, with one such partner decreeing after he has climaxed in her mouth that "Dieu a sculpté la femme à genoux aux pieds de l'homme" (1987, 151) ("God has sculpted woman on her knees at the feet of man" [1996a, 118]). Rangira Béatrice Gallimore has argued that the pattern of men stuffing their genitalia in Ateba's mouth denotes the patriarchal silencing and disenfranchisement of women (1997, 93). But through masturbation, Ateba is also able to appropriate sexual pleasure for herself, take control of her sexual pleasure, and heal from her sexual abuses. For Ateba, who has utopian visions of a matriarchal polis, self-pleasuring is about the dispensability of men, the disposability of the phallus, and the eventual dissolution of the phallic order. She refuses to "joui[r] de l'homme, de son image ou de ses gestes, de son désir retroussé, imbu d'ingéniosité et de bêtise ou de son besoin de se fabriquer un double" (1987, 22) ("come with a man, [enjoy] his image or his gestures, his curled up desire, imbued with ingenuity and foolishness or with the need to replicate himself" [1996a, 130]).

It is the lesbian yearnings of Ateba that confirm that her sexuality articulates a political dissent. Ateba nurtures a political project that reimagines the African postcolony as a lesbian continuum. This new imaginary culminates in Ateba's Fanonian act of revolutionary violence against her male lover at the end of the novel (Coly 2010, 52–54). After her lover forces her into oral sex, Ateba spits out his sperm at his feet and brings him down with a heavy copper ashtray:

> Elle s'est accroupie, a saisi la tête de l'homme et la cogne a deux mains sur le dallage. Le sang jaillit, éclabousse, souille, elle frappe, elle rythme ses coups, elle scande "Irène, Irène" et, comme elle perçoit encore la vie sous ses mains, elle ramasse un canif, et, envahie de joie, elle se met à frapper, à frapper de toutes ses forces. Enfin le dernier spasme. Ses reins cèdent, la pisse innonde le cadavre sous elle. Les yeux hagards, le souffle court, elle s'affale sur lui. (1987, 152)
>
> (She has crouched down, grabbed the man's head and with two hands she is beating it against the stone floor. The blood gushes out, splatters, sullies. She strikes, she gives a beat to her blows, scanning "Irene, Irene" and as she still notices signs of life under her hands, she picks up a knife and, overcome with joy, she begins to strike with all her might. At last the final spasm. Her kidneys give way, piss floods the corpse beneath her. With haggard eyes, she slumps on top of him, out of breath. (1996a, 118–19)]

The orgasmic subtext of this moment, described by the narrator as an apocalypse, evokes Fanon's (1961) envisioned outcome of the revolt of the colonized and firmly ties the sexual and the political together.

But the narrative indecision of the novel revokes the boldly enunciated sexual female body. In *The Pull of Postcolonial Nationhood* I have argued that Beyala backpedals on her assertion of feminine sexual pleasure through various forms of narrative ambiguity (Coly 2010, 54–55). The suggested insanity of Ateba, further reinforced by the hallucinatory ending of the novel, and her equally suggested "unafrican" ways throughout the novel discredit Ateba as a political revolutionary. The suggested cultural and mental alienation of Ateba is a narrative gesture that resignifies Ateba as a social outcast, hence a spectral nonbeing. This subtext muddles Beyala's standpoint on the politics of sexual pleasure that she has her character pursue. Similarly, in *Tu t'appelleras Tanga*, the premature death of Tanga possibly signifies the unsustainability and political naïveté of a politics of sexual pleasure. The premature death of Tanga conceptually parallels Mam's resigned homecoming to her unsatisfying husband after she runs away with her white lover in *Maman a un amant* (Beyala 1993). Beyala seems to have anticipated the critiques of some of her readership if she were to have Mam trade her marriage for her sexual well-being. Alpha Noël Malonga (2006) has congratulated Beyala for bringing Mam back to a marital home that Mam herself describes as a "port empuanti" (1993, 20) (stinking harbor). By cutting short the sexual self-actualizations of her female protagonists, Beyala revokes the enunciated sexual female body to reinscribe it in a spectral economy.

Yet Beyala's safe gesture of spectralizing the sexual female body is unlike Emecheta's, Aidoo's, and Bugul's narratives. Beyala does not write off the sexual female body. Like the specter of Marx in Derrida, the spectral sexual female bodies of Beyala leave legacies in the living present and for the future. Ateba, more so than Tanga, unravels the phallic sociopolitical order of the national community. Even Mam, who safely returns home, has planted the seeds for a sexual revolution and new gender relations in the patriarchal immigrant community of Belleville.

Yvonne Vera and Calixthe Beyala have hardly been brought together, probably because the perceived pornographic character of Beyala's writings has foreclosed comparisons with the less sexually graphic and more explicitly political texts of Vera. Critics have often missed the political tenor of the novels of Beyala, including her astute use of the sexual female body to engage with postcolonial governance and governmentalities. Female sexuality in the novels of Vera similarly takes aim at phallic governance and sabotages governmentality.

The novels of Yvonne Vera center the sexual subjectivity of her female protagonists. Vera structures her narratives around the sexual drives of her protagonists, with the yearnings of the women carrying the plot. In *Without a Name* (1994) Mazvita leaves the constrictions of her small town and her loving fiancé and sets herself on a journey toward Harare, guided by a "strong desire for her liberty" (1994, 34). When Mazvita decides that it "suited her to move forward" because she "did not care for certainties" (34), she reckons the sexuoerotic agency embedded in "her particular version of freedom" (49). For Mazvita "had loved the land. . . . She gathered from it her freedom which it delivered to her wholly and specially. If it yielded crop, then it could also free her, like the plants which grew upon it and let off their own blooms, their own scents, their own colour, while anchored on the land. She felt free like a seed released from one such plant. She could grow anywhere. Mazvita felt buoyant. Her relationship to the land involved such buoyant freedoms. She had the potential to begin again. Hope mingled with desire" (34). The desire for elsewhereness that agitates Mazvita frees the imaginary and pushes the boundaries for what the female body can do, experience, and attain. The same desire for elsewhereness guides the career ambitions of Phephelaphi in *Butterfly Burning* (2000). As "a woman who chose her own destination" (2000, 54), Phephelaphi is determined to be part of the first generation of black nurse trainees in Zimbabwe. But for Phephelaphi, "it's not being a nurse which matters, but the movement forward—the entrance into something new and untried" (60).

Judith Butler's apt reformulation of Merleau-Ponty's (1962) phenomenology of the body as a "set of possibilities to be continuously realized" (1990, 272) helps bridge Merleau-Ponty and Derrida. If Derrida's specter encodes possibilities that we actualize when we resist the impulse to exorcise the specter, Merleau-Ponty enjoins us to resist the spectralization of the body provoked by the Cartesian mind/body dichotomy. Merleau-Ponty also lends support to the resistance of Vera's protagonists against the spectralization of the sexual female body. The sexually inflected grammar of longing, yearning, and craving that coheres Mazvita and Phephelaphi's desired elsewhere enjoins them to actualize their body possibilities. Phephelaphi comes to an understanding that "she had to find what she could here, from within her own land, from her body" (2000, 70), and Mazvita is able to dislodge her lived experience of rape from her body as she "thought of him not from inside her, but from outside. He had never been inside her. She connected him only to the land. It was the land that had come towards her. He had grown from the land" (1994, 31). In Merleau-Ponty's theory of bodily intentionality the body perceives, thinks, and knows. As a result the body is not subject to the whims and dictates of the consciousness. Instead the consciousness reflects the intentionality of the body. Thus, when Vera's protagonists come to such an understanding of their body, tap into the resources of their body, and follow the leads of their body, they are able to claim custody of their sexuality. That Mazvita is able to pursue a fulfilling sexual life in the aftermath of her rape is a function of her body intentionality, meaning that "because my body can shut itself off from the world, it is also what opens me out upon the world and places me in a situation there. The momentum of existence towards others, towards the future, towards the world can be restored as the river unfreezes" (Merleau-Ponty 1962, 164–65). The trust that Mazvita and Phephelaphi place in their body to know what to do and how to do it lays the background for their sexual and erotic lives.

Vera significantly sets her novels amid Zimbabwe's fight for independence from Great Britain. *Without a Name* is set in 1977, at the peak of the second guerilla war against white rule. *Butterfly Burning* takes place between 1946 and 1948, during the general strike that mobilized African workers and nationalists against the Rhodesian state. The mirror effect between the fight for national sovereignty and the female protagonists' quest for sexual self-governance confers a political tenor to the latter quest.

The narration of the country's fight for independence from the perspective of female protagonists has political significance and clears space for the articulation of the political visions of women. This enunciating position establishes Mazvita and Phephelaphi as political visionaries. The political perspicacity of the protagonists often surfaces in their perspectives on their social and political environments. Mazvita displays political lucidity when it comes to the agendas of anticolonial freedom fighters, especially their trustworthiness to deliver the promises of postcolonial independence to the population. Her equal lucidity about the precarious lives and fates of black sharecroppers spurs her decision to leave. Her fiancé decides to stay put out of loyalty to the land, to which she contends that they "are servants paid poorly for our labours. We cannot decide which crop to grow, or when to grow it. We do not pray for the success of our crop because it is no longer our crop. We cannot pray for another's crop. There are no rituals of harvest, of planting the crop into the ground. We labour because it is our task to labour. We do not own the land. . . . We live in fear because even those who fight in our name threaten our lives" (Vera 1994, 33). Mazvita's retort amends the notion of body intentionality from the standpoint of the disempowered. Body intentionality, as seductively laid out by Merleau-Ponty, presupposes an individual in control of their body circumstances. For the enslaved body or any individual with no right to their body and whose body movements are subject to the commands of a master, body intentionality is nil. However, the foreclosure of body intentionality does not preclude such a desire and ambition from the body. It is this ambition, ultimately a sexually inflected vision for how the body can be and what the body can do, that drives the protagonists of Vera. I hang on to the notion of ambition in order to argue that the sexually inflected desires that animate both Mazvita and Phephelaphi articulate their political ambitions for the body. By being in tune with their spectralized desiring bodies, the two protagonists live out Derrida's injunction to welcome and learn to live with the specter.

Many analyses of the novels have successfully teased out the sexual drive for modernity at the core of the journeys of the two protagonists

(Palmer 2006; Gagiano 2009). But Vera's protagonists don't subscribe to a naive fascination with modernity. Annie Gagiano is correct that the protagonists are astute about the downsides of modernity, as revealed in the eyes they set on the city and its downtrodden modernity-aspiring bodies (2009, 46–47). It is precisely their belief in modernity, combined with their awareness of the pitfalls of modernity, that make them visionaries. The female protagonists of Vera are still able to envision modernity as an opportunity. Gagiano also reads the brazen spirit of the female characters in *Butterfly Burning* along similar lines. She argues that the female characters' "freer, more challenging political thoughts," in comparison to their male counterparts who hold on oppressively to their experience of colonial modernity as "humiliation," "displacement and exclusion," allow the women to confront and appropriate an otherwise destructive colonial modernity (2009, 47, 44). The decision of the female protagonists to engage the spectralized sexual body accounts for the mental liberation described by Gagiano. Embedded in Mazvita's and Phephelaphi's desire for modernity is a resolve to retool colonial modernity to suit their designs and accommodate their body intentionality. As I previously indicated, Phephelaphi's resolve to be one of the first black nurses is not about being a nurse. In aspiring to a modern profession traditionally reserved for whites, Phephelaphi resists the way "colonial modernity simultaneously uses, incorporates and excludes" (Gagiano 2009, 44–45) black bodies. Phephelaphi will not be exiled from modernity, hence from her desiring body, especially when the labor of black bodies made modernity possible. She stakes a claim to modernity and consequently to body intentionality because she is a producer of and participant in modernity. So does Mazvita, when she becomes resolute to "influence and change definitions of her own reality, adjust boundaries to her vision, banish limits to her progress" (Vera 1994, 34). Progress here means the ability to actualize the intentionality of the body.

Modernity, as understood by Phephelaphi and Mazvita, but not by the male characters of the two novels, is not Westernization. Rather, modernity is openness, a location from which one is able to engage with multiple possibilities. This conception of modernity takes us back to Merleau-Ponty's notion of body intentionality as openness to the world. Indeed the intentionality of the body posits that modernity, as a way of inhabiting the world, is always-already encoded in the body. In fact, modernity has a sexual texture and aura in the two novels. If the intentional body sets the background for sexuality, the sexual body subsequently sets the background for modernity. Sexual self-governance in the two novels rehearses Vera's political and probably utopian vision of a post-nativist and nonheteronormative postcolonial nation. Moving forward, Mazvita and Phephelaphi break away from nativist and Manichean discourses of tradition versus modernity that characterized many anticolonial nationalist movements. The movements of the two protagonists to the city and toward modernity contest the colonial political ideologies inscribed in the ideological architecture of modernity. Their mobility also challenges gendered and racial divisions of space that assign black women to rural spaces.

Mazvita and Phephelaphi are best approached as political saboteurs. The sexual and erotic underpinnings of their sabotaging activities come full force in their endeavors to unravel the heteropatriarchal nationalist discourses at the core of the political and ideological foundations of the future postcolonial nation. Vera props up sexual self-governance by writing political sabotage into sexuoerotic agency. Some of the sex scenes involving Mazvita are such occasions where Vera uninhibitedly claims sexual pleasure and agency for her protagonist in a way that departs from heteropatriarchal scripts of gender and sexuality. Two passages are of note and warrant extensive quotation:

> They had spoken, among the mushrooms. The mushrooms stood meek beneath the decaying log that was partly buried in the ground, and she had bent forward and touched them fearfully, touched their floating beauty for they seemed ready to break, seemed ready to break if they were touched. . . . Mazvita had moved from the brightness to the shadow and the shadow was so sudden and heavy like water thrown over her arms, over her whole waiting body that she shiv-

Spectral Female Sexualities 105

ered at the water that fell from the tree not in drops, but in a sudden spilling, like the mushrooms . . . The large tree glistened with wide thickly veined leaves. . . . The trunk stood firm and straight, with a smooth grey surface. The bark was wound in stiff tightening circles spiraling to the base, disappearing in a mound of weaving roots that swirled angrily from the ground. Within the roots, which formed small channels and basins, was held some water. . . . Branches grew outward, flattened, spread and created a broad dark circle, a wide shelter. . . . the shadow cleansed her. . . . She moved eagerly towards the log. . . . she reached her thumb and forefinger ever so delicately, and held the soft cushiony head, held it so gently, feeling already the grooved underneath so tender and the surface above so smooth that her finger slid over the head past the grooves and met a thin polished stem, soft, then she held that stem tight but gentle, pulled at it tight, but gentle. The ground was soft and yielding. There was nothing like pulling that mushroom. It accepted her gentle hand, followed her in a long slow quiver and the stem grew out of the ground into her palm. White. The neck was smooth and waiting and soft. She felt the softness linger between her fingers, slippery, fragile. (1994, 5–6)

Mazvita desires the landscape, and she also has the landscape quench her sexual desire and provide pleasure for her, on her own terms. Felicity Palmer has singled out this scene for its "eroticization of the landscape" and the way Vera subversively "genders the landscape as male under a female desiring gaze" (2006, 31). But I slightly disagree with Palmer's reading of the landscape as exclusively male. In her description of the landscape Vera blurs feminine and masculine imagery. As experienced by Mazvita, the landscape synthesizes normative feminine and masculine characteristics into a queer assemblage. The stiffly erect tree has basin-like roots filled with water and the mushroom evokes a "delicate phallus" (Palmer 2006, 31) but also a clitoris. That Mazvita derives pleasure from the sexually fluid landscape multiplies her sexual subject positions in a way that lends support to Elleke Boehmer's (2003) seminal queer reading of the novels of Vera. There is no penetration in this scene. There is no penetrator and penetratee in the encounter between Mazvita and the landscape. Instead, the language of embrace, as in the generous shelter offered by the branches, the cleansing shadow, and the yielding ground, articulates a feminist and equalitarian politics of pleasure. Vera reiterates this equalitarian approach in the sex scene between Phephelaphi and Fumbatha in *Butterfly Burning*, with the narrator noting that the lovers "yielded to each other" (2000, 48).

In *Without a Name* the flowing, almost liquid syntax of Vera, as she describes Mazvita's encounter with the nonnormative landscape, conveys an unconstrained, self-indulging, and emancipatory pleasure. This pleasure is in tension with the gendered sexual norms of heteropatriarchal nationalism. Vera significantly starts the scene with an apparent topos of male sexual dominance: "they had spoken among the mushrooms" (1994, 5). This opening, coupled with the brevity of the sentence, presets the interaction between Mazvita and the landscape in a phallocentric frame. But the subsequent lines, buttressed by the flowing sentences, overturn that inaugural topos of heteropatriarchal nationalism. The language of agency in the passage, when Mazvita initiates her interactions with the landscape (she bends forward, touches, moves eagerly, pulls), foreshadows and sets into place the agency she commands in her relation with her fiancé. The latter is introduced amid Mazvita's interaction with the landscape, and the sexual interaction of the two lovers is patterned after the former interaction: "Mazvita pulled Nyendezi down beneath the rocks which had been warmed by the sun, and felt the warmth rise over her naked back. She held him in a succumbing gasp, then folded his head over her chest. She felt the hardened skin of his knee over her pelvis, felt it scratch briefly beneath her navel. The knee pressed down on her, but not painfully. So she passed a tender finger though his hair. He lay between her fingers" (1994, 13). The correspondence between this passage and the first passage describing Mazvita's handling and feeling of the mushrooms is well worked out by Vera to both cast a shadow of ambiguity over the heterosexual moment and preemptively hijack the heteronormative performance from nationalist discourses of gender and sexuality. Building on my reading of Mazvita's queer interaction with the landscape, the sexual encounter between Mazvita and her nationalist lover in the same landscape seeps into the heterosexual moment. Further, as the sex scene unfolds, nature becomes a third participant in the pair's sexual intimacy. The blue of the sky and rays of the sun send "warmth rippling over her knees," he caresses her with a tongue "blue and large like the sky," the ground on which she lays feels "exquisite," then "the blue brimmed and soared around her," and she is "restored in a pleated sky" when she orgasms (1994, 3).

By having the queered landscape supplement the body of the male nationalist lover and provide sexual pleasure for Mazvita, Vera decenters the phallus and saps the core of masculinist nationalism. This decentering of the phallus echoes the dispensability of the phallus in Beyala and Bugul. Vera also infers the constriction of sexual pleasure within the heterosexual framework, and she lets the narrative of the novel suggestively locate the object of Mazvita's longings outside of the normative framework and the heterosexual economy of pleasure. Mazvita is potentially queer. So is Phephelaphi in *Butterfly Burning*. Elleke Boehmer has argued that the "open-ended longings" of Phephelaphi reflect her yearning for "a selving, that is, as other to a man, and other to the submission to desire with a man" (2003, 141). Boehmer's analysis also pertains to Mazvita in *Without a Name*.

More so than *Without a Name*, *Butterfly Burning* explicitly addresses same-sex desire. Phephelaphi is in a loving relationship with her male partner Fumbatha, but she is drawn to Deliwe, the fiercely independent female owner of a clandestine bar. I share Gagiano's and Boehmer's argument that Deliwe models a seductive modern African female personhood and independence for Phephelaphi. Upon meeting Deliwe for the first time, a smitten Phephelaphi infers, from watching Deliwe speak, that the latter possesses "some other part of Deliwe's body that only she could command" (2000, 52). Phephelaphi then "follow[s] her all the way to her house like a starved animal" (53) because "she felt that the sun rose and set with Deliwe. She admired every word which fell out of her mouth. She wanted to pick up the word and put it in her own mouth. So dearly was Phephelaphi charmed" (52). The erotic aura of Deliwe awakens

Phephelaphi to the possibilities encoded in the body. Phephelaphi, who strives for the same bodily competence as Deliwe, comes to locate independence and modernity in the intentionality of the sexual and erotic body. When she follows Deliwe home to continue her admiration, her body alights with sexuoerotic energy, with "the bliss, the ecstasy, the freedom spreading its wide wings over Phephelaphi's body as she stood watching her" (54). The graduating movement in this last sentence from sexuoerotic energy to freedom maps an embodied political understanding of sexual self-governance and foreshadows the resolve of Phephelaphi to break barriers by becoming a nurse.

Deliwe embodies a modern subjecthood that compels Phephelaphi but also sabotages her heteropatriarchal coupling with Fumbatha because the object of Phephelaphi's cravings resides outside of the pair's heteronormative relationship:

> Finding herself, that was it. Phephelaphi wanted to be somebody. Not once but twice, thrice, she visited Deliwe at her house and stood at her doorway and lingered again in the cigarette smoke, and placed her arm over her stomach where she nursed a wailing hurt, gathering there like a spring, because there was longing there, burning. Fumbatha could never be the beginning or end of all her yearning, her longing for which she could not find a suitable name. Not a male hurt or anything like it. . . . this hunger she felt was new. Not on her skin or anywhere she could touch. It was a feeling rising like tears. (2000, 64)

Phephelaphi cannot name her desire because it is queer, meaning her desire haunts and resists normative categories, trajectories, and outcomes. Hers is a dangerous desire whose violence, conveyed through the analogies of hunger and pain, unravels Phephelaphi and ferments an inner revolution, not unlike Ateba's in Beyala's *C'est le soleil qui m'a brûlée*. The comparison with a gathering spring and a rising feeling conveys the inner revolution in Phephelaphi and represents the sexual female body as a hauntology that threatens the structures of heteropatriarchal nationalism. Like Mazvita, who queerly supplements the nationalist male body, Phephelaphi, in her quest for meaning and self-actualization outside of heteropatriarchal channels, bypasses the phallus. The transformation of Phephelaphi, like Ateba's, is revolutionary and political.

The revolutionary and political nature of the sexuoerotic awakening of Mazvita and Phephelaphi is perhaps best confirmed by their acts of infanticide and abortion. Mazvita strangles her unwanted baby to death. Phephelaphi performs a self-abortion and immolates herself when she becomes pregnant again. These developments align with the protagonists' consciousness that their desired self-actualization lies outside of the frameworks of heteropatriarchy. Pregnancy and motherhood interrupt the trajectories on which they set themselves. Phephelaphi's pregnancy disqualifies her from nursing school since the school does not accept married women and pregnant women. Mazvita was resolute not to take nanny jobs, the only jobs available to African women in the city at that time, because she did not come to the city to look after other people's children. Yet she finds herself burdened with her own unwanted child. Motherhood thus constitutes a "betrayal" by the body, to use Mazvita's words. The word "betrayal" is aptly chosen because the pregnant and maternal body surrenders the female subject to patriarchy. Unwanted pregnancies mean that patriarchy has caught up with the runaway bodies of the two protagonists. Being that motherhood is a key cornerstone of nationalist ideologies and sustains the reproduction of patriarchy, nonprocreative sex represents political dissent. Infanticide sabotages the reproductive female body and operates a political sabotage of patriarchal nationalism. The desires and actions of Vera's protagonists manifest an unapologetic non-altruism that disobeys the patriarchal and nationalist ideologies of the self-sacrificing woman. The latter exists only in relation to her self-sacrificing role as wife or/and mother. Phephelaphi's project to give birth to herself, "a birth of her own" (2000, 68), is a project of political and ideological disobedience made possible by her engagement with the possibilities encoded in her spectralized sexual body.

In what appears to be a demise of the protagonists at the end of the two novels, Phephelaphi commits suicide when she has another unwanted pregnancy, and Mazvita goes back to her village to supposedly bury her child. But the demise is only apparent because the two protagonists never yield to the structures of patriarchy. Phephelaphi's self-immolation, a self-orchestrated act of "dying in her own storm" (2000, 130), is an act of agency that flaunts and theatricalizes her freedom. If pregnancy, as I argued earlier, is patriarchal nationalism's "I got you" moment, the self-immolation of Phephelaphi in front of her lover deflates the pretense of patriarchal nationalism. The open-ended conclusion of *Without a Name*, when Mazvita returns to her village to bury her child born of rape, in the same space where she was raped, suggests that Mazvita will resume her journey unburdened. The return to a land from which she had emancipated herself is thus not a movement backward. The return is part of her journey forward, especially since Mazvita returns with the knowledge that departures are not synonymous with beginnings. Instead Mazvita ponders the possibility of "a beginning even in this sorrowful finality" (1994, 42).

Vera's mode of positioning and centering the sexual female body contests both the colonial racist ideologies of the African female body and the African nationalist gender ideologies that have shaped the engagements of African women with the sexual female body. These intersecting ideologies have urged African literary and feminist discourses to gravitate toward the "mothernormativity" and "marriagenormativity" critiqued by Tamale (2006, 40). But Vera's protagonists are very present to and in their bodies. They have an acute and unapologetically non-altruistic awareness of the longings and yearnings of their bodies. This phenomenological awareness of the body, which places the sexual body at the center of Vera's literary project, endows the body with political intelligence and positions the body as an agent of change.

The novels of Yvonne Vera have echoes of the restlessness and displeasure with the gender politics of the nation that propel forward the ever-wandering protagonists of Calixthe Beyala. The two novelists share a literary project of unsettling phallic governances and reclaiming the female body from nationalist and patriarchal ideologies. Beyala, with Ateba's rejection of heterosexuality and violent murder of her male lover in *C'est le soleil qui m'a brûlée*, appears even more radical than Vera. But more so than Beyala's protagonists, those of Vera have defined political visions. The political visions of Phephelaphi and Mazvita are unlike the ambiguous dreamlike and hallucinatory register under which Beyala has her protagonist function and which then dismisses their political stature and visions. Vera's own lack of ideological inhibitions makes for a sharper break with nationalist discourses of womanhood. Additionally, Vera's protagonists, unlike Beyala's cast of prostitutes, thieves, and mentally unstable women, are not socially stigmatized figures. The sociocultural positioning of the protagonists of Beyala spectralizes them and shrouds their political voices. So does the similar positioning of Ken Bugul, whose unconventional itinerary has irremediably cast her as an alienated and eccentric figure. Still, Vera also appears to partake in the angst over the sexual female body. Her narrative choice of highly metaphorical language may at times shroud the sexual female body in opacity, if not illegibility and thus spectrality.

Yvonne Vera occupies a middle ground between Ken Bugul and Calixthe Beyala and the subsequent wave of African women's writings of the sexual body. A political thread of sexual self-governance runs through the works of the three writers, and insistently so in Beyala and Vera. Vera's recourse to metaphorical language spectralizes the sexual female body and adds to the narrative strategies used by Bugul and Beyala to spectralize the sexual female body. But in her refusal to safely cushion the sexual assertiveness of her female protagonists with mental and sociocultural stigma, Vera aligns with third-generation African women writers Léonora Miano, Lola Shoneyin, Sefi Atta, and Chimamanda Adichie.

Léonora Miano, Lola Shoneyin, Sefi Atta, Chimamanda Adichie
It comes as no surprise that Nigerian writers dominate this section of my analysis. Heather Hewett (2005) has documented the lack of inhibitions about female sexual pleasure in the writings of third-generation Nigerian women writers. While Hewitt reads this group of writers within the transgenerational category of Nigerian women's writings, I have drawn similar

conclusions when reading these writers in the context of third-generation African women's writings. Cameroonian writer Léonora Miano makes the cut, although barely.

Miano's writing is usually subdued when it comes to depictions of sex, except for one explicit sex scene in *Blues pour Elise* (2010), a novel about the love lives of young African women in Paris:

> Malaika ignorait qu'on pouvait si violemment avoir envie d'être prise. Elle ne savait pas qu'une main lui effleurant les fesses sans s'y attarder pouvait la rendre folle, que les dents lui mordillant le ventre la feraient crier dans des langages inconnus de l'espèce humaine, qu'une langue glissant sur son clitoris avant de lui fouiller la fente la propulserait tout au bord d'une falaise dont elle ne demanderait qu'à sauter, encore et encore. D'ailleurs, jamais auparavant, ce petit membre n'avait autant gonflé, durci, exigé. Lorsqu'elle avait rugi tout d'un coup, se jetant sur lui . . . Kwame avait seulement eu le temps de bafouiller: Attends jé mets lé . . . condom! (2010, 84–85)
>
> (Malaika did not know you could want so badly to be taken. She did not know that a hand touching her buttocks without lingering on them could make her go crazy, that the teeth biting her stomach would make her scream in languages unknown to the human species, that a tongue sliding on her clitoris before delving into her slit would send her to the edge of a cliff from which she would readily jump again and again. Indeed, never before had this small organ swollen, hardened and demanded so much. When she roared suddenly, throwing herself on top of him . . . Kwame had only had time to sputter: wait, let me put the condom on!)

While this scene speaks to female sexual pleasure and represents a daring sex scene in the context of African women's writings, the scene nonetheless denies Miano's female character sexuoerotic agency. Female pleasure in this scene, very much like in the sex scene in Emecheta's *The Joys of Motherhood*, reinforces the image of virile masculinity. Malaika's intense outburst of pleasure speaks to the prowess of her male lover. Like Ona in *The Joys of Motherhood*, Malaika does not initiate the sex scene. Miano has also edited *Première nuit: Une anthologie du désir* (2014), an anthology of erotic short stories by African men. This is the first project of its kind in the African context, but here again Miano foregrounds men as sexual protagonists. However, she has indicated that she is working on a parallel collection of erotic short stories by African women.[2] This collection will definitely constitute a landmark contribution to African women's writing of sexual pleasure and the sexual female body.

The positioning of African women as sexual protagonist comes through in the works of Miano's Nigerian peers, some limitations notwithstanding. Lola Shoneyin, in *The Secret Lives of Baba Segi's Wives* (2010), tackles female sexual pleasure and composes explicit scenes about women's longings for and enjoyment of sexual pleasure. Women are desiring subjects in the novel. The polygamous Baba Segi fails to meet the sexual desires of his wives. For Baba Segi, marital sex is procreative sex and is only about the satisfaction of his male desire. Iya Tope, his second wife, best relates this unsatisfactory configuration of sexual relations that spectralizes the sexual female body:

> There was no pleasure in the pleasing, no sweetness in the surrender. Baba Segi only comes to deposit his seed in my womb. He doesn't smile or tickle me. . . . he just rams me into the mattress. . . . He empties his testicles as deep into my womb as possible. It was as if he wanted to make it clear, with every thrust, that he didn't make light of his husbandly duties. He wanted to fuck me pregnant. If there was any moment when the memory of being raped became fresh in my mind, that was it. (2010, 49–50)

Shoneyin's narrative lends support to the sexual subjectivity of Baba Segi's wives. The extramarital trysts that the wives seek out for themselves position the wives as desiring subjects. Iya Tope secures the sexual services of a male lover. Her narration of the encounter foregrounds her sexual agency, and her detailed description of her gratification centers female sexual pleasure: "I let him see that I had brought more than I owed and pressed the money into his hand. I held it there and took his eyes into mine. . . . He made my body sing. He made me howl when he bent over me. He made me whimper when he sat me on his belly. And when he took me standing up, it was as if there was a frog inside me, puffing out its throat, blowing, blowing and blowing until whoosh—all the air escaped through my limbs" (2010, 95). Shoneyin's detailed description of female sexual pleasure parallels the earlier quoted scene from Miano. Through their explicit and graphic scenes, both authors boldly claim narrative space for female pleasure in ways almost unprecedented in African literatures. As a comparison, the sex scenes in Vera use subtle descriptions and metaphorical language to convey sexual pleasure while Beyala, save for *Femme nue, femme noire* (2003), is more graphic in her naming of genitalia than she is in her description of sexual encounters.

But like Miano, who holds back on her engagement with female sexual pleasure, Shoneyin also undercuts her narrative of sexual pleasure when she safely reinscribes the wives in a patriarchal economy of sexual pleasure. The narrative aborts the lesbian inclinations of the first wife and fails to disentangle sexual pleasure from motherhood. The sexual adventures of Baba Segi's wives are bound with the necessity to bear children for their husband. The children-obsessed patriarch is sterile, unbeknownst to him. When Shoneyin has the wives sacrifice the well-being of their children for their sexual desires, she invests female sexual pleasure with a symbolic negative load by suggesting the incompatibility of sexual pleasure with motherhood. In replica to Mam in Beyala's *Maman a un amant* (1993), Shoneyin has Iya Tope renounce her quest for sexual fulfillment to "become a good mother" (2010, 97) when she realizes the dire state of her neglected children. By pitting motherhood against sexual pleasure and then having motherhood triumph, Shoneyin composes a narrative that complies with patriarchal ideologies of motherhood and female sexuality. The narrative accordingly spectralizes the sexual female body. Writing more than thirty years after Emecheta and Aidoo, Shoneyin sustains the two authors' narrative gesture of rewriting the sexual female body they just enunciated as a hauntology that threatens the proper African woman.

Sefi Atta's *A Bit of Difference* (2012) also adopts the pattern of squashing the narrative of sexual independence. Deola, the narrator-protagonist, is a young Nigerian professional woman who lives in London. A single woman, she fields societal and familial pressures to settle down, but Deola deems herself an independent woman with no interest in marriage or motherhood. On a business trip to Nigeria, Deola initiates a sexual tryst with a stranger who catches her eye. The test arises when she is unexpectedly pregnant from their sexual encounter. Atta's choice of this pregnancy as a narrative denouement sends an ambiguous message about female sexual independence. We may wonder about the narrative decision to have Deola become pregnant, return home to Nigeria, and get married to the father of her child. Atta's narrative brackets off female sexual pleasure as a parenthesis by safely containing the early moments of female sexual agency on an expatriate and peripheral female body. The two sexual encounters featured in the novel symbolically occur outside of the spaces of home and homeland. The first encounter takes place in a hotel in Nigeria, and the second one happens when Deola is back in London. The framing of these vignettes of sexual autonomy neutralizes the potential ideological edge of the novel's narrative of sexual autonomy. The ending of the novel, like the proper endings of Beyala's *Maman a un amant* and Shoneyin's *Baba Segi's Wives*, falls back on the trope of marriage to redeem the stray-away female body to the national home. When Deola decides to move back home and marry her lover so that her child is born within the bond of marriage, she does the proper thing. She also becomes a conforming national female body.

In appearance Chimamanda Adichie's *Purple Hibiscus* (2003) is somewhat of a misfit in an analysis of female sexual pleasure. The novel has no sex scenes; neither does it mention sex explicitly. *Purple Hibiscus* is the coming-of-age story of fifteen-year-old Kambili, thus hardly appropriate territory for the writing of sexuoerotic pleasure and agency. Yet the novel brims with sexual tension. *Purple Hibiscus* adopts a daring approach to female sexuality by writing sexual awareness and pleasure into the coming of age of a fifteen-year-old girl. The sexual longing of Kambili for Father

Amadi, who also encourages this attraction, is a topic that potentially ventures into inappropriate terrain and elicits discomfort at times. But Adichie eases that discomfort by writing Kambili's sexual awakening as an intrinsic part of her self-actualization and healthy maturation into confident and assertive womanhood. Adichie's centering of the sexual female body is all the more militant because the sexual coming of age of Kambili happens against a landscape of patriarchal and religious repression of the sexual body. Kambili's father, Eugene, is a rigid catholic patriarch whose religious fanaticism leads him to abuse his family. Growing up under Eugene's authoritarian rule squashes Kambili's persona to the point where she possesses no voice of her own. Kambili stutters and struggles with the most basic verbal self-expressions, and Eugene's aversion for the body has his daughter develop a poor body self-image. When Father Amadi, a charismatic young priest, takes Kambili under his guidance and solicits her sensuality, the teenage girl starts to assume the intentionality of her body and grows into her own. The sexual awareness of Kambili unlocks her voice and launches her onward. At the peak of her awakening, Kambili is able to stand up to her father.

By linking voice and sexual awareness, Adichie adopts a militant approach to female sexuoerotic agency that makes sexual self-discovery a sine qua non to the development of a full-fledged feminist female subject. In so doing Adichie takes up the injunction by Charmaine Pereira (2003) to make female sexual pleasure a key point of African feminist agendas. Because the novel's narrative of family drama is a political allegory of the Nigerian nation (Andrade 2011a; Hewett 2005; Okuyade 2011), the sexual coming of age of Kambili, like the revolutionary sexuoerotic awakenings of Vera's and Beyala's protagonists, is political. Adichie joins Beyala and Vera in modeling a new female subject of the nation. The murder of Eugene by his wife, Kambili's mother, represents a feminist space-clearing gesture and paves the way for new gender politics of the nation.

As previously indicated, Adichie displays boldness by writing a sexual coming-of-age story. The same boldness carries over to *Half of a Yellow Sun* (2006) to confirm Adichie's uninhibited approach to the sexual female body. The novel is about the Biafran civil war, but detailed scenes of sexual pleasure punctuate the intense depictions of war brutalities. Tanzanian novelist Abdulrazak Gurnah (2007) has critiqued the novel for "souping-up" a serious topic with sex scenes. But Adichie's sex-filled Biafran narrative precisely drives home the point that sex is a serious and important topic. By weaving sex into her war narrative, Adichie claims space for the sexual subject. The novel's affirmation of the sexual subject pursues Adichie's exploration in *Purple Hibiscus* of the possibilities for self-actualization that sex and sexuality offer.

In *Half of a Yellow Sun*, the narrative emphasizes the sexual life of Olanna, the female protagonist, without taking away from her intellectual standing and political savvy. Her assertive sexuality informs her intellectual and political persona since, as a desiring subject, she eludes containment. Adichie asserts the sexuality of Olanna almost immediately upon her introduction to houseboy Ugwu and the reader at the end of the first chapter of the novel. Like Ugwu, the reader anticipates the arrival of Olanna in the house of Odenigbo, Ugwu's master. When we finally meet Olanna, we partake in her objectification through Ugwu's first impressions of a creature who "looked like she was not supposed to be walking and talking like everyone else; she should be in a glass case like the one in Master's study, where people could admire her curvy, fleshy body, where she would be preserved untainted" (2006, 29). Adichie pointedly unsettles that image one page later, at the end of the chapter. Ugwu listens at the door of his master's bedroom, hoping to hear Odenigbo enjoy sex with Olanna. But he only hears Olanna "moaning loudly, sounds that seemed so unlike her, so uncontrolled and stirring and throaty" (31). The brutal turn of the patriarchal topos of the proper woman from the start of the novel performs an uncompromising rejection of the topos. That Olanna first comes into being for the reader through her uninhibited sexuality shows Adichie's resolve to assert the subject through her sexuality. Her approach of sexuality as a site of subjectivation sustains the feminist politics of the novel. Kainene, Olanna's twin sister, is an assertive and highly independent woman. She is a savvy business leader who holds her own in a male-dominated industry.

When the war erupts, her leadership and political acumen save lives. She conducts an equitable and inclusive form of postcolonial governance, which is clearly an alternative to the model that has precipitated Nigeria into chaos. As with Olanna, Adichie has her narrative work out a correspondence between Kainene's robust subjectivity and sexuality.

Sex in *Half of a Yellow Sun* is built-in hermeneutics. But it takes the sex scenes involving minor characters to reveal the narrative function of sex. Sex scenes deepen our understanding of characters whose subaltern social circumstances otherwise deny them complexity and significance in the eyes of the reader. The sexual activities of the invisible subaltern women preempt their desubjectivation and spectralization by the reader. The sex scenes between Ugwu and Chinyere, the silent maid, flesh out the latter to the reader. Chinyere is the protagonist of these sexual encounters. She initiates the encounters by sneaking into Ugwu's room as she sees fit. The two lovers barely interact outside of sex, with Chinyere resolutely limiting her words to a short greeting when they run into one another. Her uninhibited agenda of sexual pleasure underpins her relationship with Ugwu and organizes the sex proceedings between the two lovers: "She was silent at first and then, hips thrashing, her hands tight around his back, she called out the same thing she said every time. It sounded like a name—Abonyi, Abonyi—but he wasn't sure. Perhaps she imagined that he was someone else too, someone back in her village. She got up and left as silently as she came. When he saw her the next day across the hedge, hanging out clothes on the line, she said "Ugwu" and nothing else; she did not smile" (2006, 161). In its function as hermeneutics here, sex allows the narrative to claim a full-fledged subjectivity for the otherwise spectral Chinyere and retrieve the voice and feminist ethos of the subaltern woman.

The inevitable scenes of sexual violence and rape as weapon of war punctuate the novel. The conspicuous ubiquity of female sexual pleasure in the narrative of war jars with the discursive conventions of war narratives. The purposive departure of Adichie from conventions forces a dissonance that performs a recuperative interruption of her narrative of war. I call that interruption a gesture of recuperation because the scenes of sexual pleasure resist the convention in war narratives to confine women to sexual violence and thereby normalize the sexual violence of war. Adichie makes sexual pleasure take center stage in such a way that sexual violence is denormalized and decentered and ultimately loses its grip on the narrative. Bibi Bakare-Yusuf helps frame the vignettes of sexual pleasure in *Half of a Yellow Sun*, especially since she also shares my reading of the possibilities that Merleau-Ponty's theory of embodied agency posits. Bakare-Yusuf is correct that from the perspective of Merleau-Ponty's "stress on the primacy of embodied agency of the subject, an overemphasis on sexual harm appears not only to malign but even to erase primarily aspects of women's sexual experience, centered around a desire for intimacy, love, curiosity, fantasy, mutuality, respect, adventure and joy. In so doing, sexual terror becomes the foundational experience of women's sexuality, rather than being seen as derivative upon an originary pleasure principle to which the body must strive to reconnect and re-attune" (2013, 30). Bakare-Yusuf's insistence on sexual pleasure resonates with the feminist agenda that drives the dissonant narrative of Adichie. Some passages in Bakare-Yusuf read like an anthem for Adichie's recuperative interruptions:

> Telling and circulating women's stories of desiring pleasures and of sexual ecstasy provides the possibility of telling a different kind of narrative that doesn't privilege domination, rape, physical harm, and violation. Such stories make it possible to recontextualize or re-embed negating or violating experiences within a redemptive discourse of new forms of storytelling. If we don't privilege the fundamentality of our capacity for joy, pleasure, love and desire towards one another, then our struggle to end sexual danger becomes futile and we lose focus on why we are doing what we are doing. We become powerless in the face of these powerful violating narratives and experiences. We come to exist in a precarious relationship to our bodies and our desires. (2013, 37)

In the context of war and amidst the pervasiveness of violence and rape, sexual pleasure represents self-care and self-reclamation. Sexual pleasure is a narrative locus where Adichie recuperates and reaffirms the war-trodden Nigerian female subject. During the war, Kainene and her fiancé Richard start a daily evening ritual of sex on their verandah. After they barely escape enemy bombs by seeking refuge in a bunker, Olanna decides she won't be an "inconsequential" casualty of war. Moving forward, "she had to matter. She would no longer exist limply, waiting to die. Until Biafra won, the vandals would no longer dictate the terms of her life" (2006, 351). The narrative executes the full return of Olanna to subjecthood when the central chapter on war-terrorized and traumatized civilians, including Olanna's household, concludes with sexual pleasure. Olanna's war-traumatized husband readily relinquishes their lives to the war and passively awaits a free Biafra to resume life. But Olanna initiates and directs a resistive and self-affirming sexual episode between the spouses in order to reposition the couple outside of the spectral status of bare life:

> She liked the way he said that, *in a free Biafra*, and she stood up and squashed her lips against his. . . . "We have more than enough for ourselves." Her lips were still against his and her words suddenly took on a different meaning and she moved back and pulled her dress over her head in one fluid gesture. She unbuckled his trousers. She did not let him take them off. She turned her back and leaned on the wall and guided him into her . . . she had no control over her own moans, over the raw primal pleasure she felt in wave after wave that ended with both of them leaning against the wall, gasping and giggling. (2006, 354)

Likewise, immediately after the couple learns of the death of their close friends, sex, which concludes again a brutal chapter, provides a lifeline away from their reduction to bare life: "When he slid into her, she thought how different he felt, lighter and narrower, on top of her. He was still, so still she thrashed around and pulled at his hips. But he did not move. Then he began to thrust and her pleasure multiplied, sharpened on stone so that each tiny spark became a pleasure all its own. She heard herself crying, her sobbing louder and louder . . . He was crying too; she felt the tears drop on her body before she saw them on his face" (2006, 491). The ability to create and experience sexual pleasure reclaims and recenters the intentionality of the body and then thrusts the subject out of paralysis and impending desubjectivation. Sex and sexual pleasure, by propelling the characters out of the condition of bare life, allow for the articulation of new imaginaries and futurities.

Farah Jasmine Griffin's analysis of the significance of female orgasm substantiates the nongratuitousness of the detailed description of sexual pleasure in *Half of a Yellow Sun*. Griffith approaches female orgasm as "a site of agency" in that "orgasm is the space where the body loses control of itself" and "moves beyond the control of itself and as such eschews control of any kind" (1996, 519). Adichie's insistence on not writing the subject outside of her sexuality asserts the link between sexual self-awareness and subjectivity. The author therefore links sexual-self-awareness and the coming into being of a feminist subject who can sidestep her interpellation into patriarchal discourses. It is probably such an astute understanding of the self-affirming possibilities of sex and the sexual subject that informs Adichie's confident handling of sex scenes and unwavering narrative allegiance to the female sexual subject throughout the novel. The narrative sustains the affirming thread of female sexual pleasure, and Adichie eschews the aborted sexual pleasure narratives of Sefi Atta and Lola Shoneyin. Unlike Miano, Adichie purposively composes her sex scenes to grant agency to her female characters. Adichie's keen understanding of the sexual subject makes for savvy and politically incisive narratives that evoke Beyala's and Vera's, more so than those of her third-generation contemporaries.

Calixthe Beyala, Frieda Ekotto, Zanele Muholi
I am singling out representations of queer sexualities in a separate category because such representations that break the silence about female sexuality and bring nonnormative sexualities out of the closet break two conventions at once. Furthermore, the queer female body troubles the conjoined ideologies of heteronormativity, marriagenormativity, and mothernormativity already discussed in chapter 2.

Chantal Zabus (2013) has provided a useful analytical survey of representations of same-sex intimacies in African women's writings. Zabus analyzes the early "implicit queer gesturing" in Ama Ata Aidoo's *Our Sister Killjoy* (1977) and Rebecca Njau's *Ripples in the Pool* (1978). The two novels pathologize the lesbian longings of the female protagonists through madness in Njau's novel and racial alterity in Aidoo's. To the two novels examined by Zabus and to open up her focus on Anglophone writers, I add Calixthe Beyala's *C'est le soleil qui m'a brûlée* (1987), in which the trope of madness serves to safely contain the lesbian longings of the protagonist. Ken Bugul's *Le baobab fou* (1982) also engages in queer gesturing, but the cultural and mental alienation of the narrator-protagonist neutralizes the queer undertones. Zabus also omits the novel *Fureurs et cris de femmes* (1989) by Gabonese author Angèle Rawiri. Rawiri's novel, unlike the queer gesturing novels of Beyala and Bugul, explicitly represents a lesbian sexual relation. But the narrative context of the relation revokes the boldness of Rawiri's representation. Jilted housewife Emilienne has a lesbian relationship with Dominique. Unbeknownst to Emilienne, Dominique is the mistress of her husband, and she initiated the relationship with Emilienne to precipitate the divorce of the couple. The function of the lesbian sexual relationship as revenge sex limits the discursive reach of lesbian sex by constructing lesbianism as a method to regain firm ground within the heteropatriarchal economy.

Another omission from the corpus of Zabus is *Chuchote pas trop* (2005) by Cameroonian writer Frieda Ekotto. The novel follows the journey of the young female protagonist, Ada, to save Affi, the daughter of her deceased mentor, from sequestration in a forced marriage. The novel is a good fit for the notion of queer gesturing. The relationship between Ada and her mentor is ambiguous and often borders on homoerotic intimacy. The only explicit same-sex relationship in the novel occurs between a female European missionary and one of the wives of the local community leader. As in Ama Ata Aidoo's *Our Sister Killjoy*, the use of the foreign woman to introduce same-sex intimacy displaces nonnormative sexualities from African contexts. The use of the foreign woman constitutes a step back to the representation, in early African literatures, of same-sex sexuality as a foreign import. The figure of the foreign woman may write off the nonnormative sexualities in *Chuchote pas trop* as an un-African foreign perversion. It is Ekotto's second novel, *Portrait d'une jeune artiste de Bona Mbella* (2010), examined in the last part of this chapter, that finally delivers the first forceful and uninhibited narrative of same-sex sexuality in Francophone African literatures.

Zabus disputes the implicit queerness that Boehmer finds in Yvonne Vera's novels on the grounds that the absence of sexual desire invalidates any claim of queerness. My own analysis of *Butterfly Burning* and *Without a Name* earlier in this chapter teased out the nuances of sexual desire in Phephelaphi's attraction to Deliwe and Mazvita's intimate rapport with the landscape. Conversely I am unconvinced by the attempt of Zabus to retrieve a suppressed lesbian thread in third-generation Nigerian writer Unoma Azuah's *Sky-High Flames* (2005). Part of the novel is set in a girls' boarding school where some of the girls are tomboys. Zabus faults Azuah, herself a lesbian, with preempting the boarding school girls "doing lesbian" (2013, 146). I rather find such preemption of lesbianism to be true for Azuah's third-generation Nigerian contemporary Lola Shoneyin. In *The Secret Lives of Baba Segi's Wives* (2010), Shoneyin aborts the lesbian inclinations of Baba Segi's first wife.

Zabus is right that both Shoneyin and Azuah write more explicitly about lesbianism in their poetry. Still, the opacity of poetic language mutes down the subversive theme. It may be that the hermetic genre of poetry provides the writers with a protective mantle and a safe conduit, not unlike the tropes of madness and foreignness in the queer-gesturing novels of first- and second-generation African women writers. Zabus lists Ugandan Monica Arac de Nyeko's short story "Jambula Tree" (2007) as another example of a current of explicit lesbianism in African women's writings. However, in this short story, the friendship between two schoolgirls leads into one incidence of sexual contact whose loose narration and immediate interruption amount to queer gesturing: "It did not occur to either of us, to you or me, that these were boundaries we should not cross nor should think of crossing. Your jambulas and mine. Two plus two jambulas equals four jambulas—even numbers should stand for luck. Was this luck pulling us together? You pulled me to yourself and we rolled on the brown earth that stuck to our hair in all its redness and dustiness. There in front of Mama Atim's house. She shone a torch at us" (Arac de Nyeko 2007). Arac de Nyeko does not allow the relation to proceed beyond that initial phase of exploration. After Mama Atim discovers the girls, the girls are separated. The age of the girls allows the reader to dismiss the incident as a passing fad, a curious exploration of sexuality in the context of puberty and coming of age. Additionally, the structure of the narrative, whereby the gossiping and prying of Mama Atim takes center stage, contributes to the decentering of the lesbian thematic.

Contra the heavy focus of Zabus on Anglophone literatures, queer female sexuality in African women's writings and cultural productions is best examined in Calixthe Beyala's *Femme nue, femme noire* (2003), Frieda Ekotto's *Portrait d'une jeune artiste de Bona Mbella* (2010), and the photography of Zanele Muholi. What singles out the novels of the two francophone Cameroonian writers is their head-on graphic engagement with queer sex, all of which matches Muholi's representation of sexually pleasured lesbian women in her photographic series *Beloved* (2005). Zabus does not mention Ekotto or Muholi but conducts a hasty and rather unsympathetic reading of Beyala that totally misses the point of the unbridled sexuality represented in the novel. Zabus argues that the orgies orchestrated by the protagonist of the novel constitute "degrading sex acts," impress an image of a "famished Africa as brothel," and feature homosexuality as a "grotesque perversity" (2013, 220). A firmer dialogue between Beyala's novel and queer theory is key to apprehending the project of Beyala in *Femme nue, femme noire*. My argument in my reading of *Karmen Geï* in chapter 2 that queerness is not an identity location but rather a process and modality of power relations pertains to the novel of Beyala.

The tour de force of Beyala's *Femme nue, femme noire* lies in its queering of "founding father" Léopold Sédar Senghor's classic poem "Femme nue, femme noire" (1945) (Nude Woman, Black Woman), a text widely read and taught across the continent. Beyala challenges Senghor's vision of a pristine Africa, a vision made possible by fixing woman in her place. In his poem Senghor feminizes and sexualizes the continent, figured alternatively as a mother and a lover. The poet's passive and desubjectified woman exists through and submits to male desire. The poet derives sexual gratification from the female body but never returns the favor because the patriarchal optic of the nationalist poem does not accommodate female desire and female sexual pleasure.

From the onset, Beyala situates her deconstructionist project against the tamed and silenced female body upheld by Senghor. The protagonist Irène specifies her disobedient and irreverent subject position:

> "Femme nue, femme noire, vêtue de ta couleur qui est vie, de ta forme qui est beauté . . ." Ces vers ne font pas partie de mon arsenal linguistique. Vous verrez: mes mots à moi tressautent et cliquettent comme des chaînes. Des mots qui détonnent, déglinguent, culbutent, dissèquent, torturent! Des mots qui fessent, giflent, cassent et broient! Que celui qui se sent mal à l'aise passe sa route. (2003, 11)
>
> ("Nude woman, black woman, clothed with your color which is life, with your form which is beauty . . ." These verses don't belong to my linguistic arsenal. Just wait and see: my own words shock and rattle like chains. Mine are words that clash, jar, tumble, dissect, and torture! My words spank, slap, break, and grind! Go your way, if you are uncomfortable.)

Irène brutally undercuts the Senghorian poem. Her refusal to complete the recitation of the foundational text and curricular staple is an act of ideological disobedience. The quick and saccadic accumulation of active verbs in the third sentence of this opening paragraph, combined with the pointed use of the word "arsenal" and the piercing incisiveness of the exclamation points, mimic an act of insubordination akin to a military assault on the gendered nationalist subject constituted by Senghor's poem. The opening of the novel thus establishes Beyala's ambition to dissolute the gendered postcolonial subject by taking down the discourses that produce and sustain that subject.

The locus of enunciation of the dissidence of Irène, from within the heteropatriarchal poem, aligns with the inside-out trajectory of queer processes detailed in my reading of *Karmen Geï* in chapter 2. Like Karmen, whose queering operations involve the interruption and hijacking of various heteropatriarchal and normative processes, Irène hijacks the Senghorian poem to introduce her model of womanhood. Irène announces that "ici, il n'y aura pas de soutien-gorges en dentelle, de bas résille, de petites culottes en soie à prix excessifs, de parfums de roses ou des gardénias, et encore moins ces approches rituelles de la femme fatale, empruntées aux films ou à la télévision" (Beyala 2003, 11) (Here, there won't be lace bras, fishnet panty hose, excessively pricy silk panties, rose perfumes or gardenias, and certainly not those femme fatale rituals borrowed from films or television). Beyala's *Femme nue, femme noire* snatches the female body from Senghor to grant it sexual agency and subjectivity.

In an unprecedented move in African literatures, the novel includes very graphic, almost pornographic-like sexual scenes. Sexual orgies and lesbian sex abound in the novel. Irène is young woman who has left home and revels in wandering without a destination. Echoing in tone and purpose the above-cited first paragraph of the novel, Irène flaunts her nonconforming womanhood to the reader when she announces that she is a kleptomaniac. When she steals, "Il me vient des sécrétions. Je suis en transe orgasmique! Je jouis. D'ailleurs en dehors du sexe, je ne connais rien d'autre qui me procure autant de plaisir" (2003, 12) (I become wet with secretions. I enter into orgasmic trance! I come. Only sex can give me that much pleasure). The convergence between theft and sexual pleasure equates the pleasure-seeking and pleasured woman to a sociocultural outlaw. The figure of the outlaw further links Irène to Karmen in *Karmen Geï*, whose outlaw activities are a modality of her queerness and sexual freedom. That Irène enjoys and snatches away the privilege of sexual pleasure that patriarchy normalizes for men elevates her petty thieveries to a revolutionary act against the law of the postcolonial African father. Irène robs the phallus when she appropriates for herself not only sexual pleasure but also sexual agency. Heterosexual encounters are always opportunities to strip heteropatriarchal masculinities:

> J'en oublie la hiérarchisation des rôles sexuels. Je revendique une morale de l'excès, de la luxure et de la débauche. Mes mains glissent sur son dos.... Je fais glisser le pantalon le long de ses cuisses ... J'ai le vertige Presque en brusquant sa virilité, en le violant Presque.... Sa bouche écume des paroles incompréhensibles. Les mots clignotent dans sa gorge et le narguent. (Beyala 2003, 22–23)
>
> (I forget all about the hierarchy of sexual roles. I claim a morality of excess, luxury and debauchery. My hands slide on his back.... I drag his pants down his thighs.... I am dizzy Almost as I assault his virility and rape him Almost.... His mouth blabbers incomprehensible sentences. The words flash in his throat and taunt him.)

Irène feminizes the male body through a normative masculine sexual act when she subjects her lover to her authority and sexual desire. She first usurps the masculine sexual grammar that enforces the sexual subjection of the female body. Proceeding forward, she appropriates the masculine sexual syntax where the desiring male subject engages specific parts of his sexual partner in an order decided by him. The male body is further feminized in this scene through aphasia and the struggle to reenter language.

But this reversal is short-lived. While on the verge of complete subject dissolution, Irène's partner is snatched back by heteropatriarchal discourses and violently regains control of the sexual interaction. One may conclude the futility of such subversive agendas as Irène's. But, as in *Karmen Geï*, the import of Irène's act lies in the ability to poke holes in the dominant structure. This ability disrupts the system by exposing the performative construction of identity, which then sets the stage for a reinterpretation of normative identities. Irène sabotages the dominant structure by laying bare its unsteady performative mechanism, unraveling its gender simulacra, and calling attention to the failure of the dominant structure to preempt resignification.

Irène is on the prey for and exploits moments of systemic failure to throw the simulacrum into disarray. In one sexual orgy that she orchestrates, Hayatou loses his erection and cannot penetrate his wife. Irène comes to the rescue by sodomizing Hayatou with a baguette. This scene finds a companion in Zanele Muholi's *Dada* (2003), a black-and-white photograph of a bare-breasted woman strapping on a dildo. The detachable piece exposes the phallus as simulacrum, allows for a disassembly and reassembly of gender, and decenters the sexual male body. Muholi's woman has very heavy breasts, and the suggestion of a breast-feeding woman and a maternal body looms in the background to evoke Judith Halberstam's (1994) notion of "queer female masculinity" that boldly expresses gender outside of the male/female binary. Irène opportunistically orchestrates a queer female masculinity that sabotages the heterosexual moment by assembling and dissembling all bodies and genders involved in the moment. Later in the novel, when Hayatou's wife is pregnant, Irène extends her sabotage of the heterosexual moment by suggesting that she is the author of the pregnancy.

Following Gilles Deleuze and Félix Guattari's (1987) notion of lines of flight as those inherent opportunities for subversion inadvertently generated by the hegemonic structure, sex is one such line of flight in *Femme nue, femme noire* because the sexual promiscuity of Irène performs subversive labor. Her self-reference as a woman "au sexe glouton" (2003, 165) (with a voracious sex) hints at such subversive labor. Irène seizes sex as a line of flight to queer heteropatriarchal frameworks and make room for female sexual pleasure. She operates through redistributions of sexual subject positions. As a flaneur, and a sexual flaneur as such, Irène, like Karmen in *Karmen Geï*, tactically infiltrates normative and normalizing spaces and reroutes geographies of sexual identity. Irène provokes sexual orgies, meaning assemblages of desires where sex is then bound to happen in a variety of configurations, and women can claim sexual pleasure for themselves.

In my reading of Beyala's *C'est le soleil qui m'a brûlée* earlier in this chapter, I argue that the demise of Ateba through the trope of madness neutralizes the subversive sexual politics of the novel. *Femme nue, femme noire* concludes with the death of Irène at the hands of a mob that accuses her of human organs trafficking. The death of Irène is unlike the death of Karmen. As argued in chapter 2, the death of Karmen obeys the ending of Bizet's *Carmen*, but director Joseph Gaï Ramaka has Karmen die a nonterminal death. Karmen dies singing a song of resistance. Her memory and queer praxis also live on through the praise song dedicated to her at the end of the film. In contrast, Beyala has Irène bludgeoned to death by an angry society. In upholding a type of murder that is meant to obliterate any trace of Irène, the narrative revokes the queer sexual female body that it has just enunciated. In fact, the violent scene of Irène's murder evokes that of Ateba's revolutionary murder of her male lover in *C'est le soleil qui m'a brûlée*. This resonance indicates that the narrative acquiesces to the brutal demise of Irène and the community's negative construction of the queer sexual female body. Likewise, the narrative decision to have an agonized Irène repent and promise that she will abide by the norms of society shows Beyala resorting again to a socially conformist conclusion.

Frieda Ekotto, in *Portrait d'une jeune artiste de Bona Mbella* (2010), rehearses the same critique of heteropatriarchy that ferments the queer praxis of Beyala's Irène. Lesbian lovers Pane and Chantou come together after the former murders the men in her adopted family for turning her into their family sex slave. Images of sexual violation and statements of sexual deprivation in the novel impress that heteropatriarchy precludes female sexual pleasure. Ekotto's women exercise subjectivity and agency by refusing to settle in and for this sexual structure. Lesbianism, as framed by Ekotto, is a subjectifying act of resistance and reclamation of female sexual pleasure. While Beyala's Irène is queer, Ekotto opts to set her characters on a trajectory of lesbian separatism. The separatism in her novels has strong resonances with the separatist feminism and lesbianism of the early novels of Beyala, especially *C'est le soleil qui m'a brûlée*. Ateba, the female protagonist of the novel, murders her male lover and symbolically unites with her girlfriend. That scene resonates to a point with the one in *Portrait d'une jeune artiste de Bona Mbella* where Pane brutally murders her sexual violators. Where the queer framework of *Femme nue, femme noire* shows that Beyala has moved away from her first-wave lesbian feminism, Ekotto's novels adhere very much to that separatist framework à la Andrea Cornwell and Adrienne Rich.

Ekotto's novel stands out for going beyond lesbian gesturing. Ekotto never shies away from explicit sex scenes. Most importantly, Ekotto makes a significant narrative decision when she does not end her novel with the demise of her lesbian protagonist. Instead, her novel brilliantly concludes with a scene of sexual intimacy that also affirms same-sex love. This conclusion is a sharp departure from the brutal demise of Irène in Beyala's novel and the socially conforming conclusions of most of the writers analyzed in this chapter. In that regard *Portrait d'une jeune artiste de Bona Mbella* aligns with Adichie's uninhibited exploration of the sexual female body in *Half of a Yellow Sun*.

With *Portrait d'une jeune artiste de Bona Mbella*, Ekotto writes a landmark-affirming and powerful same-sex love story that evokes the visual narrative of same-sex love that South African photographer Zanele Muholi puts together. Ekotto's straightforward representation of nonconforming sex is only matched by the photographic work of Zanele Muholi, specifically in her series *Beloved* (2005, fig. 5).

The series consists of five photographs of a lesbian couple in underwear, reveling in their sexual intimacy. The lovers are able to foreclose voyeuristic intrusion because they ignore the camera and the viewer in order to take in their erotic moment. The relaxed postures manifest sexually pleasured bodies. One finds a similar sexual and emotional plenitude in Ekotto's tender and serene narration of the moments of intimacy between Pane and Chantou:

> Dans les yeux de Pane, je vois le reflet des miens. Elle se lève d'un coup et me donne un baiser sur le front. Je lui tends la main, elle l'embrasse avec douceur. Nous passons la nuit à nous câliner et à nous raconter de petites histoires, unies comme deux portions d'un même cerveau. A l'image des enfants, nous nous enlaçons à l'intérieur du même corps spirituel. (2010, 82–83)
>
> (In the eyes of Pane, I see the reflection of my own. She gets up at once and kisses me on the forehead. I hold out my hand, she kisses it gently. We spend the night cuddling and sharing stories while united

5. Zanele Muholi, *Beloved V*, 2005. © Zanele Muholi. Courtesy of Stevenson, Cape Town/Johannesburg, and Yancey Richardson, New York.

like two parts of the same brain. Just like children, we embrace inside the same spiritual body.)

The evidence of sexual intimacy, pleasure, and love outside of normative frameworks stands in query of heteropatriarchal discourses of sexuality and gender.

The querying mode, which is in fact a queering modality, has been adopted with various results by the different works examined in this chapter. African women's writings of the sexual female body and female sexual pleasure stand in query of patriarchal discourses of gender while at the same time being queried by the postcolonial corporeal angst over the female body. With very few exceptions, this angst has constrained and overwritten the expressions of female sexual pleasure in the texts I have analyzed. In the next chapter I examine the types of risks that African female visual artists take in their work on the female body.

4

Subversive and Pedagogical Hauntologies

THE UNCLOTHED FEMALE BODY IN
VISUAL AND PERFORMANCE ARTS

Risky Business: The Black Female Body in Visual Representation
I am writing this chapter in May 2014, amid a controversy surrounding the latest work of African American artist Kara Walker, on exhibit from May 10 through July 6, 2014, at the former Domino Sugar factory in Brooklyn. Walker has eloquently entitled her massive installation *A Subtlety, or the Marvelous Sugar Baby, an Homage to the Unpaid and Overworked Artisans who have Refined our Sweet tastes from the Cane Fields to the Kitchens of the New World on the Occasion of the Demolition of the Domino Sugar Refining Plant*. The installation consists of a sugar-coated giant female Sphinx, measuring approximately eighty feet long by forty feet high, and several life-size childlike figures dubbed attendants. The female figure immediately convenes the attention of the viewers, but not only because of her size. The heavy-set woman is unclothed, except for a mammy headscarf. She is crouched in a sexually suggestive way, with her exaggerated bottom pushed upward and her genitals exposed. To the competent eye, even in the absence of the explicit title of the installation, the perturbing and unsavory history of sugar evoked in this installation is immediate and sobering. Who better than Walker's mongrel mammy/sex object/breeding slave to represent the sordid history of sugar, being that the history of sugar involved the reproductive labor of enslaved African women in the plantations, kitchens,

and beds of their enslavers? As Derrida (1994) would have it, the return of the mammy from an exorcised American past both forces the present to attend to the past and calls for an ethical memorialization of past histories. In Walker's installation, the creation of an ethical memory of slavery takes the form of the type of hauntology of "re-narrativization" advocated by Avery Gordon (1997). The spectralized body of the mammy comes back to haunt and rewrite the present with new narratives of the past. Walker's mammy represents a subversive hauntology that resists both the gap-filled hegemonic narratives of slavery and the spectralization of the historical figure of the mammy.

But the incompetent eye misses the full picture. Thousands of giddy visitors have flocked to the exhibition and converged swiftly on the exposed black female body for the wrong reasons. Judging by the deluge of naughty selfies on social media, the history lesson was clearly lost on many visitors. Visitors have been posting photos of themselves or friends cupping the woman's breasts, sizing up and mocking her ample buttocks, tonguing her buttocks, and simulating sexual intercourse with her. Conversely African Americans have turned to social media to express their discomfort with this transformation of a history lesson into a mockery of black womanhood. *The Root*, the premier online African American site, has seen a high volume of comments about the demeaning engagements with Kara Walker's sexual mammy. In the May 28, 2014, edition of *The Root*, Yesha Callahan reminds readers that such demeaning responses to a denuded black female body are probably inevitable because "from the days of the slave trade to even having black butts on display in music videos, the black woman's body seems to easily garner laughs and mockery, even if it's made out of sugar."

Shall we then fault Kara Walker for not knowing better? Some commentators on *The Root* have just done that, wondering what Kara Walker was thinking! Kara Walker is no stranger to controversy. Her sexualized representations of black women have earned her ostracism from some segments of the African American community, including fellow female visual artists Faith Ringgold and Betye Saar. But the problem is not with Walker's work. At issue here are the racist visual codes that frame and haunt the black female body so much so that the black female body in visual representation is always risky business. This is about the ontologies of deviance and abnormality that continue to haunt the black female body and deter black artists from working with the denuded black female body.

This chapter asks what the colonial hauntology of the black African female body predicates for African female artists who themselves inhabit haunted black female bodies. For, Avery Gordon writes, "to be haunted and to write from that location, to take the condition of what you study, is not a methodology or a consciousness you can simply adopt or adapt as a set of rules and an identity" (1997, 22). What does it mean to work from a site of hauntology and with a haunted body? What visual discourse of the female body is available to African women? Can African female artists use the same strategies as white female artists when engaging in feminist body praxis? What are the peculiarities, vicissitudes, and distinctive modalities of the African feminist nude? What are the agendas serviced by the African feminist nude? In this chapter I bring together for the first time African female visual and performance artists who are pushing the envelope with regard to the representation of the black African female body. Nathalie Mba Bikoro (Gabon), Julie Djikey (DRC), Angèle Etoundi Essamba (Cameroon), Wangechi Mutu (Kenya), Zanele Muholi (South Africa), Grace Nditiru (Kenya), Valérie Oka (Côte d'Ivoire), Tracey Rose (South Africa), and Bernie Searle (South Africa) are African female artists who work against the grain of the postcolonial African representational economy of the female body and dare unclothe the female body. Following Avery Gordon's argument that to be haunted means to develop a critical awareness of a "something-to-be-done" (1997, 16) and Derrida's advocacy of a critical openness toward specters, I analyze how the selected artists appropriate hauntology as an enabling and emancipatory epistemology of the black African female body. The artists develop subversive and pedagogical hauntologies of the African female body that strive to make space for the nude African female body as an artistic and aesthetic endeavor.

Postcolonial African artists have generally been subject to the colonial hauntology of the black African female body. Art historians of Africa have documented the presence of the denuded and erotic female body in classical African arts. With the few exceptions discussed in this chapter, the tradition in postcolonial African visual discourses has been to cover up, desexualize, and de-corporealize African womanhood. There has been to date no sustained investigation of the female nude in postcolonial African visual arts. A detour through the relevant African American context offers a conceptual framework for such a study and suggests that conjoined hauntologies of the black female body and pedagogies of black female respectability shape black visual treatments of the female body. The postcolonial African visual counternarrative of the clothed and respectable African female body (Coly 2010) evokes that of the New Negro that Deborah Willis and Carla Williams reconstitute in *The Black Female Body: A Photographic History* (2002), a study that stretches from the colonial disrobing of the black African female body to contemporary African American visual artists. The dearth of female nudity in the substantial African American artistic corpus covered by the book substantiates the point by many art historians that the female nude has not been an ideologically correct artistic pursuit for African American artists. Lisa Collins, among other scholars who have commented on the rare occurrence of the nude in African American visual arts, has elaborated that "the avoidance, as well as the rare depiction of the nude reveal histories of anguish and pride that continue to surround the Black female body" (2002, 100).

The pregnant maternal figure has been one of the early strategies that African women artists have used for denuding the female body. Nigerian artist Elizabeth Olowu seems to be a precursor of this tradition. *Zero Hour* (1986) is a life-size cement sculpture that represents a seated pregnant woman, her body unclothed except for a small waistcloth to cover her genitalia area. Olowu's daughter, Peju Layiwola, has followed in the footsteps of her mother and represents pregnant nudes. Maternity offers these artists an opportunity to denude the female body by providing a positive cultural trope and a safe point of entry into nudity and sexuality. As a celebration of the cultural vocation of motherhood, the pregnant nude reconciles the women's personal ambitions to be artists with the cultural and often prohibitive prescriptions that women be mothers. These prescriptions underlie the ideologies of "mothernormativity" and "marriagenormativity" described by Tamale (2006, 40). Since the maternal image is an icon of African nationalist discourses, it is a particularly apt trope for African female artists. Willis and Williams write that when African American photographers in the 1960s and 1970s focused on the pregnant nude, they "celebrated not only the black woman's beauty but her pivotal role as perpetuator of the race. Such images of the pregnant black female nude align the body in a positive context with its procreative properties, celebrating nothing less than black life itself" (2002, 159–60). The trope is all the more strategic for African women artists because it intervenes in debates about population control in Africa, the negative modernization of African women, and their corruption by feminism and Western values. Hence the African pregnant nude is a resistive symbol. The embrace of maternity firmly positions African female artists on solid postcolonial identitary ground by projecting an anti-feminism that may appeal African cultural nationalist audiences.

But the pregnant nude is both accommodation and resistance to the prescribed cultural roles of women. A comparison with the traditional nude figure in classical African arts (usually made by men) shows how the pregnant nude by female artists tactically leans on that artistic visual precedent only to subvert it. The traditional African nude, with its emphatic round hips and full breasts, is usually a prescriptive celebration of the fertile female body. In contrast, the pregnant nude shows the women artists reclaiming the female body for themselves. In Olowu's piece, the pregnant woman tenderly hugs her belly and sports a contented facial expression of sexual plenitude because she is reveling in the sensuality of her body. One only needs to consider Olowu's early representation of the female body to appreciate the opportunity for a full expression of the female body that the maternal theme allows. Her earlier sculpture, *Acada* (1979), represents Olowu as a student. She is fully covered and has a nun-like expression and bodily restraint that stands in sharp contrast with Olowu's pregnant nude. For her part, Cameroonian photographer Angèle Etoundi Essamba turns her camera on her fully denuded pregnant body. Her enhancement of her sensually rounded pregnant belly, aesthetically enhanced to evoke a piece of art in some shots, blends the identities of mother and artist. Essamba equates the transformation of the female body during pregnancy to a creative process. The mother here is the quintessential creator, hence the quintessential artist. Maternity provides a safe vantage point from which to elaborate an African feminist visual language of the female body. The artists appropriate the cultural capital of maternity to express the sexual female body. In so doing they reclaim the female body for women and also for feminist ends, as has been the case in Western feminist performance and visual arts.

Since female artists in the West began to lay claim to the previously male terrain of the female nude in the 1970s, there has been a prolific feminist debate on the merits and pitfalls of the nude by women. The cultural positioning of women as objects of the male gaze and the attending depersonalization of the female body have made any representation of female nudity hazardous, the revisionist and subversive encodings of the representation notwithstanding. Feminist criticism has predominantly argued that the feminist nude is doomed to failure because feminist artists of the nude are merely repositioning the female body as object of the sexualizing male gaze. But some critics contend that feminist artists are able to repossess and rewrite the female body when they problematize the spectatorship of the male viewer in a way that disables a facile consumption of the viewed female body. These insights from feminist criticism are relevant to my analysis of female nudes by African women artists. At the same time, Kara Walker's sugar woman reminds us of the shared but also very dissimilar scopophilic predicaments of the black and white female body. Despite the obvious effort to problematize the spectatorship of the viewers, including the insistent historical references to slavery, Walker's female body could barely disrupt the sexist and racist gaze of its viewers. In fact, the Free University, a collective of cultural critiques, had to organize impromptu workshops and seminars on black history to educate the viewership on how (not) to view Walker's sugar woman. This example illustrates the painstaking task of strategizing and framing that artists of the black female body have to undertake as well as the distinctive hauntologies they have to negotiate, much more so than their counterparts who work with white bodies.

How does the black African female nude exist as an artistic and aesthetic category or as a feminist statement in light of the lingering legacies of the colonial unclothing and hypersexualization of the black female body? The viability of the black African female nude first entails an unraveling of the colonial statement of the grotesque African female body. Such a discursive operation, which Stuart Hall (1997) has identified in his typology of black countersignifying practices as a contestation of stereotypes from within, presents limitations. Hall's oft-quoted "Encoding/Decoding" (1980), a pioneering essay about the involvement of the viewer in the production of meaning, puts these limitations into perspective. Hall traces the semantic course of images, from their "encoding" by their producers to their "decoding" by their viewers, and shows that the successful transfer of the intended meaning requires that the two parties share compatible sociocultural and ideological codes. Therefore, in cases of incompatibility the intended meaning is lost on the viewer. Hall's analysis suggests caution regarding the effective resignification of African female nakedness because viewers may employ codes that void this resignification. Hegemonic codes perpetually haunt operations of resignification. Although my use of haunting encompasses the Derridean definition that stresses the disruptive traces of past meanings in new meanings, the notion goes beyond Derrida's definition to include the condition of being semantically overdetermined from without. As a result, the project of an African female nude that counters the colonial statement of the grotesque and naked African female body is an uncertain project. The gap between the moments of encoding and decoding dictates the pedagogical vocation that I tease out in the female nudes of the African artists examined in this chapter.

While Hall posits that encoding and decoding represent two autonomous processes, the African artists interlock the two processes. The artists simultaneously encode and decode their works in an effort to have their nudes supply their own reading instructions, teach a new visual code of the African female body, and host subversive and pedagogical hauntologies. The new hauntologies push further Derrida's and Gordon's prescriptive advocacy of specters and ghostly matters. The artists develop hauntologies that affirm the spectralized subject and assert agency for the subject haunted by the colonial statement of the African female body. I have noted in chapter 1 that Derrida glosses over and also further spectralizes subaltern specters. Derrida suggests that the only way out of their spectral condition of victims of abusive power systems depends on the willingness of hegemony to extend hospitality. Because Derrida is unable to affirm subaltern specters in the same way he reckons with the dominant domineering specters of King Hamlet and Marx, he cannot imagine agency for subaltern specters. In contrast, Gordon focuses on subaltern specters and the abusive systems of power that produce and haunt these specters. Gordon nonetheless asserts agency for subaltern specters because she reckons with their ability to haunt dominant structures. Yet this agency is derivative and represents an agency by designation. In Gordon's schema subaltern specters haunt on the basis of their ability to lead the "new" scholar, a ghost follower, to subjugated knowledges that stand in query of hegemonic ontologies:

> A haunted society is full of ghosts, and the ghost always carries the message—albeit not in the form of the academic treatise, or the clinical case study, or the polemical broadside, or the mind-numbing factual report—that the gap between the personal and social, public and private, objective and subjective is misleading in the first place. That is to say, it is leading you elsewhere, it is making you see things you did not see before, it is making an impact on you; your relation to things that seemed separate or invisible is changing. (1997, 98)

Gordon's affirmation of specters remains prescriptive. Like Derrida, who calls for "another scholar" (1994, 13), Gordon advocates a new way of producing knowledge that would account for spectral others and ghostly matters. She thus joins Derrida in making the presence of the subaltern specter contingent on the willingness of hegemony to extend hospitality. In contrast, the female artists examined in this chapter have the subaltern specter force herself into and reconfigure the hegemonic field of vision. To that effect, the subaltern specter has to be a strategist and pedagogue.

I have described earlier in this chapter the use of the maternal body as a safe gateway to the genre of the female nude. A new generation of African female visual artists has stretched this early visual language by incorporating new strategies that permit further exploration and expression of the African female body. The artists examined in this chapter have tackled the genre of the female nude with unabashed zeal and gusto while displaying an acute sensitivity to the colonial history of the African female body. As a new taxonomy of the black African female body, the African female nude resignifies a figure overburdened by the racialized and racist inscription of grotesquerie and sexual aberration on the African female body. Like Kara Walker, whose black female nudes gesture to slavery and the racist underpinnings of capitalism, the African female nude intervenes in and disrupts past and present discourses about race, morality, and aesthetics. Each artist discussed below has developed a distinct artistic and discursive strategy that allows her to explore the African female body without reinstalling it within a colonial visual economy.

The Aesthetic Nudes of Photographers Angèle Etoundi Essamba and Zanele Muholi

Despite leaning on the trope of motherhood for some of her representations of the female body, Angèle Etoundi Essamba takes her unclothing of the female body further than Olowu. The pregnant nude by Essamba is part of her catalog of black African female nudes entitled *Noirs* (2001). In the African context *Noirs* finds a parallel in *Flesh* (2005), a series of lesbian nudes by South African photographer Zanele Muholi. The two collections represent an aesthetic project of showcasing and celebrating the beauty of the African female body. The artists aim to wrench the African female body away from its colonial confinement to nakedness and ugliness and claim its space in the aesthetic and artistic category of the nude. Kenneth

Clark (1956) has famously overlaid the distinction between the naked and the nude on the nature-culture dichotomy. Feminist art scholars have critiqued Clark's distinction for uncritically idealizing the transformation of women into objects of the male gaze. Annette Kuhn has notably argued that "the transition from naked to nude is the transformation of woman into object" (1985, 11). But Muholi's and Essamba's celebratory nude projects show that the nude has a different significance and substantiate a different agenda for African female artists. In Western arts, with very few exceptions, nudity was never bestowed on black female bodies. Colonialist aesthetic conventions meant that black women could only be naked. The Western artistic tradition of juxtaposing a denuded white female and a fully clothed black female servant, most iconic in Manet's *Olympia* (1863), Gerome's *The Great Bath at Bursa* (1885), and Titian's *Diana and Actaeon* (1556–69), confirmed the inaptness of the black female body for nudity, vouched for the ugliness of the black female body, and spectralized the black female body in aesthetic discourses. The black female body in Western arts exists as the "defining negativity" (Butler 1993, 190) of the white female subject. In her reading of Manet's *Olympia* Lorraine O'Grady has argued that the represented black female lies outside of womanhood. As a result the male gaze can only see the white female body while the black female body is "made opaque by a blank stare" (1992, 14).

Kenyan performance artist Grace Ndiritu, whose work I analyze in the next segment, addresses the racist exclusion of the black female body from the category of the nude. In *Lying Down Textile* (2007, fig. 6), a video performance, Ndiritu puts a spin on the traditional white female nude by wrapping and concealing her body in African textiles. Ndiritu adopts the eye-catching pose of the nude, but the full coverage of her body conveys the inability of the black female body to catch the eye of the viewer. The black African woman cannot be a nude because she is invisible as a beautiful body. Posing as a nude, Ndiritu is accordingly absent in her presence and invisible in her visibility.

Scholars of colonial discourses have noted the aesthetic dimension of European racism whereby blackness and Africanness mediate the beautiful

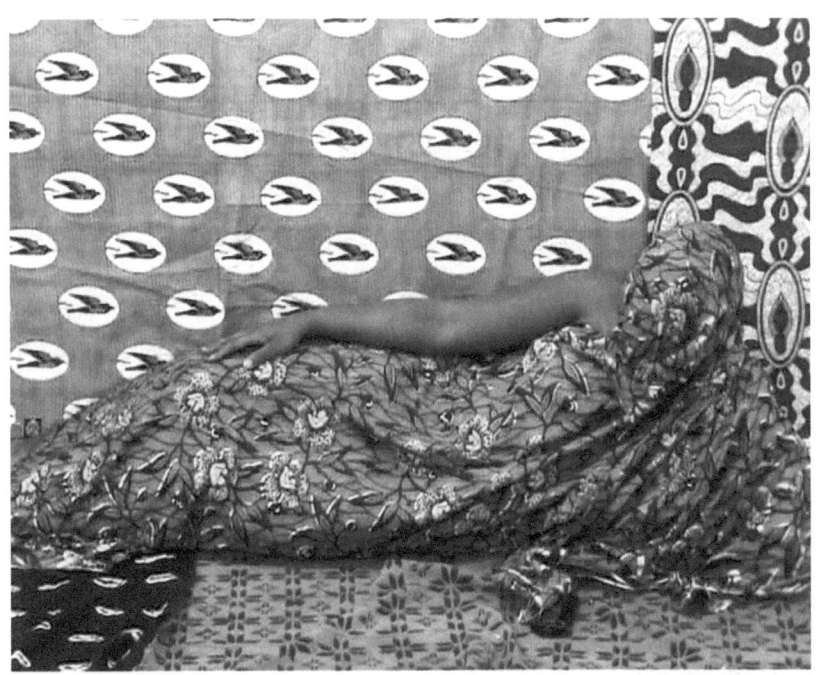

6. Grace Ndiritu, *Still Life: Lying Down Textiles*, 2007. Courtesy of Grace Ndiritu.

in the Western artistic and philosophical traditions (Gikandi 2003; Nutall 2007). According to Kobena Mercer, "distinctions of aesthetic value . . . have always been central to the way racism divides the world into binary oppositions in its adjudication of human worth" (1994, 249). The construction of the black female body as ugly poses a different conundrum for African women artists with regard to the nude, unlike the discontent their white counterparts have over the status of the white female nude as a passive muse and model. Lynda Nead has applauded the dedication of contemporary female visual artists to "challenge the aestheticization and sanitation of the female body within patriarchal culture and open the boundaries of this regime of representation to reveal woman's body as matter and process as opposed to form and stasis" (1992, 63). But the aesthetic black female nude is a subversive figure and resistive art that counter the spectralization of the black female body by Western aesthetic discourses.

Perhaps much more than the nudes of Essamba, Zanele Muholi's *Reclining Figure* (2006, fig. 7) parodies and disrupts the Western tradition of the female nude. Muholi's nude is a lesbian woman with an overabundant figure, unlike the toned and slender bodies of Essamba's nudes. Muholi's lesbian nude is a figure of excess through which the artist effects a radical displacement of the traditional nude and rebuts the normative and universalized Western racist conventions of beauty. In refusing to conceal and spectralize the denuded African female body, Muholi counters the colonial hauntology of the black female body with a hauntology of subversion that threatens Western aesthetic norms and the aesthetic hegemony of the white female body. This hauntology of subversion is also a hauntology of affirmation, unlike the spectralizing hauntology of the black female body produced by colonial discourses and generally sustained by postcolonial discourses. The full-figured lesbian nudes of Muholi resist the sociocultural invisibility of black lesbians through an excessive corporeality that unapologetically runs counter to globalized aesthetic ideals.

The nude project of Angèle Etoundi Essamba does not partake in the feminist de-aestheticization of the female body advocated by Nead. Essamba is exclusively pursuing an aesthetic project of showcasing and celebrating the colonially depreciated beauty of the African female body. Essamba has stated "a need, a call to immortalize the black woman and to celebrate her inner and outer beauty. . . . Aesthetics is my instrument to attract attention and to enable the viewer to see beyond stereotypical forms and familiar references" (quoted in Thompson 2008, 190). The toned and statuesque African female bodies in *Noirs* project classic grace, elegance, dignity, and confidence, all enhanced by the clean lines and sharp angles of the black-and-white glossy shots (fig. 8).

The full-figured nudes of Zanele Muholi (fig. 9), also shot in black-and-white but photographed in soft and sensuous angles, are a jarring departure from Essamba's and the now globalized Eurocentric norms of beauty. The full-figured nudes exude security in front of the camera. The soft and sensuous angles of the shots compliment the models and please

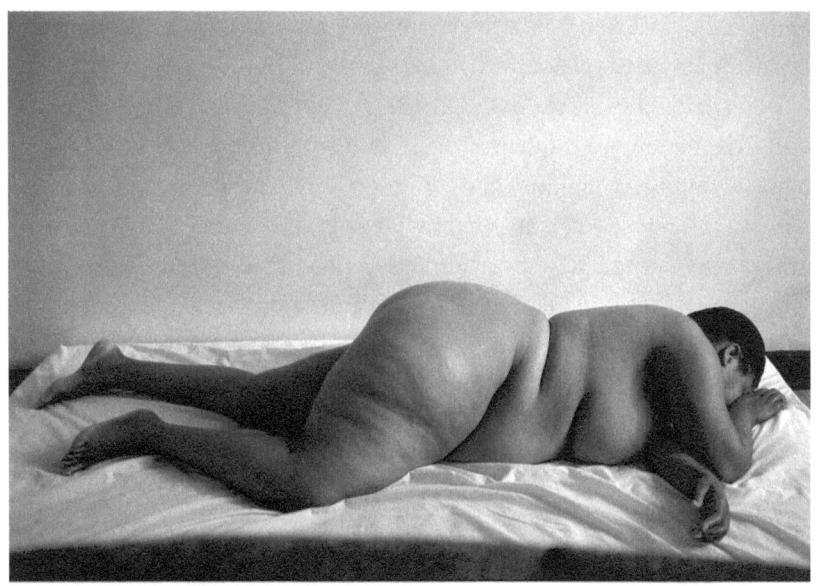

7. Zanele Muholi, *Reclining Figure*, 2006. © Zanele Muholi. Courtesy of Stevenson, Cape Town/Johannesburg, and Yancey Richardson, New York.

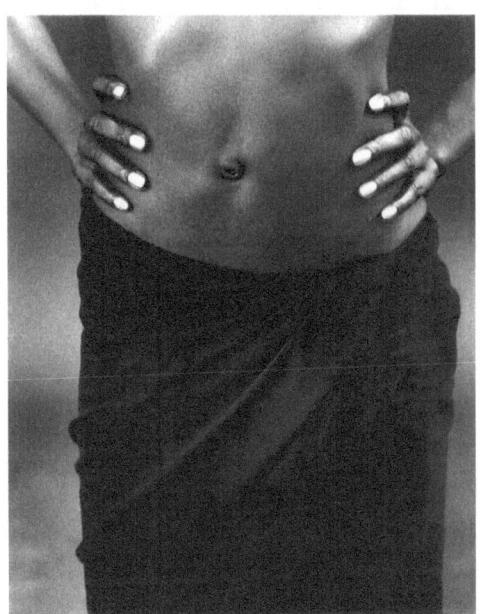

8. Angèle Etoundi Essamba, *Noirs*, 2001. Courtesy of Angèle Etoundi Essamba.

the eye of the viewer. The models' embrace of their nonconforming body types commands appreciation of their beauty.

In claiming a space for black African female bodies in the genre of the nude, the two photographers reposition the African female body from a haunted body to a haunting body. The African female bodies of Essamba and Muholi refuse to be haunted by the colonial statement. Instead they are now haunting and subverting Western aesthetic norms. For Avery Gordon, it is precisely the refusal of spectralization that allows the specter to engage in subversive hauntology, meaning "that moment (of however long duration) when things are not in their assigned places, when the cracks and riggings are exposed, when the people who are meant to be invisible show up without any sign of leaving, when disturbed feelings cannot be put away, when something else, something different from before, seems like it must be done" (1997, 16). Nudity, as used by Essamba and Muholi, troubles the colonial hauntology of the black female body because it gives lie to the colonial statement of the abnormal African female body. The two photographers' use of nudity is therefore rhetorical. Michael Bennett and Vanessa Dickerson's argument about the invisibility of the material body of the black woman illuminates the rhetorical function that I attribute to nudity in the works of Muholi and Essamba. Bennett and Dickerson distinguish between the material body of the black woman and the "discursive body society has created for the Black woman—savage, strong, and ugly," adding that in the lived daily experiences of black women the discursive body routinely supplants and conceals the material body (2000, 2). By laying bare the African female body to reveal its stark materiality and normality, the two African artists unclothe it of its grotesque colonial costume and unravel the hauntology of the black female body. Hence the importance of Muholi showcasing her models in mundane rituals such as bathing and grooming their bodies. Muholi has stated her goal to "re-write/re-visualize/re-present black queer bodies in an amicable way" so that people can see "likeness" (2011, 45). Seeing "likeness" in the denuded black African woman means that she is no longer trapped in the visual regimes of absent-presence and invisible-visibility. The spectralizing gaze

9. Zanele Muholi, *Flesh I*, 2005. © Zanele Muholi. Courtesy of Stevenson, Cape Town/Johannesburg, and Yancey Richardson, New York.

has been disabled, and the African female body now subversively haunts the hegemony of Western aesthetic norms.

The gesture of unclothing the African female body conceptually links the two photographers to African American abolitionist Sojourner Truth. The conceptual link affirms the rhetorical function of nudity in the works of the two female artists and magnifies their pedagogical hauntologies of the African female body. Reflecting on the two artists' rhetorical deployment of nudity, I am reminded of Truth's historical gesture of baring her breasts to her audience during her 1851 "Ain't I a Woman?" speech. Truth felt compelled to show her breasts in order to prove her femininity to her skeptical white audience. Bob Meyers writes that Truth's gesture illustrates the predicament of the black female body, which is that the overdetermination of the black female body precludes the visibility of the black female subject:

> Truth realized that, before one could deal with her as a democratic practitioner, one first had to recognize her humanity: that she possessed capacities exactly like her peers. What Truth struggled for on that podium was her own subjectivity. White people had already figured her out, determined her limits, and so she had to figure out a way to maneuver against the tide of information on which her constituencies entered into the room; she had to figure out some tactic which would expose their support system as weak and unstable. They had, in effect, annihilated her subjectivity, and she had to reclaim it by any means. Truth has therefore before her the near-overwhelming task most dark people and women have: How do I make you understand—as well as convince myself—that I am indeed a subject, not merely an object in the world? (1997, 31)

Essamba and Muholi carry on the pedagogical gesture of Truth. The title of Muholi's exhibition, *What don't you see when you look at me?*, echoes Truth's "Ain't I a Woman?" According to Pumla Dineo Gqola, the concern with normalizing black lesbians has led Muholi to totally lay bare the black lesbian body. Muholi's series *Period* (2006) is a graphic representation of menstrual blood, with shots of stained sanitary pads, red splats on the grass, and a stained white ceramic bathtub. Gquola is right on point that by showing lesbians going through the normal female experience of "bleeding uncontrollably, messily and stickily," Muholi "normalizes Black lesbians as women" (2006, 86). Muholi and Essamba sustain Truth's endeavor to remove the opaque veil that race and gender imprint on the African female body. The three black women unveil and accordingly banalize the African female body in order to bare the African female subject. Banality demystifies the African female body by unburdening it of the spectral opacity that both obfuscates the embodied subject and challenges the audibility and intelligibility of the African female subject. If banality gets the body out of the way, nudity, according to John Berger, provides a straight way to such an end because "at the moment of nakedness first perceived, an element of banality enters" (1972, 59).

Still, the gap between the moments of encoding and decoding evoked earlier in this chapter means that the two photographers have to train the competent viewers of their nudes in order to disable the pornographic gaze that traditionally haunts the black female body. Reader-response criticism, the Iserian strand in particular, helps theorize the artists' methods toward subversive and pedagogical hauntologies that produce competent viewers of the African female nude. While acknowledging the importance of the reader, Wolfgang Iser (1980) has argued that the authorial intent restrains the readers' decoding, offering them only gaps to fill. Within this Iserian hermeneutical strand David Trotter's *The Making of the Reader* (1984) has been most useful for my analysis of the pedagogical undercurrent of the African female nudes examined in this chapter. Trotter relates that a reader of Paul Valery's *Charmes* filled the wide margins of the book with his own reflections. When presented with this annotated copy of his book, Valery turned it into a special edition in order to show how the juxtaposition of the handwritten and typed text "presents to the eye the secret complement of the text [and] shows the reader's function" (Trotter 1984, 5). For Trotter, this example illustrates that although texts are exposed to multiple interpretive and semantic possibilities, some texts can nonetheless control their semantic range:

After all, the handwriting appears only in the space left for it by the typography; it takes its form from the blocks of print around which it flows ... the philosopher's commentary occupies only the semantic space left for it by the poems. Readers may make sense, but they do so in a rhythm and a circumstance prescribed by the text. For the rhetorical devices of the text will be aligned in such a way as to allow their secret complement only a certain space in which to appear; they will provoke their secret complement into making sense, but on their own terms; they will encourage it to make a certain kind of sense. (1984, 5)

In light of the overdetermination of the black African female body as grotesque and hypersexual, Essamba's and Muholi's representation of the African female body entails a "process of making competence out of assumed incompetence" (Trotter 1984, 5). The modalities of their African female nudes, meaning the way the artists thoughtfully and tightly release their nudes into the visual field, illustrate an implicit pedagogical praxis that is informed by the colonial history of the African female body.

Muholi and Essamba's photographs feature denuded body parts but never use a pornographic mode of address. Whereas pornography conveys desirability and accessibility, the two photographers convey desirability and inaccessibility. The stern gaze and self-absorbed stiffness of Essamba's photographic models defy possession of their bodies and secure a distance between viewer and viewed. The guarded and resolved look of the models opposes the nonchalant and absent-minded looking female nudes of the European tradition. The nudes of Zanele Muholi also neutralize the objectifying and pornographic gaze by turning their back on the viewer and pursuing their own mundane rituals. Her models are not posing for the viewer. The dismissal of the viewer shows a lack of concern for the pleasure of the viewer. This is instead about the model's own pleasure and well-being in her body. Much more than Muholi, who relies on one strategy to protect her nudes, Essamba uses a broad range of strategies and maintains a tight grip on the viewer of her nudes. The gaze of her nudes, her aesthetic of the fragment, and her use of space and color constitute techniques through which her audiences become competent viewers of her nudes. She is also able to subvert the spectralizing colonial hauntology of the African female body with a pedagogical hauntology that reteaches the African female body.

The same intense, omniscient, and haunting gaze recurs on Essamba's photographic models (fig. 10). The gaze of Essamba's African women is a directorial and disciplinary gaze that dares viewers to look at the featured bodies through pornographic or colonialist lenses.

The deactivation of inadequate visual codes for the African female body destabilizes the authoritative subject position of the viewer and claims an embodied subjectivity for the nudes of Essamba. South African performance artist Bernie Searle uses the gaze in similar fashion in her *Colour Me* series (1998), a collection of digitally enlarged photographs of her nude body covered in spices. Searle wards off objectification through her confrontational gaze.

Essamba and Searle's confrontational and pedagogical deployment of the haunting gaze joins in similar strategies by other black artists to police and humble the viewers of their nudes. *Yo Mama* (1993), an installation by Jamaican American artist Renee Cox, is a conceptual counterpart to the gazing nudes of Essamba and Searle. Cox has her nude black woman taunt the viewer with "Baby do you want to fuck me? Baby do you want to fuck with me?" The gaze of the nudes of Essamba and Searle translates into the commanding language of Cox's nude. Gazing then becomes a way of talking down to the spectator and a strategy that modifies the conventions of the traditional objectified female nude. The latter is usually muted and made to be looked at by the male spectator whose fantasies it services. In the work of Essamba, the gaze relocates the African female body from an object of visual intercourse to a subject of discourse. The gaze counteracts the vulnerability of the African female nudes since the forceful point of view of the viewed encroaches on the viewer's decoding moment. Additionally, the fierce and discomforting gaze, in counterpart to the blunt speech of *Yo Mama*, communicates an unequivocal message to the viewer. The gaze of the viewed controls the gaze of the viewer,

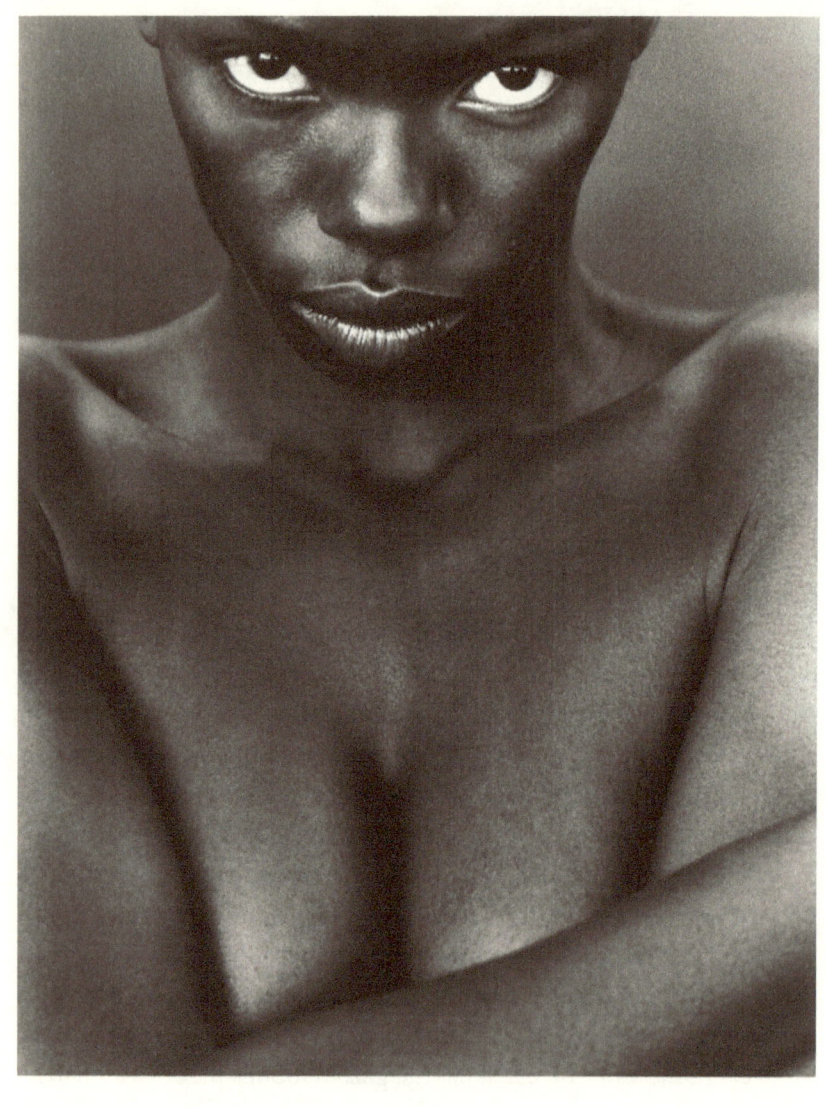

10. Angèle Etoundi Essamba, *Noirs*, 2001. Courtesy of Angèle Etoundi Essamba.

dictating how and what the viewer sees. Essamba, like Searle, utilizes the gaze to enable and disable specific readings of the African female body.

Essamba's use of space, color, and lighting reinforces the authority of the gaze. The photographer shoots in black and white, and the dominance of the black color enhances the gaze. Bernie Searle also makes her gaze stand out by having her whole face, except her staring eyes, covered in spices. The blank background of Essamba's photos adds to the strong visual presence of the gaze. There is a merging between the background and the foreground; both are inanimate spaces. These visual techniques draw viewers inside and implicate them in the artistic work. With the gaze thus standing out, and in the absence of any visual clutter to distract the gaze of the viewer, the pared-down aesthetic of Essamba's piece relates to the pedagogical imperative of artistic works that aim to be read unequivocally. According to narratologist Philippe Hamon, the realist novel is one such example of works with a "pedagogical desire to transmit a piece of information . . . and thus to avoid as far as possible any 'noise' that would interfere with the communication of that information and the transitivity of the message" (1982, 134). By paring down her visual vocabulary, Essamba holds the viewer captive with her own agenda as a postcolonial photographer and the gaze of her African women. The photographs offer the viewer no temporary space of comfort. There is no disengagement from the haunting gaze of each African woman. Being forced to sustain the gaze, the viewer is ultimately forced to hear and listen to the African woman. Additionally, the repetition of the intense gaze throughout Essamba's catalog creates an atmosphere of surveillance, more precisely a Foucauldian policing of the viewer. The latter feels dissected by the pervasive gaze of the nude. Essamba therefore operates a redistribution of subject positions and power relations between viewer and viewed. As the viewer walks through Essamba's photo exhibit, the subversive hauntology of the viewed has the viewer experience haunting, in conformity with Avery Gordon's description of haunting as "those singular yet repetitive instances when home becomes unfamiliar, when your bearings on the world lose direction, when the over-and-done-with comes alive, when what's been in your blind spot comes into view" (1997, 16).

Essamba's cognizant handling of the African female nude extends to the absence of full body shots in *Noirs*. The fragmented reveal of the denuded female body participates in the reformation of the visual code of the viewer. As a technique that visually edits the photographic model, fragmentation substantiates Susan Sontag's point that photographs "teach us a new visual code" by "alter[ing] and enlarg[ing] what is worth looking at and what we have a right to observe. They are a grammar and, even more importantly, an ethics of seeing" (1977, 3). The close-up shots of Essamba target selected selections of the body and exclude the genitals and buttocks. The editing out of these two areas sharply counterpoints colonialist ways of seeing the African female body. While the colonialist visual code, in its focus on breasts, genitalia, and buttocks, can only apprehend the African female body in terms of pornographic gratification, Essamba pursues aesthetic gratification. The close-ups focus the eye of the viewer on the aesthetic attributes of the African female body. The intended effect is to elicit aesthetic pleasure and make for new ways of seeing and knowing the African female body. The teaching of a new visual code works by repositioning the eye of the viewer in such a way that the viewer acquires a new viewpoint on the African female body.

The technique of fragmentation conceptually disassembles and reassembles the female body. The sequencing of the represented body parts binds the viewer to a new syntax of the African female body and wrestles the body from its colonial signification. Returning to Trotter's argument about the interpretive space made available to the reader, Essamba offers the viewer very minimal interpretive space. By not providing full access at once to the female body, she controls the gaze of the viewer and denies them (interpretive) agency over the represented body. The artist tightly accompanies the gaze of the viewer. She clearly refuses to let their gaze and imagination run loose over the African female body. Fragmentation breaks down the viewed for the viewer and positions the latter as a student of the African female body. Through fragmentation, the viewer relearns the African female body.

Essamba concerns herself with installing the African female body as a source of aesthetic gratification as opposed to colonialist pornographic pleasure. She thus solicits an aesthetic point of view on the African female body. She seeks aesthetic visibility for the African female body. While I want to be persuaded by the precautions and strategies adopted by Essamba to evade the reinscription of her aesthetic female nudes within a colonial and patriarchal visual economy, I cannot ward off Peggy Phelan's skepticism of visibility politics. Phelan has warned against the politics of visibility pursued by visual artists from marginalized communities:

> Visibility is a trap. It summons surveillance and the law; it provokes voyeurism, fetishism, the colonialist/imperial appetite for possession. Yet it retains a certain political appeal. Visibility politics have practical consequences; a line can be drawn between a practice (getting someone seen or heard) and a theory (if you are seen it is harder for "them" to ignore you, to construct a punitive canon); the two can be reproductive. While there is a deeply ethical appeal in the desire for a more inclusive representational landscape and certainly underrepresented communities can be empowered by enhanced visibility, the terms of this visibility often enervate the putative power of these identities. (1993, 7)

As much as I am allured by and champion the projects of Essamba and Muholi, I also understand that the trap of visibility may haunt the female nudes of the two photographers. Like Phelan, I question the terms under which these bodies are visible. For sure, the category of the nude pursued by Essamba and Muholi is about to-be-looked-at-ness. What does it mean to be visible as a nude and to gain aesthetic visibility? This is a nil project, Phelan argues:

> If representational visibility equals power, then almost-naked young white women should be running Western culture. The ubiquity of their image, however, has hardly brought them political or economic power. Recognizing this, those who advance the cause of visibility

politics also usually call for "a change" in representational strategies. But so far these proposals are rather vague. What is required in order to advance a more ethical and psychically rewarding representational field, one that sidesteps the usual traps of visibility: surveillance, fetishism, voyeurism, and sometimes, death? How are these traps more or less damning than neglect and utter ignorance? There is an important difference between willfully failing to appear and never being summoned. (1993, 11)

This is where limitations emerge in applying Phelan to the visibility politics of projects from marginalized communities. Visibility is not necessarily about power, or at least not about power as strictly defined by Phelan. I have documented earlier the importance of creating narratives of beauty for the African female body. The white female body has narratives of beauty that it may choose to sidestep, in a willful act of resistance. Invisibility for the white female body then becomes a subversive representational strategy. For the always-already invisible and spectralized African female body, invisibility was never a choice. Returning to Avery Gordon's earlier referenced point about "people who are meant to be invisible" showing up uninvited and turning "home" into an "unfamiliar" place (1997, 16), resistance here may lie in willfully appearing when you were never summoned or expected in the first place. Kenyan collage artist Wangechi Mutu perfectly summarizes this position as she relates how "beauty" was a taboo term in the art classes she took at Yale:

> But we would have discussions about art and one of the worst words you could say in class was "beautiful." I remember thinking, what in heaven's name is wrong with this word and why do people get a rash every time they hear "beauty" or "beautiful"? I went from questioning to resenting why no one was willing to discuss why we couldn't utter the word. I believe the reason is because beauty was actually available to them, their culture decides for the whole world what is beautiful, how beauty should evolve, where it begins

and ends. So they were rebelling against the very thing that had protected them. They didn't want to use the term "beauty" because they owned it. Maybe "beauty" is a sensitive and politicized word for people who have a hard time describing their own culture at this particular point because of the hierarchy colonization has set for things. It's not something they want to reject because they're still fighting to have it. If your entire history of art and your language and your culture are considered to be primitive, maybe you'll fight for the idea of something being beautiful. (quoted in Enright 2008)

Visibility for black women can function as a subversive representational strategy that counters the colonial hauntology of the black female body. White and black female bodies are positioned differently in the field of vision. Because the politics of visibility and invisibility play out differently for white and black female bodies, representational visibility has different stakes. Representational visibility has other goals beyond political or economic power. Visibility does not have to be about power, and power does not have to be about political or economic gains. So what if visibility does not translate into power, as narrowly defined by Phelan? Other benefits and rewards may be at stake. Laura Mulvey (1989) argues that there is also pleasure in being looked at and seen. She suggests that the complex workings of desire mean that the relationship between viewer and viewed may not be as unbalanced and exploitative as many feminists have theorized. Thinking that way about desire may allow us to recuperate the desiring viewed nude as both sexual object and subject.

However, Phelan's politics of invisibility finds support in Bernie Searle's *Traces* (2000), an installation of huge photographs that depict alternately the artist's naked body covered by layers of spices and the imprint that her now absent body left on the spice-covered sheet. The body of Searle totally eludes the viewer. The spice-smothered naked body remains invisible although present. Meanwhile, the visibly absent and therefore invisible body manages to be forcefully present, as its traces speak volume and bring the absent body to compelling presence.

The Nude Performance Art of Grace Ndiritu, Julie Djikey, Valérie Oka, Nathalie Mba Bikoro, Bernie Searle, and Tracey Rose

Women's performance art heeds the concerns of Phelan and many feminist critics about the sexism of the system of representation. But performance art, perhaps much more so than photography, seems to offer a position of control to female artists. The live presence of the viewer allows the artist to check in on her audience's decoding activity and maintain a tighter control on her intended message. Amelia Jones writes that "putting the artist's body—as female body—in movement radicalizes the painterly female nude, denying that it is necessarily only the object of a 'male gaze'" (2000, 24). British performance artist Catherine Elwes also explains that performance art allows the female performer to be "author, subject, activator, director and designer. . . . She is both signifier and that which is signified" (1985, 165). If, following Simone de Beauvoir (1984), the body is a situation and not a thing, performance art therefore acts out and on that situation in a way that is transformative for viewer and viewed. The potential of performance art for resignification and resituation of the female body may explain why many African female artists who work with the denuded female body have gravitated toward performance art.

Unlike Essamba, who is in pursuit of looked-at-ness and whose endpoint is the body, the examined performance artists use nudity as a medium for different agendas. They are interested in problematizing and exposing the colonialist gaze. Theirs is a pedagogical hauntology that seeks to expose invisible systems of oppression and foster critical thinking around the questions of race and gender. To all indications the performers are leery of the gaze, any gaze on the female body, including the aesthetic gaze sought by Essamba and Muholi. Bernie Searle, Tracey Rose, Julie Djikey, and Nathalie Mba Bikoro engage in gestures of de-aestheticizing and, in the case of Rose, defeminizing their bodies. Searle often coats her denuded body with messy and repellant substances such as flour or an unappetizing combination of spices. Djikey covers her body with a dark and greasy mixture of engine oil and ashes from burned tires (Figure 13). Bikoro draws scars on her body with red oil pastel and covers her body with gold dust and clay. Thus transformed, the defamiliarized and abjectified body disinvites the leeching gaze. The sticky and messy situation that is the body fends off any attempt at possession, lest the viewer finds himself stuck in an unfamiliar territory beyond his control, a messy situation so to speak.

Tracey Rose often shaves her head as a way of unbeautifying and de-objectifying herself. The video *Ongetititeldl* (1996) shows Rose shaving all her hair and letting it drop to the floor. In *Span II* (1997), a performance created for the Second Johannesburg Biennale, a fully shaved Rose sits inside of a large glass display case. She is perched on a television set that is displaying Rose as a reclining nude. The juxtaposition of the two bodies for the viewer allows Rose to act out and on the situation of the female body as object of the male gaze. Rose, unlike the reclining nude displayed on her television set, resituates herself not to be looked at. She attempts to remove herself from the patriarchal field of vision.

The agendas of these performance artists pertain to Rebecca Schneider's notion of "feminist explicit body performance":

> First, much explicit body performance replays, across the body of the artist as stage, the historical drama of gender or race (and sometimes, brilliantly, gender and race). Second, these artists critically engage ways of seeing, specifically perspectivalism, which has inscribed women as given to be seen but not as given to see. Third, these artists often tug at the plumb lines marking bodies for gender, race, and class in order to expose their link with representational structures of desire in commodity capitalism. And fourth, feminist explicit body work talks back to precedent terms of avant-garde art transgression, raising questions about modernist "shock value" and the particular fascination with a "primitive," sexual, and excremental body. (1997, 3)

Feminist explicit body performance is pedagogical in its use of the body as a teaching tool. The difference with Essamba, who also incorporates a pedagogical approach, is worth reiterating. Essamba uses nudity to teach viewers a new visual code for the African female body, whereby viewers can see the African female body as beautiful. In contrast the performance artists use nudity as a pedagogical medium to address the patriarchal and racist structures of the field of vision. Their pedagogical hauntologies consist in having the denuded African female body convene, per Avery Gordon's description, abusive systems of power that are "supposedly over and done with (slavery, for instance)" or whose "oppressive nature is denied (as in free labor or national security)" (1997, 16). In forcing temporal cracks into the linear living present, the African female body hijacks the present of the viewer and refuses to let the viewer indulge in an unburdened contemporaneity of the living present. The specter "demands its due, your attention" (Gordon 1997, 16), because the present owes the specter a "debt" (Derrida 1994). The pedagogical hauntologies of the performers lead the viewer of the performing African female body into an acknowledgment of repressed pasts, an interrogation of what is really past about these pasts, and finally an unsettling interrogation of the subject positionalities of the viewer vis-à-vis the convened histories. Indeed, to be in commerce with the specter means to pay one's ethical debt of reparative and representational justice to the specter, according to Derrida (1994, 29). Living with specters is also about self-transformation and the reconfiguration of one's social positionalities, writes Gordon (1997, 22).

Grace Ndiritu, in her feminist explicit body performances, takes her viewers on such a journey toward transformative self-questioning but also ethical accountability to repressed histories and spectralized individuals. Ndiritu never solicits an aesthetic gaze. Her performances strive to make viewers uncomfortably conscious of their subject positioning vis-à-vis the African female body and histories of desubjectification. *Still Life* (2005–7) is a four-screen video installation where Ndiritu reimagines the odalisques of Matisse in order to confront her viewers with their own voyeurism. The performance artist uses African fabric to conceal and reveal her nude body in ways that make viewers uncomfortably aware of their colonialist subject positions with regard to the African female body. The first screen (fig. 6) shows Ndiritu as a reclining nude, but fully draped in fabric except for one arm. On the second screen, Ndiritu sits up straight on a chair; this time her body is fully draped from head to toe. The next two screens

11. Grace Ndiritu, *Still Life: White Textiles*, 2005–7. Courtesy of Grace Ndiritu.

show Ndiritu naked behind the fabric. She is erotically playing with the fabric to tease her audience. She alternatively reveals and conceals parts of her denuded body and caresses her nude thighs (fig. 11).

The juxtaposition of the four performances mimes the invisibility of the African female subject and invites viewers to reflect on how they look at and see the African female body. This is a case of the specter returning to disturb and ask questions of the present. Fully covered and confined to immobility in the first set of screens, Ndiritu is a nonsubject. In the second set she only comes to existence as a sexual object.

Ndiritu accepts her interpellation into that scopic regime only to resist and unravel it. Ndiritu lures in her viewers with a promise of pornographic gratification only to displace them onto the stage and deconstruct them. Rebecca Schneider calls this strategy "counter-mimicry" or a "turn upon the historical representation of the native, upon colonial mimicry of native identity" (1997, 169–70). Mimicry quickly becomes countermimicry in Ndiritu's performance. Ndiritu exposes the voyeuristic intent of her viewers and their fraught relationship with the African woman by acting out, hence mimicking, the reasons for their presence in the audience: the viewers are merely and only present as eager would-be viewers of a denuded black female body. Ndiritu thus turns the table on her viewers, making a spectacle of their voyeurism. The gaze of the viewers and not the nude black body on stage becomes the object of the performance. Per Catherine Elwes, the viewer's "cloak of invisibility has been stripped away and his spectatorship becomes an issue within the work" (1985, 173). The viewers look at themselves looking at the nude female body. They are voyeurs, a subject position enabled by their compliance with and perpetuation of racist and patriarchal power structures. For Elwes, successful feminist performance shocks and scares away the objectifying viewer by exposing the male spectator "to the fearful proximity of the performer and the dangerous consequences of his own desires" (173).

Ndiritu, unlike Essamba, does not reveal her gaze. Her face, as in Muholi's nudes, is made unavailable to her viewers. While Muholi's women purposefully turn away from and ignore the viewers, Ndiritu performs for and faces the viewers. She engages the viewers but keeps her face covered, in a move Derrida associates with haunting specters and calls the "visor effect." Derrida describes the ghost of Hamlet's father looking at his son from within the armor, with his eyes concealed by the visor:

> This Thing meanwhile looks at us not see it even when it is there. A spectral asymmetry interrupts here all specularity. It de-synchronizes, it recalls us to anachrony. We will call this the visor effect: we do not see who looks at us. . . . This spectral someone other looks at US, we feel ourselves being looked at by it, outside of any synchrony, even before and beyond any look on our part, according to an absolute anteriority (which may be on the order of generation, of more than one generation) and asymmetry, according to an absolutely unmasterable disproportion. Here anachrony makes the law. To feel ourselves

seen by a look which it will always be impossible to cross, that is the visor effect on the basis of which we inherit from the law. (1994, 6–7)

Derrida captures the reversal of subject positionings and the ensuing unraveling of viewers that the pedagogical hauntology of Ndiritu produces. In the moment of pedagogical hauntology, viewers lose authority and are subject to the law of the viewed or the spectral other.

By purposefully concealing her face, Ndiritu is also confronting her viewers with their own refusal to see and know the viewed as a subject. Her viewers are made to confront in the open, hence uncomfortably, their fantasies of a desubjectified sexual partner. In short, Ndiritu is countermimicking her status as sex object. As she controls the movement of the fabric on her body, Ndiritu puts her nude body back in control by controlling what, when, and how viewers see. The fragmented reveal of her nude body, a conceptual counterpart to Essamba's technique of the fragment, controls the audience's visual access to her body.

In *Desert Storm* (2004), Ndiritu lies on a map of the world with her legs spread and her crotch exposed. A transparent white muslin cloth faintly covers her nude body and her face. As in *Still Life*, she plays sex object and initiates a game of strip tease with her audience. Ndiritu twists her body seductively on the map while constantly moving the white cloth on her body to suggest the possibility of seeing her completely naked. At some point, she partially rewards the expectant viewers with a quick reveal of her vagina. But here, unlike in *Still Life*, Ndiritu uses her nude body to make a pointed political intervention about the patriarchal gender politics of global warfare. Again, as in *Still Life*, mimicry becomes countermimicry. It turns out that the performance artist is securing the attention of her viewers to deliver an important message about rape as a weapon of war. A text starts to scroll on the screen with the names of countries where raped women were casualties of war: Sudan, East Timor, Iraq, Afghanistan, Rwanda, Bosnia, Kashmir, Tibet, Eritrea, Kosovo, Chiapas, Algeria, Congo, Sri Lanka, Guinea Bissau, Indonesia. Before the eyes of the viewers, the object of their pornographic fantasies transforms into a victim of rape. By undercutting the pornographic gratification of her viewers, Ndiritu messes with their decoding schema for the female body. It appears to the now discomfited viewers that the object of their sexual attention was not twisting seductively but rather twisting in pain. But perhaps more discomfiting to the viewers is their suggested complicity with the operations and mechanisms of rape. At the core of both rape and voyeurism lie a sexual objectification of women, a predatory relation to the female body, and a patriarchal sense of entitlement to the female body. Rape and voyeurism have a similar point of view because voyeurs also fantasize about raping their target. Ndiritu unequivocally aligns viewer and rapist when she ends her performance by tearing the veil away from her face and staring accusingly at the viewer-turned-voyeur-turned rapist.

The scopic regime of patriarchy consigns women to speechlessness. Women are to be seen and not heard. In order to develop her political message, Ndiritu develops a strategy of luring and holding her viewers hostage with the promise of nudity. The strategic use of the sexualized female body has two implications. The strategy becomes a commentary on the silencing of women by patriarchal scopic regimes on the one hand. On the other hand, the strategy suggests the possibility of a feminist unsilencing of women within that same patriarchal scopic regime. In theory, this is a seductive practice. The possibility of beating the system at its own game—playing with in order to play the system, so to speak—is along the lines of Luce Irigaray's mimesis (1985). Irigaray invites women to speak "unfaithfully" from their cultural positionings in order to call the stereotypical views of women into question. According to Irigaray, the very fact of repeating the stereotype unfaithfully deconstructs it and repositions the stereotyped as subject.

The theoretical appeal of Ndiritu's feminine body talk is undeniable, especially when one considers the corporeal angst that has been crippling African feminist discourses. However, I am not fully convinced that a conventional audience, meaning a nonspecialist audience not acquainted with the history of the black female body, would be attuned to the deconstructionist agenda of Ndiritu. For instance, would the juxtaposition of the striptease act and the scrolling text make sense to an audience not informed about world politics? What if Kosovo, Congo, Algeria, Iraq, Timor, and so forth carry no resonance to the viewer and, as a result, cannot clue them in on the message? The game of association that Ndiritu initiates could not proceed in these circumstances. In that event Ndiritu would fail to take control of the decoding process of her audience. So while I remained seduced by Ndiritu's performance, I am concerned that her pedagogy is inconsiderate of the clueless and incompetent viewer. Unlike Essamba, who, I argue, maintains a tight grip on her audience, Ndiritu gives too much leeway to her viewer. I also wonder whether the analogy between rape as a weapon of war and voyeurism does not make for a convoluted message, too theoretical and opaque for a performance act? I can anticipate a repeat of the faulty reception of Kara Walker's *Sugar Baby* installation where the history-challenged audience failed to pick up on the clues.

Images and evocations of rape sometimes play into patriarchal and masculine fantasies of male supremacy. I am thus all the more concerned that the co-framing of the acts of rape and striptease creates a fantastical scene that colludes with these fantasies. Race is an additional and decisive factor here. Because of the hypersexualized image of black women, I am apprehensive that the audience will totally misread the performance of Ndiritu. The metaphor of rape is even trickier to handle when it comes to black women. The rape of black women does not generate the same outrage as that of white women. Race is an interpretive lens in the reading and naming of sexual violation. Can we trust the audience to recognize and be outraged by the sexual violation of the black female body?

Wangechi Mutu's *Pinup* series (2001), which also uses looked-at-ness as a strategy to lure in the viewer, makes for a good comparison with Ndiritu. But Mutu's piece strikes me as a more successful endeavor. The message of Mutu is brutally straightforward once the lured viewer comes forward. Like Ndiritu, Mutu's pinup tells a story of a Western-fueled war and its subsequent creation of the violated African female body and her Western savior. The series consists in twelve images of topless women posing like calendar girls. Once the viewers get close enough, they realize that these are severely traumatized bodies. The women are amputees from the blood-diamond war in Sierra Leone.

Ndiritu, like all female artists of the nude, takes considerable risks on behalf of the female body. The questions raised in my analysis of her performance probably betray my own angst about the sexualized and denuded black female body in representation. But my questions also speak to the trickiness and tenuousness of the sexual black female body as a springboard for deconstructive discourses and sociopolitical activism. The ill-fated *Sugar Baby* installation and my own ambivalence about Ndiritu's performance leave me wondering whether the sexual black female body is not too overdetermined and weighted to be put to political use without a companion educational piece on the intersecting discourses of race, gender, and sexuality.

Sans nom (Without a name) (2015), a performance production by Valérie Oka from Côte d'Ivoire, is attached to *En sa présence* (In her presence) (2015), a companion educational piece that helps frame the viewing of the denuded black female body. The show was part of the 2015 exhibition *Body Talk: Feminism, Sexuality, and the Body* curated by Koyo Kouoh and featuring the works of six contemporary African female artists. The exhibition first opened on February 2, 2015, at the WIELS Center of Contemporary Arts in Brussels before traveling to the Lunds Konsthall in Lund, Sweden, and the FRAC Lorraine in the French city of Metz. Oka held a live performance at the opening of the exhibition. In *Sans nom*, the first part of the performance production, a naked black woman strolls in an open cage made of black steel bars. An erect massive white penis sits in one corner of the cage and a red fabric trapeze hangs from the top. The woman routinely engages in acrobatic dances. Oka concerns herself in this piece with the tenacity of colonial discourses of the hypersexual black African woman. The fact that the woman does not bother to step out of the open cage conveys the pervasiveness and immanence of colonial discourses. It is almost impossible to get away from the legacies of colonial discourses. As a standalone piece, this performance would definitely raise my concerns about the incompetent viewer. The latter may view the piece

12. Valerie Oka, *En sa présence*, 2015. Courtesy of Sophie Thun. From the exhibition *Body Talk: Feminism, Sexuality, and the Body in the Work of Six African Women Artists*, curated by Koyo Kouoh.

as an invitation to view the exposed black female body through the very colonial discourses the performance sought to unravel. But Oka appears to anticipate her incompetent viewership. *En sa présence*, her companion performance, is a dinner party where Oka invites eleven guests to address a question posed in bright neon letters on the wall: "Tu crois vraiment que parce que je suis noire je baise mieux?" (You really think that because I'm black I fuck better?). The guests write down their responses on the tablecloth, and a discussion about the sexual objectification of black female bodies ensues. After the opening night of the exhibition, a video recording of the first performance was featured while the companion performance was displayed, with the neon text hanging over the vacated table and the responses of the guests scribbled on the tablecloth (fig. 12).

The idea of coupling the two performances is brilliant pedagogy. Oka's project nonetheless presents some logistics problems. First, for the perfor-

Subversive and Pedagogical Hauntologies 167

mance to work, the same audience has to remain throughout the two performances. Second, the two pieces are now available online. But in the digital age the two pieces won't always circulate together. In this case, the much-needed work of contextualization that the second performance does is lost.

My visit on January 13, 2016, to the Body Talk exhibition at the FRAC Lorraine in Metz substantiated for me the intricate thought that went into framing Oka's representation of black female nudity. The exhibition was spread out over several rooms and floors in the main building of the FRAC. Oka's piece was on the top floor and would be the last one the spectator would visit, after going through less risky and more abstract pieces in terms of their presentation of nudity and sexuality. Those were pieces by Billie Zangewa, Zouleika Bouabdellah, Tracey Rose, Marcia Kure, and Miriam Syowia Kyambi that coached the viewers to think critically about race and gender and that did prep work for the installation of Oka. At the entrance of the room to Oka's installation, a warning sign read "déconseillé aux mineurs" (not recommended for minors). The installation was arranged into an L shape and consisted in a video projection of the discussion dinner at Wiels, a red neon sign on an adjacent wall reading "Tu crois vraiment que parce que je suis noire je baise mieux?" (You really think that because I'm black I fuck better?), and, on the perpendicular wall, a video projection of the nude woman in the cage. Whereas at Wiels, the audience got to see the nude performance first before proceeding to the dinner scene, the sequencing of events was different at the FRAC. Upon entering the room, viewers immediately face the video of the dinner discussion and the red neon sign, with the latter sign immediately grabbing their attention first and almost taunting them like Essamba's gaze and Cox's *Yo Mamma*. The viewers then proceed to watch the debate on the video, which takes up the question raised by the neon sign. The debate brings together a group of women and men of different races. The last stop of the viewers is the video of the nude woman, for which they had already been prepared by the previous two sequences and the pieces of Oka's co-exhibitors. In that way Oka and show curator Koyo Kouoh do an effective job of framing and protecting the exposed black female body.

For provocative performances like Ndiritu's and Oka's to realize their political potential, their audiences need to have acquired competency on how not to read the denuded black female body. Oka, much more so than Ndiritu, astutely anticipates and remedies the incompetence of her audience. So what happens once the performers remove the element of sexuality?

Enter Tracey Rose, Bernie Searle, Nathalie Mba Bikoro, and Julie Djikey. All four women routinely perform in the nude but take the precaution of desexualizing and defeminizing their nudity. Does this precaution ward off the voyeuristic and objectifying gaze? Is the sexualizing gaze kept in check by this strategy? What does the viewing eye see? Does the defeminized or desexualized nude facilitate the feminist use and resituation of the female body as a medium for critical discourse? Of course, I would be naive to assume that one is in control of the perception of one's body as feminine and sexually appealing. Still the sexual body and the feminine body are also somewhat of an act. Does the refusal to perform the act matter? Or, is the female body already so predisposed to be sexualized that it stands no chance in the nude?

Snow White (2001) is a video performance by Bernie Searle projected on two opposite mural-size screens. One screen offers a bird's-eye view of the performance while the other shows the performance at eye level. When the performance starts, a denuded Searle is kneeling on a black floor. But viewers can barely make out Searle until flour starts pouring from above to gradually cover the entire body of the artist and then bring the flour-covered body to visibility. However, the nudity of the artist is not available to viewers because the white flour only reveals the contours of the body but totally conceals its nudity. Searle thus preempts any distraction from her overall message. Viewers only see a white shape at work. Searle is busy kneading the flour that has collected around her into dough. She subsequently destroys the dough. Olu Oguibe (1997) has explained that Searle's performance enacts being "whited-out," in reference to the colonial erasure of indigenous populations. I extend Oguibe's analysis to suggest that Searle also suggests the failure of the colonial project. Searle stages a colonial scene whereby her play on visibility and invisibility mimics for her viewers the colonial "discovery" of lands and bodies. The viewers whose point of view Searle astutely aligns with the colonial gaze strive to but can never see the performer. The work of Anne McClintock (1995) on the interrelated mechanisms of colonial visuality and knowledge is a companion to Searle's piece. Viewers are made to first peer hard through the darkness where they barely make out a shadowy presence. They then see a ghostly apparition when the flour pours on Searle. Searle emerges as a ghostly apparition. McClintock writes that colonial scenes are redundant with shadows and monstrous visions that betray colonial anxieties about not being able to know the other (1995, 26–28). Searle's performance positions her curious audience alongside the scopic and visual regimes of colonialism to suggest that the viewed African female body of the performer, like the othered body of the colonial native, is no more than a colonial visual effect. In the end the othered body, a colonial simulacrum and mirage, remains invisible and unknowable to the colonial eye and Searle's audience. The performer exposes the blindness of the colonial eye, meaning the colonialist illusion of seeing and knowing the other. In sum, seeing the other is mere colonial egotistic pretense and fantasy.

In *Snow White*, probably more so than in her *Traces* installation analyzed earlier in this chapter, Searle makes Peggy Phelan's politics of invisibility and remaining unmarked her own. Refusing to be seen and to be known, Searle shares Phelan's warning that visible representation allows society to "name and thus to arrest and fix the image of that other" (1993, 2). Of course, in the context of South Africa, from which Searle hails, remaining unmarked defies the arbitrary racial classifications imposed by the Apartheid state. Searle's mistrust of visibility further plays out as she chooses to shake but not wipe the flour off her. She leaves just enough flour to allow her contours to be defined. In so doing she claims agency by allowing herself to be visibly unmarked or markedly invisible. Her visibility is on her own terms. Searle also allegorizes her choice to be unmarked by collecting and then shaping into dough the flour that has settled around her. She never allows the dough to settle into an identifiable and nameable staple. She eventually breaks the dough apart. The dough, like Searle's body, retains an elusive identity.

The flour is dumped onto Searle from above to suggest that her body is caught in a situation not of her making. But the dough, a product of her labor, signifies resistance and agency. By shaping and breaking the dough at her will, Searle conveys her ability to reclaim ownership of her body and resituate her body as she sees fit. The nude laboring body of Searle cuts a sharp contrast with the conventional reclining nude. The immobility and passivity of the latter ensure that it never rises above its situation as an object of the male gaze. The laboring body is able to distract viewers from its nudity because the attention of viewers is also solicited by the labor underway. The male gaze is most certainly deterred by the fact that the nude woman is all absorbed in and by her task. Unlike in Ndiritu's performance, where the gaze of viewers is actively solicited and the artist pointedly performs for the sexual gaze, Searle starkly ignores her audience and pointedly conveys her sexual unavailability.

Tracey Rose also uses the laboring nude as a representational strategy. In *Span II* (1997), the artist, her head freshly shaved, is in a glass case. She is deeply absorbed in knotting her shaved-off hair. The hair evokes cotton, and the scene invokes the Atlantic slave trade. The scene gets the fully clothed and cotton-dependent viewer to think about what being clothed means and entails. Rose is perched on a sideway television set on which plays an image of Rose as a reclining nude. The performance artist resituates her body by choosing to sidestep the norms of representation of the female body. She overturns the passive and languorous pose of the traditional nude. The appropriately overturned television set and her shaved-off hair represent her dissent with the patriarchal regime of representation of the female body. Like Searle, Rose emphasizes her sexual unavailability. She ignores her viewers and never bothers to acknowledge their presence. Rose further dismisses her viewers as colonial voyeurs by having them look at her as she sits in a glass display case that evokes the colonial display of non-Western people in European museums, fairs, and zoos.

Nathalie Mba Bikoro joins the two South African performers in featuring her laboring nude body in many of her performances. *(N)OnIdentity* (2011), performed in Brazil with Brazilian Wagner Tempos Rossi, revisits slavery in order to foster a critical examination of race, cultural heritage, and identity in contemporary Brazil. When the performance opens, a naked Rossi sits on a bench with his back to the audience. A tattooist is drawing a slave ship bound for the Americas on Rossi's lower back. On the opposite side of the stage Bikoro, a white sheet wrapped around her body, is washing white sheets in water and then wine before proceeding to scrubbing them. A film displaying images related to the brutal histories of race and slavery is screening at the back of the stage. The images on the screen become more violent as a panting Bikoro beats and whips the sheets over the floor to dry. Meanwhile the sheet around her body has slid to bare her upper body. Bikoro and Rossi then switch places and a fully naked Bikoro sits down to get a tattoo of a slave ship returning to Africa.

The replay of the history of slavery on both the screen and the body signifies that the story of slavery has not been told once and for all. The inscription of the history of slavery on the body, an ethics of "being-with-specters" (Derrida 1994, xix), allows for a constant "re-narrativization" of slavery. The story has to be told again and again, out of concern for a just and ethical memory of slavery and in protest of the "unresolved social violence" of slavery (Gordon 1997, 16).

The resounding frameworks of slavery and racist histories saturate the denuded body of Bikoro and potentially ward off the sexualizing gaze. Earlier in this chapter I brought David Trotter's argument about the making of readers to bear on my analysis of how Essamba tightly controls the interpretive space around her black female nudes. Likewise the histories of pain and violence that tightly frame the denuded and pained body of Bikoro help keep her audience in check. Additionally, Bikoro, like the laboring nudes of Tracy Rose and Bernie Searle, does not solicit a sexual gaze or acknowledge her audience. Neither does the nudity of the performers ground the performance, as is the case with the previously analyzed performances of Ndiritu and Oka. The fact that three focal points of interest underlay Bikoro and Rossi's performance also decenters the displayed nudity. The attention of the audience is divided between the three unfolding scenes on the stage. The performance actively solicits the critical and analytical skills of the audience to thread together the three scenes and thus make sense of the performance. As a result, the denuded black female body on stage becomes a piece of the larger puzzle that the audience is tasked with figuring out.

In *The Uncomfortable Truth* (2011), Bikoro uses again her denuded body as a pedagogical tool to magnify past and present histories of brutal objectification of the body, namely the Western exhibition and sexualization of "other" bodies, the torture of bodies at Abu Graib, and the laboring child bodies in the gold mines of Gabon. Images of these spectralized histories and bodies accompany the performance of Bikoro. As Bikoro paints red wounds and measurement marks on her denuded body and then covers her body with gold leaf and clay, she transforms her body into a site where the past and present histories projected on the screen merge seamlessly to reveal the unsettling continuities between past and present and across geographical spaces. The denuded body of Bikoro does not lend itself to sexualization because of the histories that unequivocally haunt it and self-reproduce on it. Her soiled and messy body is messed up by virtue of being at once an archival document, a site of memory, and a critical site to interrogate the present. At the end of the performance Bikoro chews and then spits out white lily flowers, a symbol of French slavery, into the audience. Bikoro echoes Frantz Fanon's revolutionary native, who "vomit[s] . . . up" the values of the colonizer (Fanon 1961, 43), and Calixthe Beyala's revolutionary Ateba, who spits out the sperm of her rapist at his feet (1987, 152). Bikoro's is a resistant body that defies objectification and spectralization.

Of the different African female performers examined in this section, Julie Djikey stands apart because her work is totally unconcerned with gender, sexuality, or race. Djikey's performance, *Ozonisation* (2013, fig. 13), sensitizes her audience to the dangers of pollution and global warming.

13. Julie Djikey, *Ozonisation*, 2013. Courtesy of Patrick Morarescu.

Djikey performs live in the streets of Kinshasa, the capital of the Democratic Republic of Congo. The online video of the performance is available on YouTube and shows a semi-nude Djikey, her body transformed into a car. She dons a gas tank on her back, a bra made from hollowed-out oil filters that barely conceal her breasts, and dark yellow-tinted sunglasses that mimic car lights. Her whole body is heavily coated with a dark mixture of engine oil and ashes from burned tires. The steering wheel in her hands connects to a tiny toy car made of discarded cans. As Djikey steers her way through the busy streets of Kinshasa, an ever-swelling crowd of onlookers trails her. Some people look puzzled, some are amused, some are taking pictures on their phones, and others can be heard exclaiming in Lingala, "Eza nini?" (What's this?). Somebody is heard explaining in French, "C'est une performance" (It's a performance). But nobody looks scandalized or offended by the nudity of the artist or the overexposed female body. Is it because the layers of darkened engine oil end up concealing her body to make her nudity less jarring? Maybe some members of her audience think that she is a madwoman in the throes of a fit? For sure, semi-naked mad people roaming around and trailed by teasing children is not that uncommon of a scene in some cities in Africa. I have witnessed more than my share of such scenes in Dakar, Lagos, and Abidjan, among other African cities where I have spent significant time.

In Djikey's performance, the nudity of her body never lends itself to sexualization. The question "Eza nini" indicates that the audience does not just see a nude female body. Neither do they see a madwoman, or they would not have bothered to ask. What they see is a "thing" whose meaning, like the meaning of Bikoro's intricate performances, they strive to elucidate. As people follow Djikey and keep on asking, they are clued in on the unfolding performance and eventually get its message. Djikey's astute use of her nude body as a canvas on which she vividly illustrates the consequences of ozone depletion ensures that her message comes across clearly. The nudity of her body becomes appropriate in this context and does not distract the audience from the message Djikey seeks to convey. As in Bikoro's performance, the nude body of Djikey is not an object, but just a tool of her performance. This is a distinction to which her audience seems to have caught on, making it possible for Djikey to deliver her message.

The Grotesques of Wangechi Mutu
I am trailing a conceptual thread from the messy body of Bernie Searle and the messed-up bodies of Valerie Bikoro and Julie Djikey to the grotesque collaged bodies of Wangechi Mutu. The disordered African female body confounds the dominant gaze by not lending itself to easy decoding. "Eza nini?" asks the puzzled audience of Julie Djikey. The disordered body

is an insubordinate body and a subversive hauntology that irreverently and unceremoniously arrests the gaze. I am including in this conceptual thread Zanele Muholi's images of menstrual blood, represented through soiled sanitary pads, blood stains, and blood-stained bathtubs. The tacky imagery of Muholi has prompted valid comparisons with Judy Chicago, but I prefer to pursue another referential framework for Muholi's messy menstruating body. Many African contexts, including South African ones, attach malefic powers to menstruation. Women have to hide menstrual blood from sight and, in some cases, keep away from sacred spaces. The bleeding female body, in societies where blood is a symbol of warrior masculinity, disrupts the patriarchal symbolic order and convenes disorder. Muholi's bleeding lesbian who flaunts both her nonconforming sexuality and her taboo feminine bodily processes is an apocalyptic discursive figure that clears a space for new discourses of the African female body.

The grotesque female bodies of Wangechi Mutu participate in this space-clearing endeavor. The grotesque is Mutu's chosen method to mess up and haunt hegemonic discourses of the African female body, including colonial notions of the grotesque African female body. Mutu works to sabotage the racial and gender binaries that sustain hegemonic discourses. The artist cuts out and collages newsprints and photographic images from magazines into watercolors. The result is a conglomerate of mongrel figures that blur the distinction between the human, the animal and the machine, the exotic and the familiar, the high and the low, the proper and the improper, the compelling and the repelling. Frances E. Connelly has built on Bakhtin's theory of the grotesque to approach grotesques as " 'trans-' modalities; better described for what they do, rather than what they are." For Connelly, "the grotesque is defined by what it does to boundaries, transgressing, merging, overflowing, destabilizing them. Put more bluntly, the grotesque is a boundary creature and does not exist except in relation to a boundary, convention, or expectation" (2003, 4).

Mutu's *Pinup* series, evoked earlier, effects this mongrelization that haunts hegemonic boundaries and categories. Mutu proceeds by uniting the clashing worlds of sexual entertainment and war. The mongrelization aims to index the grotesque cause and consequence of the war in Sierra Leone. "Diamonds are a girl's best friend," goes the song. The trade in blood diamonds in Sierra Leone fueled the country's civil war. The mutilated bodies of the populations of Sierra Leone lived on as a grotesque symbol of the Western dependence on the beauty commodity. The abjectly mutilated body subsequently haunts Western beauty to reveal the grotesque foundations that both enable and vex Western notions of beauty. Mutu exposes the grotesque splendor of Western beauty. In laying bare these foundations, her grotesque pinup lays new foundations for more complicated discourses of the beautiful female body. Beauty, as reframed by Mutu, is grotesque by virtue of being created from the promiscuous interdependence between violence and pleasure as well as horror and aesthetics. Mutu builds a new discursive framework that displaces grotesquerie from the African female body, historically apprehended as grotesque, onto the beautiful European body.

What makes the grotesques of Mutu rhetorically effective is her use of collage to jar the gaze with her act of bringing together dissonant categories and discourses into a consonant whole. The new assemblage introduces the eye to news ways of seeing and establishes concomitantly a counter-framework to unravel hegemonic discourses of the African female body. To create her collages, Mutu consistently scavenges through magazines of pornography, women's fashion, hunting, ethnography, medicine, tourism and motorcycling. The common thread to these magazines is that they typecast bodies. Mutu poaches eclectically from the represented bodies then collages her harvest into an arresting figure that eludes the taxonomy of bodies and prompts accordingly the viewer to ask the same question asked of the messy body of Djikey: "Eza nini?" (What's this?). The bodies that Mutu composes are not one thing, nor do they have a unitary meaning. The bodies of Mutu, like the Derridean specter, are many things at once. They are messy because they encode multiple and unbounded meanings. They accordingly mess up discourses by virtue of always exceeding discourse. Of relevance to Mutu's work on the body is the work of Merleau-Ponty (1964) on the corporeal schema. The notion accounts for the plasticity and expandability of the body through the capacity of the body to incorporate new instruments and thus new embodiments. The notion was understandably of some use to feminist scholars, most notably Judith Butler (1990) and Elizabeth Grosz (1994), because it potentially equips the female body with resistive possibilities. For my part and in relation to the work of Mutu, I am particularly drawn to the work of Gail Weiss (1999) for its attention to the ways in which discourses of race, gender, age, ethnicity, class, and disability create normative bodies and police corporeal schemas. For Weiss, and as seen in Mutu's engagement with typecast bodies, the corporeal schema sustains social and political inequalities but can also revert into a site of contestation, precisely because "exploring the corporeal possibilities that have been foreclosed by a given culture's own imaginary itself helps bring into being a new imaginary—one that does justice to the *richness of our bodily differences* . . . we must in turn create new images of the body, dynamic images of non-docile bodies that resist the readily available techniques of corporeal inscription and normalisation that currently define human reality" (1999, 67). The collaged bodies of Mutu suggest to the viewer a new corporeal schema, meaning a new way of seeing, thinking, and doing the body. Mutu allows her viewer to de-essentialize and imagine the body as a set of possibilities, unconstrained by race, gender, and other discursive categories.

The conceptual framework of bricolage offers another firm theoretical grip on the collages of Mutu. Where interpretations of Mutu's bodies often foreground hybridity, I favor the more proactive notion of bricolage. Where hybridity describes a condition and a location, bricolage, as conceptualized by Claude Lévi-Strauss in *The Savage Mind* (1966), captures the agency and creativity embedded in the corporeal activism of Mutu. Mutu, forever the consummate scavenger of mainstream magazines, proceeds like the bricoleur. As Lévi-Strauss argues, the bricoleur, unlike the engineer who proceeds in an abstract and methodical manner, improvises and makes do with whatever is at hand in order to adapt existing material to his or her needs and present situation (1966, 17–18). The purposefully patched and eclectic appearance of the collaged bodies of Mutu signifies

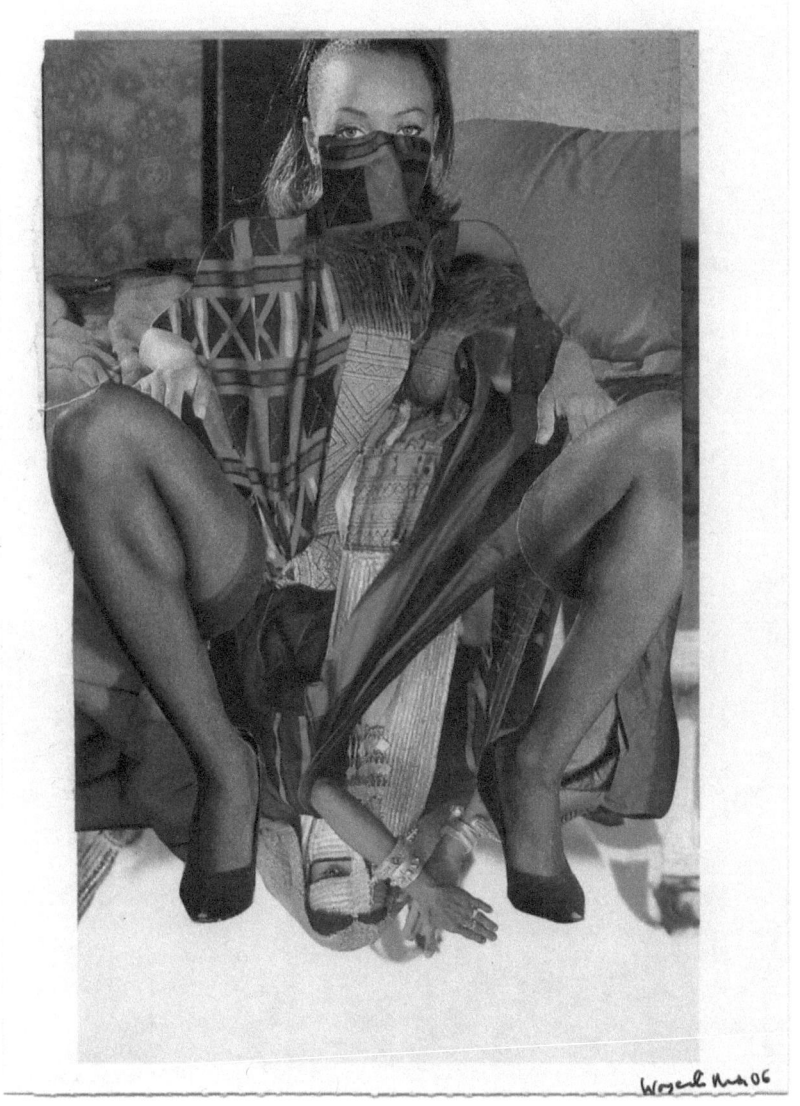

14. Wangechi Mutu, *The Ark Collection*, 2006. Courtesy of Sikkema Jones & Co., New York.

15. Wangechi Mutu, *The Ark Collection*, 2006. Courtesy of Sikkema Jones & Co., New York.

a refusal to blend in. The bodies match the cobbled and patched aspect of the finished product of bricolage, unlike the smoothness of hybridity. The flagrantly patched bodies of Mutu flaunt their heteroclite composition. In the scavenger hands of Mutu, the body becomes an intertextual and extroverted text, a fluid and mobile assemblage that sabotages received corporeal schemas. Okwui Enwezor offers an apt description of Mutu's collages, writing that the collages are "veritable landmines, always volatile, unruly, troubled" (2010, 30).

Enwezor's description dovetails with the effects of bricolage as redefined by Jean and John Comaroff (1985). The Comaroffs contend that Lévi-Strauss's bricolage "condemns the dominated to reproduce the material and symbolic forms of a neocolonial system." Having studied how the Tshidi populations of Botswana and South Africa adopt and then adapt biblical signs and metaphors in their resistance of mission Christianity, the Comaroffs overhaul bricolage as a subversion of the signifying structures and ideologies of the dominant order (1985, 261). Mutu engages in this form of bricolage in her series *The Ark Collection* (2006, figures 14 and 15). In this volume of collages she subversively cites and reframes a popular American source book on African women. Mutu turns the lenses on ethno-photography, with an eye to troubling its pseudoscientific credential and factual representations of African female bodies. She uses collage to recompose *Women of the African Ark* (1993), a popular book of ethnographic postcards by Carol Beckwith and Angela Fisher.

Ethnographic postcards grossly typecast African female bodies as antique specimens frozen in prehistoric time. Mutu adopts and then adapts the ethnographic postcard as a mode of representation. She cuts off female body parts from pornographic magazines such as *Pictorial* and *Black Tail* then grafts them onto ethnographic postcards in order to conceptualize the discursive complicity between ethnography and pornography. Mutu successfully tinkers with the ethnographic postcard, a dominant mode of representing the other, to craft a visual concept that jars the eye with the perverse coloniality of contemporary modes of representation of the African female body. Of Mutu's unsetting collages, Okwui Enwezor writes, "It is never about blunting their impact, but rather heightening the unease around them. This image can be looked at and it cannot be looked at. By confronting the salacious gaze, her work also plays on disarming the disciplinary power of the aberrant image. Here scopophilia and scopophobia are enjoined, xenophilic fascination is counteracted by xenophobic repulsion, while iconophilia and iconophobia are placed next to one another" (2010, 30). Enwezor is indeed describing how Mutu "disarms" the colonial hauntology of the black female body. Mutu also aims to unsettle the viewer with the same discomfort that Searle, Rose, Oka, Essamba, Bikoro, and Ndiritu seek to provoke through their deployments of the gaze and allusions to uncomfortable histories.

The works of the artists surveyed in this chapter show a relatively uninhibited handling of the black African female body that is seemingly freed from the postcolonial African corporeal angst over the female body. Their subversive and pedagogical hauntologies of the black female body contest the colonial statement of African womanhood. The expansive political and ideological agendas of the artists, beyond gender and sexuality, create new discursive anchorages and conceptual impetus for the representation of the black African female body. I earlier established a conceptual affiliation between Sojourner Truth, Angèle Etoundi Essamba, and Zanele Muholi. The takeaway from both this comparison and the political resonance of the female nudes of Mutu, Ndiritu, Bikoro, Oka, Djikey, Searle, Rose, and Oka is that the disrobed black female body need not only evoke Sarah Baartman. From the 1922 protest against the labor of Kenyan women on colonial coffee plantations to the 2002 protest against the Chevron Texaco oil company in the Niger Delta, African women have used their unclothed bodies as weapons against various structures of oppression. The stripping off of clothes by women, also known as "the curse of nakedness" in some African societies, offers an empowering and compelling paradigm of African female bodily praxis and helps us rethink the equation of black African female nudity with objectification, degradation, and humiliation.

5
Laying Specters to Rest?
ON BRINGING SARAH BAARTMAN HOME

In light of her embrace by African and Afro-diasporic discourses to index colonial violations of black female bodies, it seems appropriate to devote the last chapter of this book to the return of the body of Sarah Baartman to the custody of South Africa and, by extension, all communities that claim filiation to Baartman. On August 9, 2002, Baartman was properly laid to rest in her native soil. Having argued in chapter 2 that the specter of Sarah Baartman in African feminist criticism manifests a postcolonial hauntology that falls short of the transformative hauntology upheld by Derrida and Gordon and pursued by the artists examined in chapter 3, I return to the figure of Baartman in this chapter to consider the following questions: What is at stake in continuing to extend hospitality to the specter of Baartman, especially when she has been laid to rest and mourned properly? How does the homecoming of Sarah Baartman converse with the hauntologies in the discourses of the female body examined throughout this book? What type of labor is the reclaimed body of Baartman doing, on whose behalf? To address these questions, I bring together literary, visual, and performance texts that converse and disagree around the work of mourning Baartman and laying her specter to rest.

"The work of mourning" is part of the subtitle of *Specters of Marx* since the notion of mourning as work anchors Derrida's hauntology. If hauntology is the condition of living with specters, mourning is the work of creating and sustaining that condition inasmuch as mourning is the work of conjuring specters and maintaining commerce with specters. I have already referenced in the previous chapters Derrida's argument that the specter is an obligatory inheritance that the receiver can nonetheless "sort out" (1994, 18) and "restructure" (67). The work of mourning then participates in what Derrida calls the "task" of inheritance (67). Derrida's proposition that mourning is work that dialectizes death by refusing to lay specters to rest revises the traditional Freudian understanding of mourning. In Freud, mourning is a process of progressive detachment from the lost object, hence a process of laying specters to rest. What is at stake in mourning Sarah Baartman one way or the other?

The first stanza of Diana Ferrus's poem "A Tribute to Sarah Baartman," written in 1998 and published in 2003, suggested the subtitle of this chapter: Bringing Sarah Baartman Home.

> I have come to take you home, home!
> Remember the veld?
> the lush green grass beneath the big oak trees?
> The air is cool there and the sun does not burn.
> I have made your bed at the foot of the hill,
> your blankets are covered in buchu and mint,
> the proteas stand in yellow and white
> and the water in the stream chuckle sing-songs
> as it hobbles along over little stones. (2003, 592)

Various sources have credited Ferrus's poem with setting the wheels for the repatriation of the remains of Baartman to South Africa in 2002, following a decade-long campaign. The dedication of the poet to building a home that Baartman will never leave again exemplifies a mourning of Baartman that endeavors to lay the specter of Baartman to rest. One finds in Ferrus's investment in the homecoming and proper burial of the remains of Sarah Baartman the processes of conventional mourning, as detailed by Derrida:

> [Mourning] consists always in attempting to ontologize remains, to make them present, in the first place by identifying the bodily remains

and by localizing the dead. . . . One has to know. One has to know it. One has to have knowledge. . . . Now, to know is to know who and where, to know whose body it really is and what place it occupies, for it must stay in its place. In a safe place. . . . Nothing could be worse, for the work of mourning, than confusion or doubt: one has to know who is buried where—and it is necessary (to know, to make certain) that, in what remains of him, he remains there. Let him stay there and move no more! (1994, 9)

Yet if Ferrus's mourning of Baartman is meant to conjure away the specter of Baartman, the poem does not seek closure and a forward motion for the mourner, as Derrida's explanation of conventional mourning would have it. Ferrus does not seek to be released from the specter of Baartman, nor does she refuse to inherit from Baartman. She seeks to release the specter of Baartman itself. The poem strives to reclaim Baartman from the postcolonial hauntologies that host the afterlife of the colonial statement of the grotesque African female body and that subsequently partake in a depersonalization of Baartman.

The reclamation of Baartman undergirds the meaning of homecoming in the first stanza of the poem. By refusing to name or even allude to Europe, colonialism, and racism in this opening stanza, the poet performs a discursive dismissal of Europe. "I have come to take you home," as opposed to "I have come to take you away from Europe" is a dismissal of Europe that shows the detachment of the poet from the discourses that have framed Sarah Baartman as the Hottentot Venus. The poem speaks of the female body in terms and within parameters set by the poet. The indigenous landscape that grounds the voice and welcomes the body of Sarah Baartman shows the endeavor of the poet to enunciate Baartman from the inside out. Laying the specter of Baartman to rest thus means emancipating the figure of Baartman from both the colonial statement and postcolonial hauntologies. Here the refusal to extend hospitality to the specter, against Derrida's and Gordon's injunction to do so, is indeed a refusal to extend hospitality to the colonial statement. For the colonial statement weaves itself into our inheritance from the specter of Baartman and corners us into being the types of perpetual respondents to colonial discourses described by Fanon (1965) and Said (1988).

I also read the homecoming that the first stanza enacts against the background of the appropriation of Sarah Baartman by Afro-diasporic communities to symbolize the black female body. This appropriation sent Sarah Baartman onto yet another exile. Zine Magubane (2001) has addressed the theoretical industry that devolved from the faulty transformation of Baartman into an icon of racial difference. Other scholars have critiqued diasporic discourses on Baartman for robbing her of her African specificities (Baderoon 2011; Gordon-Chipembere 2011). It thus matters that Ferrus brings Baartman back home to a specifically South African landscape of veld, proteas, buchu, and mint. The footnotes to the poem specify that the protea is the national flower of South Africa, and the buchu is a medicinal herb used by the Khoikhoi people, Baartman's people. The specifications are an insistent affirmation of Sarah Baartman as a South African national and a woman of Khoikhoi heritage. Laying the specter of Sarah Baartman to rest in that context means cutting short her never-ending appropriations, commodifications, and homelessness.

South African visual artist Senzeni Marasela joins in Ferrus's envisioned homecoming for Baartman. In *Beyond Booty: Covering Sarah Baartman and Other Tales* (2010), an installation at the Axis Gallery in New York, Marasela uses red thread to hand-embroider a series of cloths. The series represents the process of dressing Baartman. Marasela chooses a typical Khoi dress code for Baartman. The dress code obeys the cultural norms of Baartman's community of origin and not European notions of dress. The installation includes individual pieces such as *Changing Sarah's Story*, *Sarah Baartman Redressed*, and *Shielding Sarah from the Cold*. The Khoi blankets that Marasela uses to dress Baartman replicate the image of the blankets covered in bushu and mint that Ferrus caringly prepares for Baartman. The proactive titles of the different pieces in the series foreground the artist's agenda of "re-narrativization," to go back to the terminology from Gordon used throughout this book. Like Ferrus, Marasela suggests that the re-narrativization of Baartman entails laying her specter to rest once and for all.

The agenda of re-narrativization pursued by Ferrus and Marasela, alongside their caring engagement with the body of Baartman in their work, convey their view that laying the specter of Baartman to rest constitutes a praxis and ethics of care for Baartman. The ethics of refusing hospitality to the specter of Baartman form a counterargument to Derrida's and Gordon's affirmation of hauntology as ethics. It is not the case that Ferrus and Marasela are refusing their responsibility to inherit from and pay their ethical debt to Baartman. Instead, they are suggesting that in Baartman's case an insistence on living with the specter violates the latter. If in Derrida and Gordon the work of mourning is the task of paying an ethical debt to the specter, Ferrus and Marasela contend that the work of mourning Baartman is unethical. Laying Baartman to rest once and for all means not having her play parts in our contemporary politics, body narratives, and body dramas. Ferrus's poem preempts appropriation of the narrative of Baartman. By not tending to present-day needs, agendas, politics, and ideologies, the poem allows the pain, suffering, and grievance of Baartman to take center stage.

> I have come to soothe your heavy heart,
> I offer my bosom to your weary soul.
> I will cover your face with the palms of my hands,
> I will run my lips over the lines in your neck,
> I will feast my eyes on the beauty of you
> and I will sing for you
> for I have come to bring you peace. (Ferrus 2003, 592)

The many narratives of the story of Sarah Baartman have generally failed to individualize her and restore her to full humanity because they appropriate Baartman's name to tell other stories of abuse. As a result the narratives obliterate Sarah Baartman, the individual. This mode of appropriation makes it impossible for us to imagine the pain and humiliation of Sarah Baartman, the Khoi woman. The postcolonial and Afro-diasporic iconography of Baartman potentially reiterates her desubjectivation by colonial discourses.

Ferrus's poem, by refusing to do the work of mourning Baartman, resubjectifies Baartman and operates a restatement of the story of Baartman. Restatement, far from repeating a statement, is in this specific case a pointed refusal to repeat the original statement, where the work of mourning Baartman would entail a repetition of the colonial statement. Ferrus's restatement and refusal to do the work of mourning Baartman interrupt the afterlife of the colonial statement. Her poem refuses to extend the story of Baartman into the present or recycle it as a framework for the racist violations of African female bodies. The poem mentions the fate of Baartman in the hands of Cuvier in the shortest stanza, placed between two stanzas that focus on subjectifying Baartman. By mentioning the episode only to decenter it immediately, Ferrus strives to cut short the life of the colonial statement. The statement will not be referenced again. The nonrepetition of the colonial statement deems it into obsolescence.

Repetition inscribes and actualizes. But following Butler (1990) on repetition as "resignification" and Stuart Hall (1980) on repetition as "transcoding," repetition can also perform the type of restatement that Ferrus achieves through nonrepetition. Tracey Rose's installation *Ciao Bella* (2001), made a year before the repatriation of the remains of Baartman, grapples with the possibilities and pitfalls of repeating the colonial statement when doing the work of mourning Baartman. *Ciao Bella* adapts both Leonardo da Vinci's *The Last Supper* (1498) and Judy Chicago's *The Dinner Party* (1979) in an effort to explore the repetition of female archetypes across time and space. Rose convenes thirteen women around her table, including Marie Antoinette, Lolita, a topless mermaid with an afro, a nun, a rubber-clad bunny girl, porn star Cicciolina, and Sarah Baartman. The full installation consists of thirteen large-scale photographs and a triple-screen video projection. The photographs are portraits of Rose's own impersonation of the thirteen female archetypes. The ability of Rose to conduct a seamless impersonation of each archetype is an effective illustration of gender performativity.

For her impersonation of Baartman, Rose is photographed naked in a bush setting. The landscape of hills, lush green grass, oak trees, and proteas evoke the South African resting place and home where Ferrus seeks to repatriate Baartman. Like Ferrus and Marasela, Rose reattaches Baartman to South Africa. Rose's Baartman is not posing but appears instead to be hunted and on the lookout for her aggressor. But Baartman's defensive posture in the post-apartheid South African landscape that frames Rose's restatement potentially queries the type of home that contemporary South Africa is for South African women. This is a question that South African dancer and choreographer Nelisiwe Xaba takes up in *Sakhozi Says Non to the Venus* (2008). In this solo dance piece Xaba, as Baartman, returns to South Africa only to long to go back to France because of the xenophobia and gender oppression in post-apartheid South Africa. Conversely, the assertive body language of Rose's Baartman, as she appears ready to fight back and defend herself, reverses her passive demeanor in her European representations and unpositions her as a victim. Rose's Baartman also has a determined look. Because we don't see the target of her gaze, she appears to be peering into the future. By equipping her defensive and assertive Baartman with a future-oriented gaze, Rose brings Derrida's notion of the specter as "revenant" and "arrivant" to bear on her restatement of Baartman. Armed with knowledge of the past, Rose's Baartman is able to preempt a repetition of the past and of new forms of subjugation of her body.

Rose's performance of the archetypes also deconstructs Baartman as an icon of black womanhood. The repetition of the colonial statement in a new context that aligns Baartman with female archetypes across time and space takes the burden of singularity off Baartman. The new context disclaims Baartman as the historical freak that colonial discourses have made her to be and that postcolonial and Afro-diasporic counterdiscourses have unwittingly reified. When Rose fits Baartman into a transhistorical, transracial, and transgeographical corporeal assemblage, she reclaims Baartman as Everywoman and reallocates across groups the symbolic trauma that black women appropriate for themselves.

In the companion video to the photographic series, the women interact and come to life. But the developments in the video revoke the suggestion in the photographic impersonation act that repetition and the work of mourning may present possibilities for restatements. The women in the video bicker, then the bunny character shoots all the women. Baartman is the only one to be resurrected, but she is reincarnated as labia in a jar. The return of Baartman as labia shows the futility of engaging the colonial statement while her defensive posture in the post-apartheid South African landscape calls for feminist vigilance with regard to the postcolonial nationalist reclamation of Sarah Baartman. The inconclusive presence of Baartman in Rose's installation is an interrogative strategy that poses the work of mourning Baartman not as an agenda but as a question.

Zoë Wicomb takes up the question of the work of mourning Baartman in *David's Story* (2002), where she concerns herself with the types of agendas and discourses that the work of mourning Baartman services. In *David's Story*, a novel set at the time of Nelson Mandela's release from prison in 1991, David Dirske, a guerrilla fighter for the armed wing of the African National Congress, hires a woman amanuensis to write his biography. The project leads David on a quest for his roots as a colored South African. He traces his ancestry back to the Khoisan people and Sarah Baartman. But to the dismay of David, the amanuensis plots his biography to be a story about women. Among the women whose stories she chooses to foreground are those of David's wife, Sally, and his ANC comrade and love interest, Dulcie Oliphant. She reluctantly includes Sarah Baartman, upon the insistence of David, but she occasionally overrides some of David's entries on Baartman. The fleeting and elusive presence of Baartman, compared to the foregrounded presence of the first two women, is a refusal to represent Baartman. By devoting very minimal space to Baartman, the amanuensis signifies her refusal to partake in the nationalist positioning of Baartman as mother of the post-apartheid nation. She crafts a narrative that interrogates what is at stake in the nationalist work of mourning Baartman and who is benefiting from that work.

David's inclusion of Baartman is gestural, appropriative, and ultimately opportunistic. The reader is cued in on David's agenda at the start of the novel. David insists on the presence of Baartman in his story because, in his words, "one cannot write nowadays . . . without a little monograph on Baartman; it would be like excluding history itself" (2002, 1). In the aftermath of the repatriation of the remains of Baartman to South Africa, she became one of the mothers of South Africa. Meg Samuelson (2007) has examined the symbolic subject positions available to South African women in the post-apartheid era and concluded that women are either silent and normative mother-symbols or dissident and disruptive figures who need to be controlled. As the designated mother of the nation, Baartman serves the purposes of the nationalist male autobiography that David is putting together. As a mother figure, Baartman is a prop to the male autobiographical subject. Her presence in the nationalist text does not overshadow the male hero since she solely functions to anchor his birth in an indigenous body and legitimize his status as son and narrator of the nation. Further, as a mother instead of a daughter of the nation, Baartman is not only tamed—she is desexualized. It is symptomatic of the postcolonial angst over colonial discourses of the female body that her postcolonial reappropriation entails her desexualization. Her integration into the national pantheon as a respectable woman of the nation is contingent on her desexualization.

The presence of Baartman in David's nationalist autobiography reflects the gender and sexual politics of post-apartheid nationalism. The maternal figure of Baartman allows national discourses to incorporate women while containing them. The elevation of Baartman as the symbol of colonially victimized black African womanhood mobilizes postcolonial solidarities around her victimization and against the structures of colonialism, Eurocentrism, and white hegemony. Postcolonial African patriarchies are thus off the hook for their own gender violations. In fact, postcolonial African patriarchies can use the figure of Baartman to engage in feminist posturing, as is the case with David Dirske and the duplicitous post-apartheid political leadership that he is made to represent in the novel.

The narrator exposes the duplicity in the nationalist work of mourning Baartman by teasing out David's actual contempt for the real-life Sarah Baartman. According to the narrator, the notes that David jots down on Sarah Baartman stress Baartman's "foolish vanity" and show a superficial understanding of her predicament (2002, 134–35). David views Baartman as the sexualized and grotesque Hottentot Venus. Nor does he have any sympathy, compassion, or empathy for her, even as he reads about her dissection by Georges Cuvier. He does not grieve over her fate, and he cannot even muster anger or outrage at Cuvier. His fascination with the scientific genius of Cuvier, the ultimate act of treason to Sarah Baartman and South African women, exposes his hypocrisy and the disingenuousness and duplicity of his fellow male nationalists when it comes to women's issues. Wicomb thereby invites distrust for the post-apartheid nationalist reclamation of Sarah Baartman.

In an intended echo to Marlowe's "keep the woman out of it" in Joseph Conrad's *Heart of Darkness* (1899), Wicomb has David chide his amanuensis for writing a story filled with women. The correspondence between the sexist Marlowe, whose journey to the Congo is made possible by women, and David, whose nationalist masculinist narrative is secured by Sarah Baartman, is apropos. The analogy reiterates to the reader the misappropriation of Sarah Baartman as a launch pad for post-apartheid patriarchal narratives. The comparison also serves to expose the fraught gender politics of post-apartheid nationalism and the masculinist anxieties about women that informed the post-apartheid nationalist idolization of Sarah Baartman. Baartman is not a resistant woman. Her lack of agency and historical voice makes her an ideal female icon for patriarchal nationalism. Plus, her post-apartheid repatriation fits a masculinist savior narrative that showcases the heroism of the sons of the nation. Having Sarah Baartman stand as Everywoman is a way to "keep the women out of it" by repressing the voices of the women of the nation through fraudulent substitution and feminist posturing. David's insistence on the presence of Baartman and his anxiety over the many women in his story reflect a fraudulent patriarchal feminism that can only accommodate the silent presence of women because it wants undisputed narrative custody of the nation.

The decision of the amanuensis to claim narrative space for other women at the expense of both Baartman and David is an act of dissent from the nationalist work of mourning Baartman. The amanuensis manages to turn David's story into the story of David's comrade in the ANC, Dulcie Olfiant, and David's wife Sally, also a former ANC cadre. The two women are foils for Baartman since the post-apartheid mythologization of Baartman has served to mask the contributions of South African women to the fight against apartheid. Dulcie is a point of anxiety for David, who struggles to make sense of his feelings for her. David does not know how to relate to Dulcie because she exceeds the categories of the woman and the freedom fighter. In David's description of Dulcie, the latter is grotesque by virtue of being an unfeminine woman yet not so unfeminine as to fit into the masculine category of the guerilla fighter. His romantic attraction to Dulcie may be a way to contain her and reassure himself that she can be domesticated like his wife Sally. Dulcie rises to the rank of senior officer in the movement, which is testimony to her fortitude and competence. However, as punishment for resisting domestication and being out of place, she is abused and humiliated repeatedly by her male comrades, including David. In counterpoint to Dulcie, David's wife Sally allows herself to be domesticated though marriage and motherhood. Sally also experienced sexual abuse while in the movement, and she traded her participation in the movement for the normative role of unfulfilled housewife. She then symbolically developed Baartman's condition of steatopygia, a metaphor for her containment by the structures of patriarchy and her loss of control over her body. Sally, often referred to by the amanuensis as "Steatopygious Sally," also goes by Sarah, having changed her name from Saartjie. This is a further connection to Baartman, who was born Saartjie and renamed Sarah.

The experiences of abuse and torture of the two women at the hands of the very men that repatriated the remains of Sarah Baartman and rescued her from colonial abuse expose the fraudulent gender politics of post-apartheid nationalism. In this context the work of mourning Sarah Baartman deflects the past and present violation by South African nationalists of the rights of South African women. The dissenting narrative of the amanuensis aligns the colonial abusers of Sarah Baartman with her post-apartheid saviors in order to invite suspicion if not disavowal of the post-apartheid work of mourning Baartman. The theme of betrayal and lack of solidarity, evoked earlier through David's admiration of Cuvier, carries over to David's betrayal of Dulcie. David takes part in the torture of Dulcie. The resonance between the mutilated body of Baartman in Cuvier's hands and the tortured body of Dulcie shows a haunting correspondence if not filiation between Cuvier and David. The amanuensis refuses to represent Sarah Baartman's violated body, yet she crafts a detailed and graphic description of the horrific mutilation of Dulcie's body by her ANC comrades. The theme of betrayal also conveys the betrayal of Sarah Baartman through the political recuperation of her painful story by the self-serving male nationalist establishment in post-apartheid South Africa. The theme carries over to the betrayal of South African women by a post-apartheid nation that misappropriates Sarah Baartman to further put down the women of the nation.

More than a refusal to share narrative space with the women of the nation, the erasure of women from the nationalist story is also a result of the unrepresentability of their violated bodies. It is about the inability of the nation to confront its own history of violence toward its women. When David tries to represent Dulcie, he can only produce a "mess of scribbles" about Sarah Baartman (2002, 135). The amanuensis is able to tease out the specter of Dulcie that haunts and threatens to unravel the nationalist representation of Sarah Baartman because Dulcie's name "is written several times and struck out. Then there are beginnings scattered all over, and at various angles that ignore the rectangularity of the paper, as if by not starting at the top or not following the shape of the page he could fool himself that it is not a beginning" (2002, 135). David's subsequent attempt produces "a page without words" but with "dismembered shapes of a body," leading the amanuensis to conclude that "it is Dulcie who lies mutilated on the page" (2002, 205).

Christa Baiada (2008) compares David's narrative mutilation of Dulcie to Cuvier's mutilation of Baartman. In fact, the parallel between the two speaks to the violence of representation, especially when representation is in the service of a larger narrative. Cuvier dissected and rearranged the body of Baartman to fit scientific racism. David fragments Dulcie because he attempts to have the story of Dulcie serve his nationalist heroic narrative. In the end Sarah Baartman displaces Dulcie in another injurious act to the body of Dulcie. Here Dulcie's injury stems from the fact that David is trying to force her persona into the premade nationalist mold of Sarah Baartman. In the process David also shatters the nationalist mold when his story about Baartman becomes a "mess of scribbles." The superimposition of the fragmented bodies of Baartman and Dulcie, as David tinkers with each story, creates a disconcerting continuity between past and present that challenges any discontinuity between the colonial and postcolonial treatment of the female body. The South African nationalist mold made for Sarah Baartman is also violence to Baartman and her story, thus a perpetuation of Cuvier's disassembly and reassembly of Baartman. In contrast to David, the amanuensis refuses to represent Baartman and instead privileges Dulcie, who is ultimately unrepresentable. In so doing, the amanuensis crafts a postcolonial feminist narrative that is mindful of centering the story of postcolonial violations and trivializing the story of colonial violations. Postcolonial feminist vigilance means that the amanuensis is aware of the potential neocolonial recuperations of her story of postcolonial violations. Such a story that deflects or disguises colonial violations of the female body would be a disservice to Baartman.

Wicomb has stated her discomfort with the reclamation of Sarah Baartman (quoted in Meyer and Olver 2002). While *David's Story* refuses to partake in the post-apartheid work of mourning Sarah Baartman, the motif of steatopygia in the novel reveals Wicomb's more nuanced relationship to the inheritance from Sarah Baartman. The motif pervades the novel as most women in the novel, including the amanuensis, turn out to have steatopygia. As mentioned earlier, David's wife Sally develops steatopygia once she becomes a housewife and mother. But steatopygia is more of a multilayered metaphor that writes back to colonial discourses of the African female body and exposes postcolonial violations of female bodies.

Wicomb has shared in interviews her objective to reclaim the ridiculed body part from colonial discourses. Wicomb rewrites colonial discourses that associate steatopygia with aesthetic deformity and moral deformity. The novel attempts to endow the ridiculed feature with desirability and power. Significantly, both David's wife and his love interest Dulcie have steatopygia, and David revels in the anatomical feature that "offer[s] warmth and well-being" (2002, 16–17). Andrew le Fleur, David's ancestor, marries his wife Rachel Susanna because he finds "in the swell of her full-grown steatopygia a spirit moving him to husbandhood" (2002, 46). Large posteriors are also strategic political assets. When le Fleur dreams of an impending betrayal by some of his men, he enlists his wife to hide strategic documents "in the curve of her back, in the generous space shaped by steatopygia where it would never be found" (2002, 55). The women selected as "rain sisters" or "queens of steatopygia" are "blessed with the most bountiful behinds" and "had been shaped by God into perfect vessels . . . to carry water to the Promised Land" (2002, 153).

But Wicomb is not successful in her attempt to resignify the ridiculed body part. She tries to endow the part with positive meaning, only to further objectify the steatopygous women. The body part has desirability and sexual appeal only through the male gaze, but the women themselves don't revel in their bodies. The discomfort of Sally with her body further compromises the aesthetic reclamation attempted by Wicomb. Sally subjects her body to the torture of spandex undergarments and calls herself a "clumsy, steatopygous woman" who "cannot help but feel a sense of shame" at her inability to walk a straight path" (2002, 201). Wicomb's attempt to endow steatopygia with power and importance is also fraught. Rachel le Fleur surrenders her body to her husband to aid in his nationalist designs, and the rain sisters are no more than vessels of patriarchy.

The metaphor of steatopygia works most efficiently, meaning in a feminist manner, when it engages the postcolonial condition of women. Here, steatopygia becomes a condition that women suffer from, and the steatopygous female body bears the marks of the continuity between past and present. There are a lot of references in the text to the hampered mobility of the steatopygous characters. Steatopygia may as well signify that Baartman has ultimately become a burden for post-apartheid women because her elevation has been at their expense. The nationalist construction of the homecoming of Sarah Baartman as a liberation of South African women makes the specter of Baartman stand in the way of the liberation of South African women. Hence steatopygia in the novels induces stasis or slows down women. Therein lies the urgency for South African women of laying the specter of Sarah Baartman to rest once and for all.

The importance of *David's Story* has to be appreciated in the context of the previously mentioned Afro-diasporic reclamations of Sarah Baartman. Like Ferrus, who brings Baartman home to a South African landscape, Wicomb brings Baartman home to a South African political and social landscape. As a result, the novelist raises new questions: What does it mean to bring Baartman home to South Africa as opposed to the black diaspora? What does it mean to remember her through and in the bodies of South African women as opposed to the bodies of Afro-diasporic women? The novel's answers to these questions strongly suggest that the work of mourning Baartman by women in the African diaspora approximates an act of cultural appropriation. *David's Story* shows that the work of mourning Sarah Baartman became a burden for South African women, and living with the specter of Baartman has social, political, and ideological consequences for South African women. The work of mourning Baartman in Afro-diasporic contexts does not come with a burden.

53 cm (1999) by Sandrine Bessora, a writer of Gabonese and Swiss parentage, takes up the question of the significance of the work of mourning Baartman in an Afro-diasporic context. The novel, dedicated to Baartman, stages an undocumented biracial immigrant woman of African and European ancestry in 1990s France. The protagonist's meaningful name, Zara, already signals the type of transposition of Baartman to an Afro-diasporic body that Ferrus, Marasela, and Wicomb question. Arguably, the lived experience of Baartman in France as an exotic curiosity and her transformation into a scientific specimen by French scientifico-cultural ideologies of race is an important frame to consider in relation to Bessora's project in *53 cm*. I particularly take note of Lydie Moudileno's useful reading of the important work of recontextualization, memorialization, and homing Baartman, hence the work of mourning Baartman, that *53 cm* performs:

> Bessora's fiction performs an important recontextualisation of Baartman's story, transforming it from the exclusive narrative of an exhibition into a story of migration. In this process, the body becomes less of an icon of radical difference, as Gilman conceived of it, than an archetypal transnational/transcontinental migrant body travelling from Africa to Europe and back. Thus, as a novel which provides closure to a trajectory of homelessness, loss and wandering, *53 cm* emerges as a memorialising gesture which stages a transfer from the European museum to a diasporic space that transcends national affiliations. Ultimately the dismembered, exiled colonial ghost of the Hottentot Venus is re-historicised, re-named and re-patriated into a collective imaginary. (2009, 206)

Moudileno is right to frame the discussion of Bessora's diasporic reappropriation of Baartman in the context of transnational migration. This is how *53 cm* departs from the pattern in Afro-diasporic works of only invoking Baartman in relationship to the hypersexualization of black female bodies. In contrast, the return of Baartman back to contemporary France in Bessora's novel aims to make Baartman speak to additional histories. This return also aims to create a new narrative for Baartman, beyond the reappropriations that have unwittingly helped cement her identity as a grotesque body. At fault in these reappropriations that keep on repeating the colonial statement has been the failure to treat inheritance as a task, and henceforth the failure to approach mourning as the type of work that Derrida describes. Bessora's re-narrativization of Baartman and pointed intervention into French immigration politics through Baartman bear out a thoughtful engagement with the story and legacy of Baartman. Bessora makes hers Derrida's notion that to do the work of mourning is to inherit responsibly, by which Derrida means that one must "filter the inheritance" in order to "keep this rather than that" (1994, 69).

In *53 cm* the protagonist's undocumented status in 1990s France and her failed quest for regularization, during the same time France was refusing to return the remains of Baartman to South Africa, is fodder for an exploration of the afterlife of Baartman in postcolonial France. The tedious journey of Zara through the maze of French immigration bureaucracy, especially her subjection to an obligatory medical examination, underscores the racial and colonial ideologies of normal and different bodies at the core of contemporary French immigration and naturalization laws. Bessora writes the scene detailing the minute inspection of Zara's body by the French immigration physician to evoke the treatment of Baartman by Georges Cuvier. Zara relates that the physician "examine tous mes millimètres" (1999, 14) (examines all my millimeters) and that he subsequently writes down the information he collects from her body.[1] This recorded information represents knowledge about Zara and determines whether she will stay or leave France. Of note is that *53 cm* is a parody of Cuvier's *Règne animal distribué d'après son organisation* (1817), and the titles of Bessora's chapters mimic Cuvier's. In addition to the parody of Cuvier, the mimicry also suggests that Cuvier's book has been recuperated as a manual for French immigration policies to aid in their sorting of bodies. Bessora accordingly mocks the absurdity and backwardness of these policies. Furthermore, these official decisions about Zara, based on the scientific taxonomy of her body, are occurring in the backdrop of France's refusal to repatriate the remains of Baartman because Cuvier's nineteenth taxonomy of her body deemed that her abnormal body was a scientific specimen.

Zara's quest to stay and belong in France is in limbo for most of the novel. Her undocumented status means that she is yet to receive classification, unlike Baartman, whose classification maintained her legally on French territory as scientific data. While the developed posterior of Baartman was the basis of her classification and legal status in France, Zara is biracial and has a small posterior. This combination poses challenges to her classification. Zara's 53 cm posterior is above white European norms and below black African norms, which places her in a limbo since "la fesse fait la race" (1999, 157) (your rear end defines your race). A prominent posterior would have confirmed her African origins and helped sort out her legal status in France. Steatopygia, the scientific name for prominent buttocks, was the reason Baartman entered and remained in France.

Throughout the novel Zara meets skepticism when she asserts her African origins. This disbelief based on anatomy shows the legacies of nineteenth-century ideologies of the black female body and Sarah Baartman in contemporary France. The opening scene of the novel is set in a gym where the owner tries to classify the racially ambiguous Zara, based on the measurements of her posterior. In another instance Zara is told that "53 centimètres . . . c'est peu. Cuvier n'en croirait pas son mètre de couturier: dans quelle race classer un individu présentant un si faible périmètre fessier?" (1999, 168) (53 cm . . . that's too small. Cuvier would never have believed his tailor's tape. What is the racial classification of somebody with such a small rear end?). The reference in the quotation to Cuvier as a tailor is purposive and feeds into Bessora's deconstruction of scientific knowledge. This deconstruction also unravels the racist construction of Baartman. Scientists such as Cuvier are products of a colonial and racist regime of truth, a point that the novel reinforces by bringing attention to the mutual dependence of anthropological and scientific discourses. References to colonial anthropologists and their racist theories about African and primitive bodies, including their anthropometric and voyeuristic gaze on these bodies, merge seamlessly with Cuvier's treatment of the black female body and his tailoring of a scientifically authoritative truth about black bodies. As noted earlier, *53 cm* is a parody of Cuvier's book. The successful parody of the book through the literary genre of the fictional novel underscores the shared narrative strategies between science and fiction. The apt juxtaposition between scientific and fictional texts not only interrogates notions of scientific disciplines as sites of absolute truth and knowledge but also draws attention to science as a historically, ideologically, and culturally situated narrative.

The use of satire and humor in *53 cm* magnifies the absurdity of such colonial constructs as Baartman and even more so the enduring legacies of colonial discourses of the African female body in contemporary France. In the novel Zara turns into a reverse anthropologist and documents her ethnographic observations about contemporary France as she wanders through Paris. The resulting comical observations and outlandish conclusions urge the reader to draw similar conclusions about the findings of anthropological texts that participated in the construction of Sarah Baartman and continue to inform the perception of African female bodies in contemporary France. The reverse anthropology of Zara in *53 cm* turns the tables on French immigration policies by exposing their foundations in colonial anthropology and scientific racism. The absurd backwardness of French immigration laws thus exposed allows Sarah Baartman and her African female descendants in France to have the last laugh, even if symbolically, at the expense of contemporary France.

If we return to the questions urged by Diana Ferrus, Senzeni Marasela, Tracey Rose, and Zoë Wicomb of what it means to mourn Sarah Baartman, the reluctance of the four South African women to rally around postcolonial and Afro-diasporic reclamations of Baartman has merits. The uses to which Sarah Baartman is put through these reclamations is a politically resonant question. The political and ideological commodification of Baartman as an icon for black sufferings and a stepping stone for acts of postcolonial writing back, and often lazy ones as such, is a fact. It is pertinent for South Africans to interrogate what Wicomb calls the transformation of Baartman into a "postcolonial icon" (quoted in Meyer and Olver 2002) and Zine Magubane (2001) describes as a theoretical commodification of Baartman. These questions pertain to the types of memories and imaginaries that the specter of Sarah Baartman enables both in and out of South Africa.

Yet if Diana Ferrus and Senzeni Marasela pointedly remind us that Sarah Baartman belongs to South Africa, and her homecoming and mourning need to be a South African affair, Bessora offers an important reminder that France is a crucial site, probably as crucial as South Africa, for the work of mourning Sarah Baartman. After all, Baartman as the world, including South Africa, came to know of her has French origins. Bessora further reminds us that Baartman lives a rich afterlife in contemporary

France. In my essay "Housing and Homing the Black Female Body in France: Calixthe Beyala and the Legacy of Sarah Baartman and Josephine Baker" (Coly 2008), I explore the ways Sarah Baartman shaped French attitudes toward black female bodies, paved the way for Josephine Baker's popularity in France in the 1920s and 1930s, and contributed to shaping "the spaces available for negotiating black womanhood in contemporary France" (262). As a result Baartman appears as a trope in the works of French women of African descent, most notably Calixthe Beyala and Fatou Diome (Coly 2010, 84–85, 118–19).

I have referenced earlier in this chapter Nelisiwe Xaba's *Sakhozi Says Non to the Venus* (2008) for its interrogation of the type of South Africa where the remains of Sarah Baartman return. The performance, already analyzed in the introduction to this book, joins Bessora's *53 cm* in interrogating French anti-African immigration policies and the perception of the African female body in contemporary France. Whereas Xaba's Baartman longs to return to France, Xaba asserts in her solo dance at the museum that her return would be to the museum as Sakhozi is adamant that he can only grant her a visa for the museum. Xaba successfully merges her own story as a black female artist perceived and welcomed as an exotic black female body in France with the itinerary of Sarah Baartman from South Africa to France. Like Bessora in *53 cm*, Xaba concerns herself with exposing the persisting colonialist ideologies of the black female body in France and the Sarah Baartman–inflected spaces available to black women in France.

Sakhozi Says Non to the Venus expands on Xaba's *They Look at Me and That's All They Think* (2006), a solo dance that exposes the sexualizing gaze that Europe still casts on the black female body and more specifically the continuing influence of Sarah Baartman on European points of view on black female bodies. Xaba performs in a white hoop skirt that overtakes her body and centers the gaze on the skirt and away from her body. When the audience first meets Xaba, she is kneeling down at the center of the stage and her face is hidden from view. She is just a depersonalized black female body. Xaba then throws her skirt over her head and sends her legs into the air by positioning her body upside down. The audience is treated to a reveal of Xaba's rear end, clad in bright yellow underpants with the inscription "beach girl" across the cheeks. The arrangement of Xaba's body, with the overturned white skirt, muted orange tights, and dainty high heel shoes visually propping up her yellow-clad rear end, evokes a precious floral arrangement for the sensuous delight of her audience. By offering herself in that way to her audience, Xaba seemingly invites the objectification and sexualization of her body. Her propped-up rear end anchors the sexualizing gaze and reinscribes the buttocks as a metonym of the hypersexual black female body, following colonial discourses. As the performance proceeds, Xaba comes back on her feet and dances around while her billowing skirt takes the shape of protruding buttocks. Brandi Wilkins Catanese (2010, 48) has argued that the hoop skirt is meant to invoke the backside-enhancing crinolines that mid-nineteenth-century European women donned and the surgical buttock implants and enhancements of the twenty-first century. These various enhancements point to a Euro-American history of appropriating the physical features of black women while mocking black women for these very features. Xaba proceeds to take off and set up the skirt as a cinema screen. At this point the performer turns the tables on her audience, as the skirt becomes a critical text. Xaba corners her audience into self-reflexive critical thinking in a manner that evokes the strategy of countermimicry presented in my analysis of performance artist Grace Ndiritu in chapter 4. The skirt-turned-screen displays the painstaking attempts of a black woman to straighten her hair, a commentary on the legacies of colonial discourses on black female bodies. A significantly overblown Xaba then dances behind the screen. She has transformed herself into a Baartman look-alike, with large buttocks and breasts. She emerges from behind the screen and deflates her costume. By displacing the gaze of the audience from her body to the screen that acts as an overlay of the displayed black female body, Xaba confronts her audience with their own fantasies and inability to see the black female body. What they see when they look at the black female body are projections of their own racist and sexual thoughts. In other words Xaba is lecturing her audience that "what you see when you look at my body is not my

16. Breeze Yoko, *Ode to Sarah Baartman*, 2015. Courtesy of Sebastien Casters.

body but your own perverted thoughts." Xaba's restatement of the story of Sarah Baartman in France and to French audiences joins texts such as *53 cm* and other Afro-French novels in imposing Baartman into French national memory.

Black French dancer Chantal Loial from Guadeloupe offers another example of the creation of a national memory for Baartman in France. Since 2011 Loial has been performing her solo dance show entitled *On t'appelle Venus* (They call you Venus) throughout France, in an effort to create French awareness of the unknown story of Baartman. Loial herself only came to read about the story of Baartman five years earlier. In the reading material distributed to her audiences before the show, Loial, like Bessora and Xaba, links the story of Baartman to contemporary French immigration debates. She also positions the story of Baartman in relation to French colonialism and claims its place in French history.

As I conclude this chapter on July 13, 2015, South African visual artist Breeze Yoko was also claiming space for Baartman in French history by creating a French site of memory for Baartman. Yoko designed a mural about Sarah Baartman on rue Oberkampf, in the eleventh arrondissement of Paris. The mural, titled *Ode to Sarah Baartman* (fig. 16), was completed on time for Bastille Day, the French National Day, on July 14.

The Oberkampf mural is an outdoor space that changes regularly, so Yoko's work can no longer be found in the Parisian neighborhood. This was the only central and public French space available to host the memory of Sarah Baartman, and the spectral character of the Baartman mural speaks to the willed French amnesia about the history of black bodies in France. At the same time, the nonpermanent mural of Sarah Baartman signifies that the repressed French past cannot be erased. An embodiment of that past, the figure of Sarah Baartman remains just below the surface and may surge up anytime, even if momentarily. Baartman represents a hauntology as much for African discourses as for French discourses. In the end the highly symbolic and self-explanatory mural centers Sarah Baartman in French history. In redirecting the specter of Baartman toward France, the South African artist brings Baartman back to bear more so on the history of France than the history of South Africa. As a matter of fact, Sarah Baartman tells us more about France than she does about South Africa.

Conclusion

Some may argue that notions of a colonial hangover in twenty-first-century Africa, fifty years after independence, are antiquated and misguided. Evan Mwangi (2009) has thoughtfully questioned the current relevance for African literatures of the paradigmatic notion of "writing back to the center." Likewise, examinations of postcolonial African anxieties surrounding the female body most readily index anxieties about a perceived erosion of male privileges in the face of growing female agency. This latter approach falls in line with Mwangi's injunction that scholars of postcolonial African discourses need to step away from the writing back to the center paradigm and tease out the "internal heteroglossia" of African postcolonialities (2009, 4). In Mwangi's reading of contemporary African literatures, postcolonial African discourses, more often than not, are writing back to themselves and are unconcerned with responding to colonial discourses.

I am concerned that the above mode of reading does not pay due attention to the workings of statements and the tenacity of colonial statements in particular. The Foucauldian injunction to focus on the statement not as a descriptive utterance but as a discursive event with performative effects, means that we engage in modes of reading that are attentive to the various and often hidden ways in which statements continue to operate and their lives are prolonged. These insidious workings and afterlives of statements are what this book has identified as postcolonial hauntologies. Mwangi sees in the themes of gender and sexuality in postcolonial African literatures instances of the self-reflexivity and dialogic heteroglossia of postcolonial African discourses. But the various discourses of the African female body examined in this book dispute this so-called inward turn of postcolonial African discourses of gender and sexuality.

Nelisiwe Xaba, whose dance performance opened this book, is helpful in closing it. Xaba's performance theorizes the tenuous, if not impossible, inward turn of postcolonial discourses of the female body. In overlaying her own twenty-first-century itinerary from South Africa to France with Baartman's, Xaba connects colonial and postcolonial Western discourses of the African female body to reveal what Joaquín Barriendos (2011) calls "the coloniality of seeing." In other words, the contemporary Western gaze still subjects African female bodies to colonial ways of seeing the African female body. Henceforth, Nelisiwe Xaba's act of effectively conjuring the specter of Sarah Baartman back to the present and into the bodies of twenty-first-century African women acts out the tenacious afterlife of colonial discourses of the African female body. And, most importantly, her performance also acts out the inevitable continuing antagonist position of postcolonial discourses of the female body, as these latter discourses are compelled to confront the persisting coloniality of seeing the African female body. Hence, once again, the tenuousness of the inward turn about which Mwangi writes.

Having said this, I have certainly, throughout this book, expressed concern with the writing-back paradigm at the core of the discourses examined in this book. I have been particularly concerned that the lack of an inward turn limits the discursive horizon of African women's discourses of the female body. But my selected corpus of discourses, consisting in African discourses that are meant to circulate in Western spaces or anticipate a Western audience, probably limits my conclusions. Arguably, these discourses cannot but write back to the center. Mwangi's injunction is therefore best modified to suggest that scholars of postcolonial discourses stop privileging Western-oriented discourses as sites for the studies of postcolonial identities and expressions. It is of significance that the silences about the sexual female body in the discourses examined in this book jar with the full-fledged expressions of the sexual female body to be found in some of the verbal arts of African women. The location of these silences in globalized postcolonial discourses is of significance. The silences about the sexual female body pertain to the location of these postcolonial discourses in global networks of signification that remain saturated by colonial discourses.

In my analysis of *Karmen Geï* in chapter 2 I agreed with Jeremy Weate's (2003) critique of Achille Mbembe for sidelining the vernacular in his account of the postcolony. Weate correctly argues that Mbembe's focus on "official culture" blinds him to forms of vernacular or ordinary resistance and consequently skews his conclusion about the futility of resistance in the postcolony. Like Mbembe, my book focuses on nonvernacular discourses of the female body. Yet my focus is purposeful. The corpus examined in my book represents but one set of postcolonial African women's discourses of the female body. At the same time, the enunciation of this set of discourses from official sites and in official languages, forms, and modalities has turned them into authoritative sources for scholars of postcolonial discourses. But their reinvented African female body, haunted as it is by colonial discourses, signals that the types of sources privileged in postcolonial studies may not be the most comprehensive and culturally authoritative sources when it comes to the study of postcolonial societies, experiences, and subjects. A follow-up project to this book would thus investigate African women's vernacular expressions of the female body. The scholarship of Thomas Hale (1998), Hale and Aissata Sidikou (2013), Lisa McNee (2000), Sidikou (2001), and Marame Gueye (2010, 2011, 2013) has already laid the groundwork for such studies by establishing African women's verbal arts as a rich site for the exploration of women's self-understanding, self-assertion, and resistance to patriarchy. Likewise dance and dress also offer inroads into examining African women's discourses of the female body.

In Senegal, the focus of some of my research, the sabar dance and the erotic underskirt known as the bethio express the sexual female body in ways not found in the literary texts of Senegalese women. As already discussed in my analysis of *Karmen Geï* in chapter 2, the sabar dance is a female space where women perform sexually explicit dances for other women. In the space of the sabar, women coax each other to explore their sexual body and express their sexual self. Hélène Neveu-Kringelbach (2013) provides a vivid depiction of a sabar dance that highlights a confident owning of sexuality, a creative engagement with the possibilities of the sexual body, and an assertive self-fashioning:

> Later in the evening, the energy level rises along with the sexual suggestiveness of the dances. . . . The women encourage each other to be daring, to roll the buttocks generously and to perform creative steps drawn from the sabar repertoire and from the popular mbalax genre. The high level of energy is palpable and there is frantic to-and-fro movement. Chairs are taken and quickly left again to perform in the central space for a few seconds to half a minute. The few women who refuse to dance at least once, lacking confidence in their skills, are made to pay a symbolic fine. Some of the dancers walk across the space and playfully lift their wrapper to reveal their beeco, or underneath wrapper, and their tiny thongs decorated with motifs, such as a sunflower or a cat's head. Revealing one's latest underwear design is part of the fun, and outbursts of laughter resound with every skirt being lifted. One of the women, standing with her back to the musicians at the very edge of the circle, beats her friends in boldness and reveals the full extent of her female anatomy. "You know what we, women, say," my friend tells me, "the bigger, the better!" Others remove their wrapper and go on dancing in their beeco, bare legs beating the air. Some of the beeco are made of white cotton painted with bawdy inscriptions. (78)

A similar expression of the sexual female body is at work in the bethio or beeco, an erotic underskirt crafted by women for other women. The underskirt is often hand-embroidered with graphic sexual designs representing favorite sexual positions or erotic one-liners. The designs may be commissioned by the customer or independently created by the designer.

Finally, African women are increasingly appropriating digital media to carve out new narrative spaces for themselves. What discourses are emerging from digital spaces? Does the relative anonymity provided by some digital online platforms help foster uninhibited discourses of the female body? In 2009 Ghanaian feminists Nana Darkoa Sekyiamah and Malaka Grant founded the interactive blog "Adventures from the Bedrooms of African Women" in order to create a safe space where African women could talk openly about sex and sexuality. The blog hosts fiction and nonfiction submissions from women from all over the continent. All submissions are open to comments. The blog "Holaa," founded in 2012 by Kenyan feminist activist Tiffany Kagure Mugo, publishes fiction and nonfiction stories by queer African women. The stories in both blogs affirm the sexual female body in ways similar to the bold and uninhibited affirmation of the sexual female body in vernacular spaces such as the sabar dance and the bethio. Further research, beyond this book, may explore the potential for African female digital spaces to re-create the vernacular environments of some African women's discourses.

Notes

1. The African Female Body

1. #MyDressMyChoice was initiated after the assault of a young woman in Kenya. The march in Uganda protested a 2014 law against miniskirts.
2. Edward Said has made similar remarks in *Orientalism* (1978). Gaurav Desai (2001) has also written about the tendency in studies of colonial discourses about Africa to read for sense rather than for rhetoric.
3. I have singled out Mudimbe because of the place of his scholarship in studies of colonial discourses about Africa, to the point where his work has been said to be the African counterpart of Edward Said's *Orientalism* (1978). Additionally, *The Idea of Africa* (1994) and *The Invention of Africa* (1988) remain, to date, among the very few studies with a marked endeavor to attend to colonial discourses about Africa.
4. For a history of dress and cloth in Africa, see Hendrickson (1996), Mack and Boyd (2000), Perani and Wolff (1999), and Renne (1995, 2013).
5. This also applies to African cinema. Alexie Tcheuyap (2005) offers an insightful discussion of the careful treatment of female nudity in African cinema.
6. See, for instance, the analyses by Ambroise Kom (1996) and David Ndachi Tagne (1990).
7. The figure of the veiled woman has become a rhetorical trope in the Western construction of Moslem societies as backward and in need of reformation.

2. Haunted Silences

1. See Lisa Wade (2012) for a review of African feminist responses to Western engagements with the practice of female circumcision.
2. See Carina Ray (2009), Brenna Munro (2010), Tavia Nyong'o (2010), and Neville Hoad (2010).
3. See Higginbotham (1994), White (2001), and Thompson (2008).

4. See, for instance, Yuval-Davis and Anthias (1989), McClintock (1995), and Yuval-Davis (1997).

3. Spectral Female Sexualities
1. All translations are mine unless noted otherwise.
2. In 2015 Miano published *Volcaniques: Une anthologie du plaisir*, a collection of erotic short stories by women of African descent. Time constraints did not allow me to include an analysis of the collection in this book.

5. Laying Specters to Rest?
1. All translations are mine unless otherwise noted.

References

Adichie, Chimamanda. 2003. *Purple Hibiscus*. Chapel Hill NC: Algonquin Books of Chapel Hill.

———. 2006. *Half of a Yellow Sun*. New York: Knopf.

Agamben, Giorgio. 1998. *Homo Sacer: Sovereign Power and Bare Life*. Stanford CA: Stanford University Press.

Aidoo, Ama Ata. 1977. *Our Sister Killjoy*. London: Longman.

———. 1991. *Changes: A Love Story*. New York: CUNY, Feminist Press.

Aken'Ova, Dorothy. 2013. "Better Sex and More Equal Relationships: Couple Training in Nigeria." In Jolly, Cornwall, and Hawkins, *Women, Sexuality, and the Political Power of Pleasure*, 76–92.

Allman, Jean, ed. 2004a. *Fashioning Africa: Power and the Politics of Dress*. Bloomington: Indiana University Press.

———. 2004b. "'Let Your Fashion Be in Line with Our Ghanaian Costume': Nation, Gender, and the Politics of Clothing in Nkrumah's Ghana." In Allman, *Fashioning Africa*, 144–65.

Amadiume, Ifi. 1987. *Male Daughters, Female Husbands: Gender and Sex in an African Society*. London: Zed Books.

———. 1997. *Re-inventing Africa: Matriarchy, Religion, and Culture*. London: Zed Books.

———. 2008. "African Women's Body Images in Postcolonial Discourse and Resistance to Neo-Crusaders." In Thompson, *Black Womanhood*, 49–69.

Ampofo, Akosua Adomako, and Signe Arnfred, eds. 2009. *African Feminist Politics of Knowledge: Tensions, Challenges, Possibilities*. Uppsala: Nordic Africa Institute.

Andrade, Susan. 2011a. "Adichie's Genealogies: National and Feminine Novels." *Research in African Literatures* 42, no. 2: 91–101.

———. 2011b. *The Nation Writ Small: African Fictions and Feminisms, 1958–1988*. Durham NC: Duke University Press.

Arac de Nyeko, Monica. 2007. "Jambula Tree." In *African Love Stories: An Anthology*, edited by Ama Ata Aidoo, 9–19. Boulder CO: Lynne Rienner.

Arnfred, Signe, ed. 2004. *Re-thinking Sexualities in Africa*. Uppsala: Nordic Africa Institute.

———. 2009. "African Feminists on Sexualities." *Canadian Journal of African Studies* 43, no. 1: 151–59.

Atta, Sefi. 2012. *A Bit of Difference*. Melbourne: Spinifex Press.

Azuah, Unoma. 2005. *Sky-High Flames*. Baltimore: Publish America.

Baderoon, Gabeba. 2011. "Baartman and the Private: How Can We Look at a Figure That Has Been Looked at Too Much?" In *Representation and Black Womanhood: The Legacy of Sarah Baartman*, edited by Natasha Gordon-Chipembere, 65–83. New York: Palgrave Macmillan.

Baenga, Bolya. 2002. *Afrique, le maillon faible*. Paris: Le Serpent à Plumes, 2002.

Bagnol, Brigitte, and Esmeralda Mariano. 2011. "Politics of Naming Sexual Practices." In Tamale, *African Sexualities*, 271–87.

Baiada, Christa. 2008. "On Women, Bodies, and Nation: Zoë Wicomb's Feminist Critique in *David's Story*." *African Studies* 67, no. 1: 33–47.

Bakare-Yusuf, Bibi. 2003. "Beyond Determinism: The Phenomenology of African Female Existence." *Feminist Africa* 2. http://www.agi.ac.za/agi/feminist-africa/02.

———. 2011. "Nudity and Morality: Legislating Women's Bodies and Dress in Nigeria." In Tamale, *African Sexualities*, 116–29.

———. 2013. "Thinking about Pleasure: Danger, Sexuality, and Agency." In Jolly, Cornwall, and Hawkins *Women, Sexuality, and the Political Power of Pleasure*, 28–41.

Barriendos, Joaquín. 2011. "La colonialidad del ver: Hacia un nuevo diálogo epistémico." *Nómadas* 35:13–29.

Bastian, Misty. 2005. "The Naked and the Nude: Historically Multiple Meanings of Oto (Undress) in Southeastern Nigeria." In *Dirt, Undress, and Difference: Critical Perspectives on the Body's Surface*, edited by Adeline Masquelier, 34–60. Bloomington: Indiana University Press.

Beauvoir, Simone de. 1984. *The Second Sex*. Trans. H. M. Pashley. Harmondsworth: Penguin.

Becker, Carol. 1998. "The Second Johannesburg Biennale." *Art Journal* 57, no. 2: 86–107.

Beckwith Carol, and Angela Fisher. 1993. *Women of the African Ark*. San Francisco: Pomegranate Art Books.

Beidelman, T. O. 1968. "Some Nuer Notions of Nakedness, Nudity, and Sexuality." *Africa* 38, no. 2: 113–31.

Bennett, Jane. 2011. "Subversion and Resistance: Activist Initiatives." In Tamale, *African Sexualities*, 77–100.

Bennett, Jane, and Charmaine Pereira, eds. 2013. *Jacketed Women: Qualitative Research Methodologies on Sexualities and Gender in Africa*. Paris: United Nations University Press.

Bennett, Michael, and Vanessa Dickerson, eds. 2000. *Recovering the Black Female Body: Self-Representations by African American Women*. New Brunswick NJ: Rutgers University Press.

Berger, John. 1972. *Ways of Seeing*. London: Penguin.

Berlant, Lauren, and Michael Warner. 1995. "What Does Queer Theory Teach Us about X?" *PMLA* 110:343–49.

Bessora, Sandrine. 1999. *53 cm*. Paris: Serpent à plumes.

Beyala, Calixthe. 1987. *C'est le soleil qui m'a brûlée*. Paris: Stock.

———. 1988. *Tu t'appelleras Tanga*. Paris: Stock.

———. 1993. *Maman a un amant*. Paris: Albin Michel.

———. 1996a. *The Sun Hath Looked upon Me*. Trans. Marjolijn de Jager. Oxford: Heinemann.

———. 1996b. *Your Name Shall Be Tanga*. Trans. Marjolijn de Jager. Oxford: Heinemann.

———. 2003. *Femme nue, femme noire*. Paris: Albin Michel.

Bhabha, Homi. 1983. "The Other Question." *Screen* 24, no. 6: 18–36.

———. 2004. *The Location of Culture*. London: Routledge.

Boehmer, Elleke. 2003. "Tropes of Yearning and Dissent: The Troping of Desire in Yvonne Vera and Tsitsi Dangarembga." *Journal of Commonwealth Literature* 38, no. 2: 135–48.

Brooker, Peter. 1999. *A Concise Glossary of Cultural Theory*. London: Hodder Arnold.

Bugul, Ken. 1982. *Le baobab fou*. Dakar: Les Nouvelles Editions Africaines.

———. 1991. *The Abandoned Baobab: The Autobiography of a Senegalese Woman*. Trans. Marjolijn de Jager. Charlottesville: University of Virginia Press.

———. 1994. *Cendres et braises*. Paris: L'Harmattan.

———. 1999. *Riwan ou le chemin de sable*. Paris: Présence Africaine.

———. 2008. *Mes hommes à moi*. Paris: Présence Africaine.

Burke, Timothy. 1996. *Lifebuoy Men, Lux Women: Commodification, Consumption, and Cleanliness in Modern Zimbabwe*. Durham NC: Duke University Press.

Butler, Judith. 1990. *Gender Trouble: Feminism and the Subversion of Identity*. London: Routledge.

———. 1993. *Bodies That Matter: On the Discursive Limits of Sex*. London: Routledge.

Callahan, Yesha. "Reactions to Kara Walker's *A Subtlety* Prove a Black Woman Will Be Sexualized Even in Art." *The Root*, May 28. https://thegrapevine.theroot.com/reactions-to-kara-walker-s-a-subtlety-prove-a-black-wom-1790885464.

Camara, Fatou Kiné. 2010. "La renaissance africaine? Épître pour redonner son sens à un mot chargé d'histoire et porteur des enseignements du passé." *Walfadjri*, January 5.

Catanese, Brandi Wilkins. 2010. "Remembering Saartjie Baartman." *Atlantic Studies* 7 (1): 47–62.

Certeau, Michel de. 1984. *The Practice of Everyday Life*. Berkeley: University of California Press.

Cessou, Sabine. 2009. "Les colosses de Dakar." *Libération*, December 17.

Child, Hortense. 1974. "Q&A: Questions and Answers." *New Era, December 1974:* 12–13.

Clark, Kenneth. 1956. *The Nude: A Study in Ideal Form*. New York: Pantheon Books.

Collins, Lisa. 2002. "Economies of the Flesh: Representing the Black Female Body in Art." In Wallace-Sanders, *Skin Deep, Spirit Strong*, 99–127.

Coly, Ayo. 2008. "Housing and Homing the Black Female Body in France: Calixthe Beyala and the Legacy of Sarah Baartman and Josephine Baker." In Thompson, *Black Womanhood*, 259–77.

———. 2010. *The Pull of Postcolonial Nationhood: Gender and Migration in Francophone African Literatures*. Lanham MD: Lexington Books.

Comaroff, Jean. 1985. *Body of Power, Spirit of Resistance*. Chicago: University of Chicago Press.

———. 1996. "The Empire's Old Clothes: Fashioning the Colonial Subject." In *Cross-Cultural Consumption: Global Markets, Local Realities*, edited by David Howes, 19–38. New York: Routledge.

Comaroff, Jean, and John Comaroff. 1997. *Of Revelation and Revolution: Dialectics of Modernity on a South African Frontier*. Chicago: University of Chicago Press.

Connelly, Frances E. 2003. *Modern Art and the Grotesque*. Cambridge: Cambridge University Press.

Conrad, Joseph. 1899. *The Heart of Darkness*. London: William Blackwood and Sons.

Cronin, Jeremy. 1999. "Over the Rainbow: By Way of Reply to Okwui Enwezor." In *Grey Areas: Representation, Identity and Politics in Contemporary South African Art*, 95–100. Johannesburg: Chalkham Hill Press.

D'Almeida, Irène. 1994. *Francophone Women Writers: Destroying the Emptiness of Silence*. Gainesville: University Press of Florida.

Decker, Alicia Catharine. 2007. "Beyond the Barrel: Women, Gender, and Military Rule in Idi Amin's Uganda, 1971–1979." Diss., Emory University.

Deleuze, Gilles. 1989. *Cinéma 2: The Time-Image*. Minneapolis: University of Minnesota Press.

———. 1994. "Désir et plaisir." *Magazine littéraire* 325:59–65.

Deleuze, Gilles, and Félix Guattari. 1986. *Kafka: Towards a Minor Literature*. Minneapolis: University of Minnesota Press.

———. 1987. *A Thousand Plateaux: Capitalism and Schizophrenia*. Minneapolis: University of Minnesota Press.

Derrida, Jacques. 1994. *Specters of Marx: The State of the Debt, the Work of Mourning and the New International*. London: Routledge.

———. 2001. *The Work of Mourning*. Chicago: University of Chicago Press.

Desai, Gaurav. 2001. *Subject to Colonialism: African Self-Fashioning and the Colonial Library*. Durham NC: Duke University Press.

Diallo, Rackie Diankha. 2008. *Petit pagne*. Online video. http://www.agencetopo.qc.ca/dakarweb/dakar/Petit_Pagne/index.html.

Diouf, Makhtar. 2002a. *L'Afrique dans la mondialisation*. Paris: L'Harmattan.

———. 2002b. *L'endettement puis l'ajustement: L'Afrique des institutions de Bretton-Woods*. Paris: L'Harmattan.

Ekotto, Frieda. 2005. *Chuchote pas trop*. Paris: L'Harmattan.

———. 2010. *Portrait d'une jeune artiste de Bona Mbella*. Paris: L'Harmattan.

Elwes, Catherine. 1985. "Floating Femininity: A Look at Performance Art by Women." In *Women's Images of Men*, edited by Sarah Kent and Jacqueline Moreau, 164–93. London: Writers and Readers.

Emecheta, Buchi. 1979. *The Joys of Motherhood*. London: Allison and Busby.

English, Darby. 2007. *How to See a Work of Art in Total Darkness*. Cambridge MA: MIT Press.

Enright, Robert. 2008. "Resonant Surgeries: The Collaged World of Wangechi Mutu," Interview. *Border Crossings* 105 (February). http://bordercrossingsmag.com/article/resonant-surgeries-the-collaged-world-of-wangechi-mutu.

Enwezor, Okwui. 1997. "Reframing the Black Subject: Ideology and Fantasy in Contemporary South African Representation." *Third Text* 40:21–40.

———. 2010. "Weird Beauty: Ritual Violence and Archaeology of Mass Media in Wangechi Mutu's Work." In *Wangechi Mutu: My Dirty Little Heaven*, edited by Freidhelm Hütte and Christina Merz, 26–39. Stuttgart: Hatje Cantz.

Essamba, Angèle Etoundi. 2001. *Noirs*. Arnhem, The Netherlands: Museum voor Moderne Kunst.

Etoké, Nathalie. 2006. "Ecriture du corps féminin dans la littérature de l'Afrique francophone: Taxonomie, enjeux et défis." CODESRIA *Bulletin* 3/ 4:41–44.

Fabian, Johannes. 1983. *Time and the Other: How Anthropology Makes Its Object*. New York: Columbia University Press.

———. 2000. *Out of Our Minds: Reason and Madness in the Exploration of Central Africa*. Berkeley: University of California Press.

Fanon, Frantz. 1961. *The Wretched of the Earth*. New York: Grove Press.

———. 1965. *A Dying Colonialism*. New York: Grove Press.

———. 1967. *Black Skin, White Masks*. New York: Grove Press.

Ferrus, Diana. 2003. "Tribute to Sarah Baartman." *Feminist Studies* 29, no. 3: 592.

Foucault, Michel. 1972. *The Archeology of Knowledge*. New York: Pantheon Books.

———. 1977. *Discipline and Punish: The Birth of the Prison*. Harmondsworth: Penguin.

———. 1980. *Power/Knowledge: Selected Interviews and Other Essays 1972–1977*. New York: Pantheon Books.

———. 1990. *The History of Sexuality*. Vol. 1, *An Introduction*. New York: Vintage.

Gagiano, Annie. 2009. "Buried Hurts and Colliding Dreams in Yvonne Vera's *Butterfly Burning*." *Maringá* 31, no. 1: 41–52.

Gallimore, Rangira Béatrice. 1997. *L'oeuvre romanesque de Calixthe Beyala*. Paris: L'Harmattan.

Geary, Christraud. 2003. *In and Out of Focus: Images from Central Africa, 1885–1960*. London: Philip Wilson.

Gikandi, Simon. 2001. "Globalization and the Claims of Postcoloniality." *South Atlantic Quarterly* 100, no. 3: 627–58.

———. 2003. "Picasso, Africa, and the Schemata of Difference." *Modernism/Modernity* 10, no. 3: 455–80.

Gordon, Avery. 1997. *Ghostly Matters: Haunting and the Sociological Imagination*. Minneapolis: University of Minnesota Press.

Gordon-Chipembere, Natasha, ed. 2011. *Representation and Black Womanhood: The Legacy of Sarah Baartman*. New York: Palgrave Macmillan.

Gquola, Pumla Dineo. 2006. "Through Zanele Muholi's Eyes: Re/Imagining Ways of Seeing Black Lesbians." In *Zanele Muholi: Only Half the Picture*, edited by Zanele Muholi and Sophie Perryer, 82–89. Cape Town: Michael Stevenson Gallery.

———. 2010. *What Is Slavery to Me? Postcolonial/Slave Memory in Post-Apartheid South Africa*. Johannesburg: Wits University Press.

Griffin, Farah Jasmine. 1996. "Textual Healing: Claiming Black Women's Bodies, the Erotic and Resistance in Contemporary Novels of Slavery." *Callaloo* 19, no. 2: 519–36.

Grosz, Elizabeth. 1987. "Notes towards a Corporeal Feminism." *Australian Feminist Studies* 2, no. 5: 1–16.

———. 1994. *Volatile Bodies: Towards a Corporeal Feminism*. Bloomington: Indiana University Press.

———. 1995. *Space, Time and Perversion: Essays on the Politics of Bodies*. London: Routledge.

Gueye, Marame. 2010. "*Woyyi Céet*: Senegalese Women's Oral Discourses on Marriage and Womanhood." *Research in African Literatures* 41, no. 4: 65–86.

———. 2011. "Laabban Song." In Tamale, *African Sexualities*, 633–36.

———. 2013. "Wolof Women Break the Taboo of Sex through Songs." In *Women's Songs from West Africa*, edited by Thomas Hale and Aissata Sidikou, 9–33. Bloomington: Indiana University Press.

Gurnah, Abdulrazak. 2007. "Post-Nation Depression." *Financial Times*, April 13.

Guy-Sheftall, Beverly. 2002. "The Body Politic: Black Female Sexuality and the Nineteenth-Century Euro-American Imagination." In Wallace-Sanders, *Skin Deep, Spirit Strong*, 13–35.

Halberstam, Judith. 1994. "F2M: The Making of Female Masculinity." In *The Lesbian Postmodern*, edited by Laura Doan, 210–28. New York: Columbia University Press.

Hale, Thomas. 1998. *Griots and Griottes: Masters of Words and Music*. Bloomington: Indiana University Press.

Hale, Thomas, and Aissata Sidikou. 2013. *Women's Songs from West Africa*. Bloomington: Indiana University Press.

Hall, Stuart. 1980. "Encoding/Decoding." In *Culture, Media, Language: Working Papers in Cultural Studies, 1972–1979*, 128–38. London: Hutchinson.

———. 1997. "The Work of Representation." In *Representation: Cultural Representations and Signifying Practices*, edited by Stuart Hall, 1–74. London: Sage.

Hamon, Philippe. 1982. "Un Discours Constraint." In *Littérature et réalité*, edited by Gérard Genette and Tzvetan Todorov, 119–81. Paris: Seuil.

Hansen, Karen Tranberg. 2004. "Dressing Dangerously: Miniskirts, Gender Relations, and Sexuality in Zambia." In Allman, *Fashioning Africa*, 166–85.

Harper, Gil. 2005. "Editorial." *Agenda* 63:2.

Hassan, Salah M., ed. 1997. *Gendered Visions: The Art of Contemporary Africana Women Artists*. Trenton NJ: Africa World Press.

Hendrickson, Hildi, ed. 1996. *Clothing and Difference: Embodied Identities in Colonial and Post-Colonial Africa*. Durham NC: Duke University Press.

Hewett, Heather. 2005. "Coming of Age: Chimamanda Ngozi Adichie and the Voice of the Third Generation." *English in Africa* 32, no. 1: 73–97.

Higginbotham, Evelyn. 1994. *Righteous Discontent: The Women's Movement in the Black Baptist Church, 1880–1920*. Cambridge MA: Harvard University Press.

Hoad, Neville. 2010. "Run, Caster Semenya, Run! Nativism and the Translations of Gender Variance." *Safundi* 11, no. 4: 397–405.

Irigaray, Luce. 1985. *This Sex Which Is Not One*. Ithaca NY: Cornell University Press.

Iser, Wolfgang. 1980. *The Act of Reading: A Theory of Aesthetic Response*. Baltimore: Johns Hopkins University Press.

Ivaska, Andrew. 2004. "'Anti-Mini Militants Meet Modern Misses': Urban Style, Gender, and the Politics of 'National Culture' in 1960s Dar es Salaam, Tanzania." In Allman, *Fashioning Africa*, 104–21.

Jaggar, Alison, and Susan Bordo, eds. 1989. *Gender/Body/Knowledge: Feminist Reconstructions of Being and Knowing*. Newark NJ: Rutgers University Press.

Jolly, Susie, Andrea Cornwall, and Kate Hawkins, eds. *Women, Sexuality, and the Political Power of Pleasure*. New York: Zed Books.

Jones, Amelia. 2000. "Survey." In *The Artist's Body*, edited by Tracey Warr, 18–47. London: Phaidon Press.

Jones, Kima. 2014. "The Rumpus Interview with Chimamanda Ngozi Adichie." *Rumpus*, June 17. http://therumpus.net/2014/06/the-rumpus-interview-with-chimamanda-ngozi-adichie.

Ki-Zerbo, Joseph. 2003. *A quand l'Afrique: Entretien avec René Holenstein*. Paris: Editions d'en bas.

Klugman, Barbara. 2000. "Sexual Rights in Southern Africa: A Beijing Discourse or a Strategic Necessity?" *Health and Human Rights* 4, no. 2: 155–73.

Kom, Ambroise. 1996. "L'univers zombifié de Calixthe Beyala." *Notre librairie* 125:64–71.

Kuhn, Annette. 1985. *The Power of the Image: Essays on Representation and Sexuality*. London: Routledge & Kegan Paul.

Levine, Phillippa. 2008. "States of Undress: Nakedness and the Colonial Imagination." *Victorian Studies* 50, no. 2: 189–219.

Lévi-Strauss, Claude. 1966. *The Savage Mind*. Chicago: University of Chicago Press.

Lewis, Desiree. 2011. "Representing African Sexualities." In Tamale, *African Sexualities*, 119–217.

Loomba, Ania. 1998. *Colonialism/Postcolonialism*. London: Routledge.

Lugones, Maria. 2007. "Heterosexualism and the Colonial/Modern Gender System." *Hypatia* 22, no. 1: 86–209.

———. 2010. "Toward a Decolonial Feminism." *Hypatia* 25, no. 4: 742–59.

Mack, Beverly, and Jean Boyd. 2000. *One Woman's Jihad: Nana Asma'u; Scholar and Scribe*. Bloomington: Indiana University Press.

Magubane, Zine. 2001. "Which Bodies Matter? Feminism, Poststructuralism, Race, and the Curious Theoretical Odyssey of the Hottentot Venus." *Gender and Society* 15:816–34.

Malonga, Alpha Noël. 2006. "Migritude, amour et identité: L'exemple de Calixthe Beyala et Ken Bugul." *Cahiers d'études Africaines* 46:169–78.

Mani, Lata. 1987. "The Contentious Traditions: The Debate on Sati in Colonial India." *Cultural Critique* 7:119–56.

Masquelier, Adeline, ed. 2005. *Dirt, Undress, and Difference: Critical Perspectives on the Body's Surface*. Bloomington: Indiana University Press.

Maticka-Tyndale, Eleanor, Richmond Tiemoko, and Paulina Makinwa-Adebusoye, eds. 2007. *Human Sexuality in Africa: Beyond Reproduction*. Johannesburg: Action Health Incorporated.

Mazrui, Ali. 1968. "Miniskirts and Political Puritanism." *Africa Report* 13, no. 7: 9–12.

M'Baye, Babacar. 2011. "Variant Sexualities and African Modernity in Joseph Gaye Ramaka's *Karmen Gei*." *Black Camera* 2, no. 2: 114–29.

Mbembe, Achille. 2001. *On the Postcolony*. Berkeley: University of California Press.

———. 2002. "African Modes of Self-Writing." *Public Culture* 14, no. 1: 239–73.

McClintock, Anne. 1995. *Imperial Leather: Race, Gender and Sexuality in the Colonial Contest*. New York: Routledge.

McFadden, Patricia. 2003. "Sexual Pleasure as Feminist Choice." *Feminist Africa* 2. http://www.agi.ac.za/sites/default/files/image_tool/images/429/feminist_africa_journals/archive/02/fa_2_standpoint_1.pdf.

McNee, Lisa. 2000. *Selfish Gifts: Senegalese Women's Autobiographical Discourses*. New York: State University of New York Press.

Mercer, Kobena. 1994. *Welcome to the Jungle: New Positions in Black Cultural Studies*. London: Routledge.

Merleau-Ponty, Maurice. 1962. *Phenomenology of Perception*. London: Routledge.

———. 1964. *The Primacy of Perception: And Other Essays on Phenomenological Psychology, the Philosophy of Art, History and Politics*. Evanston IL: Northwestern University Press.

Meyer, Stephan, and Thomas Olver. 2002. "Zoë Wicomb Interviewed on Writing and Nation." *Journal of Literary Studies* 18, no. 1: 182–98.

Meyers, Bob. 1997. "What Is My Legacy? Transient Consciousness and the 'Fixed' Subject in the Photography of Renée Cox." In Hassan, *Gendered Visions*, 27–38.

Miano, Leonora. 2010. *Blues pour Elise*. Paris: Plon.

———. 2014. *Première nuit: Une anthologie du désir*. Paris: Mémoire d'Encrier.

———. 2015. *Volcaniques: Une anthologie du plaisir*. Paris: Mémoire d'Encrier.

Miller, Christopher. 1985. *Blank Darkness: Africanist Discourse in French*. Chicago: University of Chicago Press.

Minh-ha, Trinh T. 1989. *Woman, Native, Other: Writing Feminism and Postcolonialism*. Bloomington: Indiana University Press.

Moudileno, Lydie. 2009. "Returning Remains: Saartjie Baartman, or the 'Hottentot Venus' as Transnational Postcolonial Icon." *Forum for Modern Language Studies* 45, no. 2: 200–212.

Mudimbe, V. Y. 1988. *The Invention of Africa: Gnosis, Philosophy, and the Order of Knowledge*. Bloomington: Indiana University Press.

———. 1994. *The Idea of Africa*. Bloomington: Indiana University Press.

Muholi, Zanele. 2011. "Ngibonile—I Have Seen . . ." In *Zanele Muholi: African Women Photographers #1*. Madrid: Casa Africa.

Mulvey, Laura. 1989. *Visual and Other Pleasures*. Bloomington: Indiana University Press.

Muñoz, José Esteban. 2009. *Cruising Utopia: The Then and There of Queer Futurity*. New York: New York University Press.

Munro, Brenna. 2010. "Caster Semenya: Gods and Monsters." *Safundi* 11, no. 4: 383–96.

Mwangi, Evan. 2009. *Africa Writes Back to Self: Metafiction, Gender, Sexuality*. Albany: State University of New York Press.

Nash, Jennifer. 2008. "Strange Bedfellows: Black Feminism and Antipornography Feminism." *Social Text* 26, no. 4: 51–76.

Ndjio, Basile. 2013. "Sexuality and Nationalist Ideologies in Post-Colonial Cameroon." In *The Sexual History of the Global South: Sexual Politics in Africa, Asia, and Latin America*, edited by Saskia Wieringa and Horacio Sivori, 120–43. London: Zed Books.

Nead, Lynda. 1992. *The Female Nude: Art, Obscenity and Sexuality*. London: Routledge.

Neveu-Kringelbach, Hélène. 2013. *Dance Circles: Movement, Morality and Self-Fashioning in Urban Senegal*. New York: Berghahn Books.

Nigeria Senate. 2008a. *Lead Debate on the Bill for An Act to Prohibit and Punish Public Nudity, Sexual Intimidation and Other Related Offences in Nigeria*. Abuja: National Assembly of Nigeria.

———. 2008b. *Official Report of Proceedings at the Public Hearing on Sexual Offences Bill and the Public Nudity Bill Organized by the Senate Committee on Judiciary*. Abuja: National Assembly of Nigeria.

Njau, Rebecca. 1978. *Ripples in the Pool*. London: Heinemann.

Nnaemeka, Obioma. 1994. "From Orality to Writing: African Women Writers and the (Re)Inscription of Womanhood." *Research in African Literatures* 25, no. 4: 137–57.

———. 2004. "Nego-Feminism: Theorizing, Practicing, and Pruning Africa's Way." *Signs* 29, no. 2: 357–85.

———, ed. 2005. *Female Circumcision and the Politics of Knowledge: African Women in Imperialist Discourses*. Westport CT: Praeger.

Nutall, Sarah. 2007. "Introduction: Rethinking Beauty." In *Beautiful/Ugly: African and Diaspora Aesthetics*, edited by Sarah Nutall, 6–29. Durham NC: Duke University Press.

Nyong'o, Tavia. 2010. "The Unforgivable Transgression of Being Caster Semenya." *Women & Performance* 20, no. 1: 95–100.

Nzegwu, Nkiru. 2011. "Osunality (or African Eroticism)." In Tamale, *African Sexualities*, 253–70.

———. 2012. *Family Matters: Feminist Concepts in African Philosophy of Culture*. Binghamton NY: SUNY Press.

O'Grady, Lorraine. 1992. "Olympia's Maid: Reclaiming Black Female Subjectvity." *Afterimage* 20, no. 1: 14–20.

Oguibe, Olu. 1997. "Beyond Visual Pleasures: A Brief Reflection on the Work of Contemporary African Women Artists." In Hassan, *Gendered Visions*, 63–72.

Okoye, Ikem Stanley. 1988. "Ajuju Azu Ndu II: (or Fishy Questions) on the Body of Contemporary Izhon and Igbo Sculpture: Sokari Douglas Camp and Chris Afuba." In *Issues in Contemporary African Art*, edited by Nkiru Nzegwu, 28–29. Binghamton NY: International Society for the Study of Africa.

Okuyade, Ogaga. 2011. "Weaving Memories of Childhood: The New Nigerian Novel and the Genre of the Bildungsroman." *Ariel* 41, no. 3–4: 137–66.

Oyewumi, Oyeronke. 1997. *The Invention of Women: Making an African Sense of Western Gender Discourses*. Minneapolis: University of Minnesota Press.

———. 2015. *What Gender Is Motherhood? Changing Ideals of Power, Procreation, and Identity in the Age of Modernity*. New York: Palgrave Macmillan.

Palmer, Felicity. 2006. "Sex in the Postcolonial City: Desire, Kinship, and Freedom in Yvonne Vera's *Without a Name*." *Vienna Journal of African Studies* 11:27–44.

Perani, Judith, and Norma Wolff, eds. 1999. *Cloth, Dress and Art Patronage in Africa*. Oxford: Berg.

Pereira, Charmaine. 2003. "'Where Angels Fear to Tread': Some Thoughts on Patricia McFadden's 'Sexual Pleasure as Feminist Choice.'" *Feminist Africa* 2. http://www.agi.uct.ac.za/sites/default/files/image_tool/images/429/feminist_africa_journals/archive/02/fa_2_standpoint_2.pdf.

Petty, Sheila. 2009. "The Rise of the African Musical: Postcolonial Disjunction in *Karmen Geï* and *Madame Brouette*." *Journal of African Cinemas* 1, no. 1: 95–112.

Phelan, Peggy. 1993. *Unmarked: The Politics of Performance*. London: Routledge.

Powrie, Phil. 2004. "Politics and Embodiment in *Karmen Geï*." *Quarterly Review of Film and Video* 21, no. 4: 283–91.

Price, Janet, and Margrit Shildrick, eds. 1999. *Feminist Theory and the Body: A Reader*. London: Routledge.

Puar, Jasbir. 2007. *Terrorist Assemblages: Homonationalism in Queer Times*. Durham NC: Duke University Press.

Ramaka, Joseph Gaï, dir. 2001. *Karmen Geï*. San Francisco: California Newsreel. Videocasssette, 82 min.

Rawiri, Angèle. 1989. *Fureurs et cris de femmes*. Paris: L'Harmattan.

Ray, Carina. 2009. "Caster Semenya: 21st Century Hottentot Venus?" *New African*, no. 489 (November): 18–19.

Renne, Elisha. 1995. *Cloth That Does Not Die: The Meaning of Cloth in Bunu Social Life*. Seattle: University of Washington Press.

———, ed. 2013. *Veiling in Africa*. Bloomington: Indiana University Press.

Rovine, Victoria. 2008. *Bogolan: Shaping Culture through Cloth in Contemporary Mali*. Bloomington: Indiana University Press.

Said, Edward. 1978. *Orientalism*. New York: Pantheon Books.

———. 1988. *Nationalism, Colonialism and Literature: Yeats and Decolonization*. Dublin: Field Day.

Samuelson, Meg. 2007. "The Disfigured Body of the Female Guerrilla: (De)Militarization, Sexual Violence and Re-Domestication in Zoë Wicomb's *David's Story*." *Signs: Journal of Women in Culture and Society* 32, no. 4: 833–56.

Savarese, Eric. 2000. "Montrer la féminité, figurer l'altérité: Le corps des femmes indigènes dans l'imaginaire colonial français à partir de l'illustration (1900–

1940)." In *Le corps dans tous ses états: Regards anthropologiques*, edited by Gilles Boetsch and Dominique Chevé, 39–52. Paris: CNRS Editions.

Schneider, Rebecca. 1997. *The Explicit Body in Performance*. London: Routledge.

Sedgwick, Eve Kosofsky. 1985. *Between Men: English Literature and Male Homosocial Desire*. New York: Columbia University Press.

Sharpley-Whiting, T. Denean. 1997. *Frantz Fanon: Conflicts and Feminism*. Lanham MD: Rowman and Littlefield.

———. 1999. *Black Venus: Sexualized Savages, Primal Fears, and Primitive Narratives in French*. Durham NC: Duke University Press.

Shoneyin, Lola. 2010. *The Secret Lives of Baba Segi's Wives*. London: Serpent's Tail.

Sidikou, Aissata. 2001. *Recreating Worlds, Reshaping Worlds: The Verbal Art of Women from Niger, Mali and Senegal*. Trenton NJ: Africa World Press.

Sissako, Abderrahmane. 2006. *Bamako*. New York: New Yorker Films.

Sontag, Susan. 1977. *On Photography*. New York: Farrar, Straus and Giroux.

Stoler, Ann Laura. 1995. *Race and the Education of Desire: Foucault's History of Sexuality and the Colonial Order of Things*. Durham NC: Duke University Press.

Suleiman, Susan. 1986. *The Female Body in Western Culture*. Cambridge MA: Harvard University Press.

Tagne, David Ndachi. 1990. "Notes de lecture: Calixthe Beyala, *C'est le soleil qui m'a brûlée*." *Notre librairie* 100:96–97.

Tamale, Sylvia. 2006. "African Feminism: How Should We Change?" *Development* 49, no. 1: 38–41.

———, ed. 2011. *African Sexualities: A Reader*. Cape Town: Pambazuka Press.

Tcheuyap, Alexie. 2005. "African Cinema and Representations of (Homo)Sexuality." In *Matatu 29/30, Body, Sexuality and Gender: Versions and Subversions in African Literatures*, edited by Flora Veit-Wild and Dirk Naguschewski, 143–54. Amsterdam: Rodopi.

Thompson, Barbara, ed. 2008. *Black Womanhood: Images, Icons, and Ideologies of the African Body*. Seattle: University of Washington Press.

Traoré, Aminata. 1999. *L'étau: L'Afrique dans un monde sans frontières*. Paris: Actes Sud.

———. 2002. *Le viol de l'imaginaire*. Paris: Actes Sud.

———. 2008. *L'Afrique humiliée*. Paris: Fayard.

Trotter, David. 1984. *The Making of the Reader: Language and Subjectivity in Modern American, English and Irish Poetry*. London: Macmillan.

Vance, Carol, ed. 1982. *Pleasure and Danger: Exploring Female Sexuality*. London: Pandora.
Vaughan, Meghan. 1991. *Curing Their Ills: Colonial Power and African Illness*. Stanford CA: Stanford University Press.
Veit-Wild, Flora, and Dirk Naguschewski, eds. 2005. *Matatu 29/30: Body, Sexuality and Gender: Versions and Subversions in African Literatures*. Amsterdam: Rodopi.
Vera, Yvonne. 1994. *Without a Name*. Harare: Baobab Books.
———. 2000. *Butterfly Burning*. New York: Farrar, Straus and Giroux.
Wade, Lisa. 2012. "Learning from 'Female Genital Mutilation': Lessons from 30 Years of Academic Discourse." *Ethnicities* 12, no. 1: 26–49.
Wallace-Sanders, Kimberly, editor. *Skin Deep, Spirit Strong: The Black Female Body in American Culture*. Ann Arbor: University of Michigan Press.
Weate, Jeremy. 2003. "Achille Mbembe and the Postcolony: Going beyond the Text." *Research in African Literatures* 34, no. 4: 27–41.
Weiss, Gail. 1999. *Body Images: Embodiment as Intercorporeality*. London: Routledge.
White, E. Frances. 2001. *Dark Continent of Our Bodies: Black Feminism and Politics of Respectability*. Philadelphia: Temple University Press.
Wicomb, Zoë. 2002. *David's Story*. New York: Feminist Press.
Willis, Deborah, and Carla Williams. 2002. *The Black Female Body: A Photographic History*. Philadelphia: Temple University Press.
Wipper, Audrey. 1972. "African Women, Fashion, and Scapegoating." *Canadian Journal of African Studies* 6, no. 2: 329–49.
Wolff, Janet. 1990. *Feminine Sentences: Essays on Women and Culture*. Berkeley: University of California Press.
Yuval-Davis, Nira. 1997. *Gender and Nation*. London: Sage.
Yuval-Davis, Nira, and Flora Anthias, eds. 1989. *Woman-Nation-State*. London: Palgrave Macmillan.
Zabus, Chantal. 2013. *Out in Africa: Same-Sex Desire in Sub-Saharan Literatures and Cultures*. Suffolk: James Currey.
Zeleza, Paul. 2003. *Rethinking Africa's Globalization: The Intellectual Challenges*. Trenton NJ: Africa World Press.

Index

Page numbers in italics indicate illustrations.

abortion, 92, 110
Acada (Olowu), 137
Ada (fictional character), 123
Adaku (fictional character), 90–91
Adichie, Chimamanda, 87–88, 116–22; *Half of a Yellow Sun*, 117–22, 131; *Purple Hibiscus*, 116–18
"Adventures from the Bedrooms of African Women" (Sekyiamah and Grant), 211
aesthetics: colonial, 142; deformity reclaimed by, 196; of female body, 41, 51, 139, 141; in gaze of viewer, 158, 160; of nude in photography, 141, 144, 145, 150–51, 153, 154, 155; racist, 142, 143
Affi (fictional character), 123
Africa: colonialism in, 14, 31–32, 34, 40; female body representing, 11, 18, 20, 23–25, 135–36; feminism in, 64, 80–81, 125–26, 137; postcolonialism in, 14, 38, 43–45; Sarah Baartman representing, 56; West, comparisons with, 37
African Americans, 134, 136

African diaspora, 23–24, 55, 186, 187–88, 189, 197–98, 201
African Feminist Politics of Knowledge (Ampofo and Arnfred), 50
African Gender Institute, 81
African Gender Studies (Oyewumi), 50
African Regional Sexuality Resource Center (ARSRC), 81–82
African Renaissance Monument, 5, 9, 41–43, *42*, 44–45
African Sexualities (Tamale), 82–83
African Women and Feminism (Oyewumi), 50
Agbadi (fictional character), 87–88
Agenda (journal), 81
Aidoo, Ama Ata: *Changes*, 89–90, 91; *Our Sister Killjoy*, 123
Aken'Ova, Dorothy, 80
Algeria, 11–12
Allegory of Africa (de Vos), 18
Amadi, Father (fictional character), 116–17
Amadiume, Ifi, 23–24, 50, 52
amanuensis (fictional character), 190–94
Amateifio, Mrs., 32

Amin, Idi, 40–41, *41*
Ampofo, Akosua Adomako: *African Feminist Politics of Knowledge*, 50
anachrony, 21, 162
antagonism, 13, 14, 58–59, 208
anthropology, 200–201
anticolonialism, 11–13, 14, 53, 58, 63, 78–79
anti-nudity bill, 32–33, 34–37, 46
apartheid, 170. *See also* post-apartheid condition
Arac de Nyeko, Monica, 124–25
archetypes, female, 188, 189
The Ark Collection (Mutu), *179*–80, 181
Arnfred, Signe, 54; *African Feminist Politics of Knowledge*, 50; *Re-thinking Sexualities in Africa*, 53, 83–84
ARSRC (African Regional Sexuality Resource Center), 81–82
Ateba (fictional character), 98–100, 130
Atim, Mama (fictional character), 125
Atta, Sefi: *A Bit of Difference*, 116
Azuah, Unoma: *Sky-High Flames*, 124

Baartman, Sarah: anatomy of, 56, 197; the arts on, 29; in *David's Story* (Wicomb), 190–97; feminism and, 62, 65; in *53 cm* (Bessora), 197–201; French legacy of, 201–2, 205; as leitmotif, 3, 5, 49, 55–61; mourning of, 183–85, 187–88, 190, 193–94, 197–98, 201; poetry on, 184–88; remains of, 7–8, 183; as scientific subject, 199; as specter, 55–61, 84; visual arts on, 1–2, 188–90, 202–5

Baba Segi (fictional character), 114
Bagnol, Brigitte, 60, 83
Baiada, Christa, 194
Bakare-Yusuf, Bibi, 34, 36–38, 46, 62, 120
Baker, Josephine, 202
Le baobab fou (Bugul), 92, 123
Barriendos, Joaquín, 208
Basden, George, 24
beauty (term), 156–57
Beauvoir, Simone de, 158
Becker, Carol, 29–30
Beckwith, Carol: *Women of the African Ark*, 181
beecos (bethios), 84–85, 93, 209–10
Beloved (Muholi), 125, 131, *132*
Bennett, Jane, 53, 62; *Jacketed Women*, 81
Bennett, Michael, 146
Berger, John, 149
Berlant, Lauren, 78
Bessora, Sandrine: *53 cm*, 197–202
bethios (beecos), 84–85, 93, 209–10
Beyala, Calixthe, 28–29, 91–92, 97–101, 115, 202; *C'est le soleil qui m'a brûlée*, 98, 111–12, 123, 129–30; *Femme nue, femme noire*, 125–29; *Maman a un amant*, 100; *Tu t'appelleras Tanga*, 97–98, 100
Beyond Booty (Marasela), 186–87
Bhabha, Homi, 23
Bikoro, Nathalie Mba, 158–59, 169; *(N)OnIdentity*, 172–73; *The Uncomfortable Truth*, 173
A Bit of Difference (Atta), 116

Bizet, Georges: *Carmen*, 66
The Black Female Body (Willis and Williams), 136
Black Tail (magazine), 181
Blank Darkness (Miller), 23
blogs, 211
Blues pour Elise (Miano), 113–14
body, African female, 1–5, 7; clothing issues and, 17–18, 23–25, 31, 32–34, 36–38, 41–45, 43, 59, 96, 182; colonialism and, 12–13, 18–22, 28, 36–38, 44, 58–59, 60–61, 140, 203; feminism and, 51–55, 58–59, 61–66, 80–81; in film, 68–69, 71–72, 74, 75, 80, 84–85; hauntology and, 14–15, 46, 60–61, 135–36, 181, 182, 183; in literature, 93, 100, 103–4, 110, 111, 195–97, 198, 201–2; patriarchy and, 51–52, 84, 119; in performing arts, 158–62, 164–67; in photography, 141–42, 144, 146, 148–51, 153, 154–55; postcolonialism and, 12–13, 15–16, 28–29, 31–32, 38–39, 44–45, 46; Sarah Baartman representing, 55–58, 59, 183, 186, 188; touchiness about, 10, 23, 205; in visual arts, 133–35, 139, 141, 175–78; white artists and, 29–30. *See also* women, African
body, male, 1, 22, 109, 128, 129
body, sexual female, 49, 50, 91, 92–93, 98, 143–44, 200. *See also* body, African female
Body Talk (Kouoh), 166, 168–69
Boehmer, Elleke, 106–7, 108, 124

Brazil, 172
bricolage, 178, 181
Brooker, Peter, 71
Bugul, Ken, 91–97, 112; *Le baobab fou*, 92, 123; *Cendres et braises*, 92; *Mes hommes à moi*, 96–97; *Riwan ou le chemin de sable*, 92–93, 96
Burke, Timothy: *Lifebuoy Men, Lux Women*, 17–18, 25
Butler, Judith, 52, 101, 178, 188
Butterfly Burning (Vera), 101–4, 107, 108, 124
buttocks, 57, 113, 134, 154, 199–200, 203, 210. *See also* steatopygia

Callahan, Yesha, 134
Camara, Fatou Kiné, 44
Camp, Sokari Douglas, 28
Carmen (Bizet), 66
Cartesian dualism, 50–51, 102
Catanese, Brandi Wilkins, 203
Cendres et braises (Bugul), 92
censorship, 59, 63
C'est le soleil qui m'a brûlée (Beyala), 98, 111–12, 123, 129–30
Changes (Aidoo), 89, 90–91
Changing Sarah's Story (Marasela), 186
Chantou (fictional character), 131–32
Charmes (Valery), 149–50
Chicago, Judy: *The Dinner Party*, 188
Chinyere (fictional character), 119
Christianity, 34, 178, 181
Chuchote pas trop (Ekotto), 123–24
Chukwumerije, Uche, 35–36
Ciao Bella (Rose), 188–90

cinema, African, 213n5. See also *Karmen Gei* (film)
circumcision, female: in feminist thought, 61; reaction to, 43, 55, 58, 60; Sarah Baartman and, 6, 29, 55, 57, 60; self-circumcision, 53
Clark, Kenneth, 141–42
clitoridectomy. *See* circumcision, female
clitoris, 97–98, 106
collage, 176, 177, 178, 181–82
Collins, Lisa, 136
colonialism, 2–5; in Algeria, 11–12; in Asia, 23; clothing issues and, 24–25, 36–38, 139, 142–43; female body in, 17–18, 22–25, 96, 111, 154–55, 160–61, 181–82, 202–3; feminist criticism and, 51, 52–55, 57, 58–59, 60–62, 84; hauntologies of, 140, 144, 146, 151, 157, 158; in India, 11; patriarchal influences in, 46–41; postcolonialism affected by, 13–14, 16, 28, 31–32, 33–35, 39–40, 135–36, 195, 207–9; Sarah Baartman representing, 185–86, 188, 189–91, 195–96, 202, 204; science influenced by, 200–201; in viewers' gaze, 166–67, 169–71; violence in, 45; women's role in, 45, 104–5
Colour Me (Searle), 151
Coly, Ayo A.: *The Pull of Postcolonial Nationhood*, 94, 100
Comaroff, Jean, 39–40, 178
Comaroff, John, 39–40, 178
commandment, postcolonial, 68–69, 71–72, 73, 76, 78

Connelly, Frances E., 176
Conrad, Joseph: *Heart of Darkness*, 22, 25, 192
conscription of African female body, 4, 10, 28, 29, 30–31, 32–33, 40, 46, 63
countermemories, 47, 58
counter-mimicry, 161–62, 163
Cox, Renee: *Yo Mama*, 151
Cronin, Jeremy, 29–30
Curing their Ills (Vaughan), 23–24
Cuvier, George, 188, 192, 194–95, 199, 200; *Règne animal distribué d'après son organisation*, 199

Dada (Muholi), 129
D'Almeida, Irène, 55
David's Story (Wicomb), 190–97
da Vinci, Leonardo: *The Last Supper*, 188
death, 76, 77–79, 100, 110, 129–30, 184
Decker, Alicia Catharine, 40–41
decoding, 139–40, 149
Deleuze, Gilles, 70, 73–74, 77, 79, 129
Deleuzean smooth space, 67
Deliwe (fictional character), 108–9, 124
Demoiselles d'Avignon (Picasso), 24
Deola (fictional character), 116
Derrida, Jacques, 5–6; hauntology theory of, 16, 47, 57–58, 139–40, 187; on mourning, 183–85, 198; on specters, 28, 34, 59, 91, 101–2, 103, 140–41, 160; *Specters of Marx*, 2, 12–13, 183; visor effect described by, 162–63
Desai, Gaurav, 33, 213n2 (chap. 1)
Desert Storm (Ndiritu), 163–64

desexualization, 31, 46, 55, 59, 61–62, 91, 169, 191
desubjectivation, 119, 122, 160, 188
de Vos, Martin: *Allegory of Africa*, 18
Diallo, Rackie Diankha: *Petit pagne*, 84–85
diamond trade, 177
Diana and Actaeon (Titian), 142
Dickerson, Vanessa, 146
The Dinner Party (Chicago), 188
Diop, Corporal Lamine (film character), 74, 76
Dirske, David (fictional character), 190–95
Dirske, Sally (fictional character), 190, 193–94, 195–96
Djikey, Julie, 158, 169; *Ozonisation*, 173–75, *173*
Dominique (fictional character), 123
Domino Sugar, 133–34
dress codes, 5, 9–10, 31–33, 40–41, 186, 213n1 (chap. 1). *See also* body, African female: clothing issues and; women, African: clothing issues and

Ekaette, Eme Ufot, 33, 34
Ekotto, Frieda: *Chuchote pas trop*, 123–24; *Portrait d'une jeune artiste de Bona Mbella*, 124, 125, 131
elsewhereness, 14, 101
Elwes, Catherine, 158, 162
Emecheta, Buchi: *The Joys of Motherhood*, 87–91
Emilienne (fictional character), 123

encoding, 138, 139–40, 149
English, Darby, 31
En sa présence (Oka), 166–68, *167*
Enwezor, Okwui, 29–30, 181–82
Esi (fictional character), 89
Essamba, Angèle Etoundi: colonial hauntology disrupted by, 146, 151; gaze of models of, 150–51, 153; gaze of viewers and, 150, 154, 158, 165; *Noirs*, 141, 144, *145*, *152*, 154; nudity in photography of, 137–38, 141–42, 144, 154–55; pedagogical approach of, 148–49, 150–51, 159
ethnography, 24, 181
Etoké, Nathalie, 28
Eugene (fictional character), 117
Europe, 20–21, 22–23, 24, 25

Fabian, Johannes, 24
Fanon, Frantz: on colonialism, 25, 28, 186; on death, 77; hauntology model of, 13–14; on hegemony, 47; legacy of, 99, 173; queering and, 78–79; on veiled female body, 11–13, 16; *The Wretched of the Earth*, 78–79
Female Circumcision and the Politics of Knowledge (Nnaemeka), 57
feminism, African: body performance and, 159–60, 162; female body and, 51–52; lesbian, 130; motherhood and, 138; nego-feminism, 63–64; nudes and, 135, 138–39; pleasure and, 97, 107, 117, 120; respectability limiting, 61–66; Sarah Baartman and, 56–57

Index 235

feminism, black, 56–57
feminism, Western, 50, 51–52
Feminist Africa (journal), 81
feminist criticism, 49–53, 55, 57, 58–59, 59–60, 62–66, 81–85
Femme malgache civilisée (postcard), 25, 26
Femme nue, femme noire (Beyala), 125–29
"Femme nue, femme noire" (Senghor), 125–27
Ferrus, Diana, 184–88, 201; "A Tribute to Sarah Baartman," 184–88
53 cm (Bessora), 197–202
Fils, Charifou, 26
Fisher, Angela: *Women of the African Ark*, 181
Flesh (Muholi), 141, 147
Foucault, Michel, and Foucauldian theory, 20, 21, 25, 67, 153, 207
fragmentation in photography, 154
France, 1–2, 3, 199–200, 201–2, 204–5
Freudian understanding, 7, 184
Fumbatha (fictional character), 107, 108–9
Fureurs et cris de femmes (Rawiri), 123

Gagiano, Annie, 104
Gaugin, Paul: *Offerings of Gratitude*, 18
gaze, 150–51, 153–54, 158, 169, 182, 202, 203, 208
Gender Epistemologies in Africa (Oyewumi), 50
gender testing, 10, 55, 57

geopolitics, 40–41, 43
Gerome, Jean Lyon: *The Great Bath at Bursa*, 142
gestures, discursive: colonial, 11, 24–25, 35; postcolonial, 12, 13, 14, 22, 41
Ghana, 32
Ghostly Matters (Gordon), 15
Gikandi, Simon, 29
globalization, 43–44
Gordon, Avery: *Ghostly Matters*, 15; on haunting, 2, 4, 7, 45–46, 135, 153; hauntology theory of, 6, 14–15, 57–58, 59, 94, 135, 183, 187; on reading, 34; re-narrativization theory of, 28, 47, 54–55, 134, 186–87; spectrality theory of, 5, 140–41, 146, 156, 160, 185
Gquola, Pumla Dineo, 148–49
Grant, Malaka, 211
The Great Bath at Bursa (Gerome), 142
Griffin, Farah Jasmine, 122
Grosz, Elizabeth, 178
grotesque: as art, 175, 176–77; as perception, 16, 31, 139, 141, 150, 185, 193, 198
Guattari, Félix, 73–74, 129
Gurnah, Abdulrazak, 118
Guy-Shetfall, Beverly, 24

Halberstam, Judith, 129
Half of a Yellow Sun (Adichie), 117–22, 131
Hall, Stuart, 139–40, 188
Hamlet, King, 15, 140
Hamon, Philippe, 153

236 Index

harems, 92–94
Harper, Gil, 81
hashtag campaigns, 10, 213n1(chap. 1)
haunting, 45–46, 94, 139, 162
hauntology, 2, 4–6; of antagonism, 58; colonial, 24, 28, 13–15, 16, 60, 144, 146, 150, 157, 182; crippling, 49; critical, 47, 58; definitions of, 13–15, 57–58; as ethics, 187; of female body, 26, 32, 38, 65, 91, 135, 144, 146, 147, 151, 182; female body as, 95, 109, 115; pedagogical, 158, 163; postcolonial, 13–15, 183; of re-narrativization, 134; Sarah Baartman as, 58; subversive, 146, 153, 176; of vigilance, 59
Hayatou (fictional character), 128–29
Heart of Darkness (Conrad), 22, 25, 192
hegemony: colonial, 25; female body and, 21–22, 144, 148, 176–77; hauntings and, 14, 47, 94–95, 140–41; interference with, 70; lines of flight caused by, 129; phallic, 67; resignification and, 139; slavery and, 134
heteronormativity, 78, 122
heteropatriarchy, 70, 97, 98, 105, 107, 109–10, 126–28, 130
Hewett, Heather, 112–13
"Holaa" (Mugo), 211
hottentot apron, 1–2
Hottentot Venus, 56, 185, 192. *See also* Baartman, Sarah
Human Sexuality in Africa (Maticka-Tyndale, Tiemoko, and Makinwa-Adebusoye), 81–82

hypersexuality, 53, 55, 139, 150, 165, 166, 198

The Idea of Africa (Mudimbe), 18, 213n3 (chap. 1)
immigration, 1, 3, 199, 201, 202, 204
immolation, 111. *See also* sati (widow immolation)
infanticide, 110
inheritance, specters as, 28, 38–39, 12–13, 55, 65, 184, 186, 195, 198
inscription on the African female body, 3, 4; colonial, 10, 20, 24, 28, 31–32, 46; postcolonial, 41; racist, 141; from slavery, 172
intentionality of body, 102, 103, 104–5, 109, 117, 122
The Invention of Africa (Mudimbe), 18, 213n3 (chap. 1)
The Invention of Women (Oyewumi), 22
invisibility: in the arts, 161, 162; of black female, 142, 146, 156; colonial, 170; politics of, 157; postcolonial, 4, 9; in *Snow White* (Searle), 170; sociocultural, 144; of white female, 156
Irène (fictional character), 126–29
Irigaray, Luce, 164–65
Iser, Wolfgang, 149
Iserian strand, 149
Islam and Muslims, 40–41, 42–43, 44, 92, 213n7

jacket (symbol), 62
Jacketed Women (Bennett and Pereira), 81

Jones, Amelia, 158
The Joys of Motherhood (Emecheta), 87–91

Kainene (fictional character), 118–19, 121
Kambili (fictional character), 116–17
Karmen Geï (film), 6; death in, 76–79; feminist queering in, 6, 66, 68, 70, 71–72, 74, 80; influence of, 84; inspiration for, 66–69; postcolonial aspects of, 67–69, 70, 71–72, 73–75, 76, 78, 79–80; power shift theme of, 69–70, 71–74; sabar dance in, 67, 70–72, 74; wedding scene in, 74–76. *See also* Ramaka, Joseph Gaï
Kastell, Koumba, 68, 79
Kenya, 53, 213n1 (chap. 1)
Khoikhoi people, 55–56, 186
Khoisan people, 1–2
Kouoh, Koyo: *Body talk*, 166, 168–69
Kuhn, Annette, 142
Kwame (fictional character), 113

labia, 1–2, 60, 190
The Last Supper (da Vinci), 188
Layiwola, Peju, 136
le Fleur, Andrew (fictional character), 196
le Fleur, Rachel Susannah (fictional character), 196
lesbianism: in film, 72; in literature, 99, 123–25, 127, 130–31; in photography, 131, 141, 144, 148–49, 176

Lévi-Strauss, Claude: *The Savage Mind*, 178
Lewis, Desiree, 83–84
libertinage, 92–93
Lifebuoy Men, Lux Women (Burke), 23–24
lines of flight, 70, 72, 129
Loial, Chantal: *On t'appelle Vénus*, 204
looked-at-ness, 155, 158, 165
Lying Down Textile (Ndiritu), 142, 143

madness, 67, 76, 123, 129–30
Magubane, Zine, 55–56, 186, 201
The Making of the Reader (Trotter), 149–50
Makinwa-Adebusoye, Paulina: *Human Sexuality in Africa*, 81–82
Malaika (fictional character), 113–14
Malawi, 39
Malonga, Alpha Noël, 100
Mam (fictional character), 100
Maman a un amant (Beyala), 100
Manet, Édouard: *Olympia*, 142
Mani, Lata, 11–12, 16
Marasela, Senzeni, 201; *Beyond Booty*, 186–87; *Changing Sarah's Story*, 186; *Sarah Baartman Redressed*, 186; *Shielding Sarah from the Cold*, 186
Mariano, Esmeralda, 60, 83
Marlowe (fictional character), 192
marriagenormativity, 61–63, 91, 111, 122, 137
Marx, Karl, 13, 15, 34, 100, 140
masturbation, 97–98
Matatu (journal), 28

maternity. *See* motherhood
Maticka-Tyndale, Eleanor: *Human Sexuality in Africa*, 81–82
Mazvita (fictional character), 101–8, 109–12, 124
M'Baye, Babacar, 73
Mbembe, Achille, 14, 60–61, 64, 65–66, 67–69, 76–78, 209; *On the Postcolony*, 66–67, 75, 78–80
McClintock, Anne, 18, 22, 170
McFadden, Patricia, 51–53, 63, 64–65, 82–83
menstruation, 148–49, 176
Mercer, Kobena, 143
Merleau-Ponty, Maurice, 101–2, 103, 105, 120, 177–78
Mes hommes à moi (Bugul), 96–97
Meyers, Bob, 148
Miano, Léonora: *Blues pour Elise*, 113–14; *Première nuit: Une anthologie du désir*, 114; *Volcaniques*, 214n2
Miller, Christopher: *Blank Darkness*, 23
mimicry and countermimicry, 161–62, 163
Minh-ha, Trinh T., 54
modernity, 32, 34–35, 37–38, 40–41, 103–5
Monument de la Renaissance Africaine. *See* African Renaissance Monument
motherhood, 43–45, 59, 62–63, 82, 89–90, 110, 115, 136–37, 193
mothernormativity, 62–63, 91, 111, 122, 137
Moudileno, Lydie, 198

Mudimbe, Valentin Y., 14; *The Idea of Africa*, 18, 213n3 (chap. 1); *The Invention of Africa*, 18, 213n3 (chap. 1)
Mugo, Tiffany Kagure, 211
Muholi, Zanele, 131, 142, 144, 146, 150–51, 153; *Beloved*, 125, 131, *132*; *Dada*, 129; *Flesh*, 141, *147*; *Period*, 148–49; *Reclining Figure*, 144, *145*
Mulvey, Laura, 157
Muñoz, José Esteban, 78
murals, 204–5
Muslims. *See* Islam and Muslims
mutilation, 60, 177, 194
Mutu, Wangechi, 156–57, 175–78, 181–82; *The Ark Collection*, *179–80*, 181; *Pinup*, 165–66, 176–77
Mwangi, Evan, 207–8

nakedness: colonialism and, 18, 22–25, 39–40, 141, 142; inappropriate clothing as, 35–38; nudity compared to, 49, 142; as protest, 36, 182; resignification of, 139; in Western culture, 155. *See also* nudes and nudity
Nash, Jennifer, 56–57
nationalism: anticolonial, 43, 63; masculinist, 108; patriarchal, 107, 109–10, 110–11, 192; postapartheid, 191–92, 193–94; sexual, 63, 191–92
Ndiritu, Grace, 163–66, 169; *Desert Storm*, 163–64; *Lying Down Textile*, 142, *143*; *Still Life*, 160–62, *161*
Ndjio, Basile, 63–65

Index 239

Nead, Lynda, 143, 144
neocolonialism, 60–61, 96, 181
Neveu-Kringelback, Hélène, 209
Nigeria, 9, 32–38, 117, 119
Njau, Rebecca: *Ripples in the Pool*, 123
Nnaemeka, Obioma, 63, 90; *Female Circumcision and the Politics of Knowledge*, 57
Nnaife (fictional character), 90
Nnu Ego (fictional character), 90–91
Noirs (Essamba), 141, 144, 145, 152, 154
noise, 5, 53, 153
(N)OnIdentity (Bikoro), 172–73
nudes and nudity, 5, 7; in the arts, 134, 135–39, 142–44, 146, 148; attitudes toward, 32; bills about, 9, 32–36, 40, 70; colonialism and, 18, 139, 146; feminism and, 135, 138–39; nakedness compared to, 142, 149; postcolonialism and, 28. *See also* nakedness
Nyendezi (fictional character), 107–8
Nzegwu, Nkiru, 52, 60

objectification, 58, 118, 151, 164, 167, 173
Odenigbo (fictional character), 118
Ode to Sarah Baartman (Yoko), 204–5
Offerings of Gratitude (Gaugin), 18–19
O'Grady, Lorraine, 142
Oguibe, Olu, 29–30, 169
Oka, Valérie, 166–68; *En sa présence*, 166–68, 167; *Sans nom*, 166–68
Okoye, Ikem Stanley, 28
Olanna (fictional character), 118, 121
Oliphant, Dulcie (fictional character), 190, 193–95, 196

Olowu, Elizabeth: *Acada*, 137; *Zero Hour*, 136, 137
Olympia (Manet), 142
Olympics, 10, 29
Ona (fictional character), 87–88
Ongetititeldl (Rose), 159
On t'appelle Venus (Loial), 204
On the Postcolony (Mbembe), 66–67, 75, 78–79
oral sex, 98–99
orgasms, 80, 94, 96–97, 99, 108, 122, 127
Orientalism (Said), 213nn2–3 (chap. 1)
Our Sister Killjoy (Aidoo), 123
Oyewumi, Oyeronke, 45, 50, 51, 52; *The Invention of Women*, 22
Ozonisation (Djikey), 173–75, 174

Palmer, Felicity, 106
Pane (fictional character), 131–32
passivity, 63–64, 171
patriarchy: clothing issues and, 9–10, 15–16; fantasies of, 165; female body and, 46, 15–16, 132, 164, 193, 196; feminism and, 63–64, 192; nationalism in, 110–11, 192; postcolonial, 191; religion and, 117; in sexual matters, 84–85, 88, 95, 115, 132; silence and, 51–53, 164; vision of, 155, 159–60. *See also* heteropatriarchy
Pereira, Charmaine, 53, 54, 62, 117; *Jacketed Women*, 81
Period (Muholi), 148–49
Petit pagne (Diallo), 84–85
Petty, Sheila, 75

240 *Index*

phallic economy, 66, 68, 69, 71, 73, 74–75, 98
phallus: disabling of, 72, 98–99, 100, 108, 127, 129; landscape representing, 106–7; representing power, 64, 66, 67, 68, 69
Phelan, Peggy, 155–56, 157–58, 170
Phephelaphi (fictional character), 101–2, 103–5, 107, 108–12, 124
photography, 56, 137, 181
Picasso, Pablo: *Demoiselles d'Avignon*, 24
Pictorial (magazine), 181
Pinup (Mutu), 165–66, 176–77
poetry, 124, 125–27
polygamy, 92–94, 95–96, 114
pornography, 24, 28–29, 150–51, 154, 163–64, 181
pornotropics, 20
Portrait d'une jeune artiste de Bona Mbella (Ekotto), 124, 125, 131
post-apartheid condition, 189, 190–94, 197
postcards, 24, 25, 26–27, 181
postcolonialism, 2–6; clothing issues and, 15–16, 39, 40–41, 96; as deathscape, 76–77; female body in, 9–11, 29, 30–32, 33, 39–40, 62, 89, 93, 132; feminist criticism and, 56; future of, 76; globalization affecting, 43–44; hauntologies of, 13–15, 135–36, 183; lesbianism in, 99; patriarchal influences in, 63–64, 105; phallic economy in, 66–68, 69, 74–75, 98; power in, 68–69, 70, 71–72, 73–74; queering in, 70, 75, 79–80; Sarah Baartman representing, 196–97, 199
posteriors. *See* buttocks; steatopygia
pregnancy, 92, 110–11, 116, 129, 136–38, 141
Première nuit (Miano), 114
prison warden (fictional character), 66–67, 69, 71–73
protests, 9–10, 36, 182
Puar, Jasbir, 72
Public Nudity Bill. *See* anti-nudity bill
The Pull of Postcolonial Nationhood (Coly), 94, 100
Purple Hibiscus (Adichie), 116–18

queer gesturing, 123–24
queering, 66, 68, 70, 72, 75–76, 78–79, 125–26
queerness, 76, 77–78, 79, 124, 125, 127

Race and the Education of Desire (Stoler), 20
race issues: Apartheid and, 170; beauty and, 142–44; colonialism and, 111; feminism and, 51, 53, 60, 84; grotesquerie and, 141; as interpretative lens, 165; racial alterity in literature, 123; Sarah Baartman in, 186, 188, 195; scientific racism in, 201; sexuality and, 20; slavery and, 172; visibility in, 157, 159–60, 162; in visual representation, 134–35, 138–39
Rai, Amit, 75
Rama (fictional character), 94–95

Ramaka, Joseph Gai, 6, 77–78, 129–30. See also *Karmen Geï* (film)
rape: law and, 33, 46; in literature, 87, 89, 102, 111, 114, 128; voyeurism and, 164–65; in war, 119–20, 163–64, 165
Rawiri, Angèle: *Fureurs et cris de femmes*, 123
readers, 90–91, 92, 100, 118–19, 149–50, 191, 192, 201
Reclining Figure (Muholi), 144, *145*
Règne animal distribué d'après son organisation (Cuvier), 199
religion, 34–35, 37, 42, 63, 117
"re-narrativization," 16, 28, 54–55, 134, 172, 186–87, 198
repetition, 188, 189–90
repressed indigeneity, 37
resignification: of fictional characters, 100; of large buttocks, 196; of motherhood, 44; of nude female body, 139, 141, 158; of power structures, 71, 128; repetition causing, 188
Re-thinking Sexualities in Africa (Arnfred), 53, 83–84
Richard (fictional character), 121
Ringgold, Faith, 134
Ripples in the Pool (Njau), 123
Riwan ou le chemin de sable (Bugul), 92–93, 96
The Root (website), 134
Rose, Tracey, 158, 169, 201; *Ciao Bella*, 188–90; *Ongetititeldl*, 159; *Span II*, 159, 171
Rossi, Wagner Tempos, 172

Saar, Betye, 134
sabar dance, 67, 68, 69–72, 74–75, 209–10
Said, Edward, 43, 58; *Orientalism*, 213nn2–3 (chap. 1)
Sakhoẓi Says Non to the Venus (Xaba), 1–3, 5, 189, 202
Samuelson, Meg, 191
Sans nom (Oka), 166–68
Sarah Baartman Redressed (Marasela), 186
Sarkozy, Nicolas, 1–2
sati (widow immolation), 11, 13, 16. See also immolation
The Savage Mind (Lévi-Strauss), 178
savagery, 19
Savarese, Eric, 25
Schneider, Rebecca, 159, 161–62
Searle, Bernie, 153, 158; *Colour Me*, 151; *Snow White*, 169–71; *Traces*, 157
The Secret Lives of Baba Segi's Wives (Shoneyin), 114, 124
seduction, 71, 164
Sekyiamah, Nana Darkoa, 211
self-censorship, 59, 63
Semenya, Caster, 29, 55, 57
Senegal, 42–43, 44, 67, 85, 93–95, 209
Senghor, Léopold Sédar: "Femme nue, femme noire," 125–27
sex scenes in literature, 87–89, 91, 107–8, 113–15, 119, 121–22, 127–28
sexuality, female: African, fascination with, 57; in dance, 210; dismissal of, 61, 65, 80–81; European, 20; feminists ignoring, 50–53, 54; in

literature, 89–91, 101, 102, 105, 107, 115–16, 117–20, 122–23, 207–8; nonnormative, 123–24, 132, 176; in performance art, 169; as political dissent, 99; regulation of, 62–63; reproduction-oriented, 81–82, 136; same-sex, 124–25; in scholarly works, 81–84

sexual pleasure: female circumcision and, 60; heterosexual, 108; in literature, affirmed, 92–93, 105, 112–13, 116–19; in literature, restrained, 88, 89, 91, 94, 95, 113–14, 116; male, 85; motherhood and, 115; patriarchy and, 129, 130; political aspects of, 64–65, 80, 96–98, 100, 117; theft and, 127; war and, 119–22

sexuoerotic agency, 3–4, 6; bethios (beecos) and, 85, 93; in film, 66–67, 68, 73, 75, 80; in literature, 101, 105, 113, 117; repercussions of, 64; research on, 65–66

Sharpley-Whiting, Tracy Denean, 12

Shielding Sarah from the Cold (Marasela), 186

Shoneyin, Lola, 114–15; *The Secret Lives of Baba Segi's Wives*, 114, 124

Sierra Leone, 166, 177

silence about female sexuality, 3, 5–6; artistic, 16; as colonial phenomenon, 53–55, 59; in feminist criticism, 49–53, 58–59, 62, 65; legitimate, seen as, 50; in literature, 126; mistaken for detachment, 24; patriarchy causing, 51–53; as post-

colonial phenomenon, 31, 45–46, 55, 208–9; queer sexualities and, 122; Sarah Baartman and, 59, 62; scholarly, 16, 83

Sisterhood, Feminisms, and Power (Nnaemeka), 50

Sky-High Flames (Azuah), 124

slavery, 60, 133–34, 171, 172, 173

Snow White (Searle), 169–71

"something-to-be-done," 7, 15, 45, 59, 135

Sontag, Susan, 154

Span II (Rose), 159, 171

specters: of authority figures, 15; colonial, 12–13, 14, 47; exorcism of, 91, 101–2; haunting, 146, 162–63; Jacques Derrida on, 28; of Ken Bugul, 96; of literary characters, 194; in living present, 88, 100, 160, 161, 208; potential of, 61; of Sarah Baartman, 49, 58–59, 65, 84, 183–87, 189, 197, 201, 205, 208; of slavery, 134, 172; subaltern, 140–41

Specters of Marx (Derrida), 2, 13–14, 183–84

steatopygia, 193, 195–97, 200. *See also* buttocks

stereotypes, 17, 164

Still Life (Ndiritu), 160–62, *161*

Stoler, Anne Laura: *Race and the Education of Desire*, 20

subjectivation, 68, 118

subordination, female, 45, 52, 98

A Subtlety, or the Marvelous Sugar Baby (K. Walker), 133–34, 138–39, 165, 166

Sugar Baby (K. Walker). See *A Subtlety, or the Marvelous Sugar Baby* (K. Walker)

tactics, 70, 71, 79
Tamale, Sylvia, 54, 62, 63–65, 137; *African Sexualities: A Reader*, 82–83
Tanga (fictional character), 97–98, 100
Tcheuyap, Alexie, 213n5
temporalities, 21, 29, 67
Thackeray, William Makepeace: *Vanity Fair*, 56
They Look at Me and That's All They Think (Xaba), 202–3
Tiemoko, Richmond: *Human Sexuality in Africa*, 81–82
Titian: *Diana and Actaeon*, 142
to-be-looked-at-ness, 155, 158, 165
Tope, Iya (fictional character), 114, 115
Traces (Searle), 157
"A Tribute to Sarah Baartman" (Ferrus), 184
Trotter, David: *The Making of the Reader*, 149–50
Truth, Sojourner, 148–49
Tu t'appelleras Tanga (Beyala), 97–98, 100

Uganda, 9, 38, 40–41, 213n1 (chap. 1)
Ugwu (fictional character), 118–19
The Uncomfortable Truth (Bikoro), 173

vagina, 57, 97, 163
Valery, Paul: *Charmes*, 149–50

Vance, Carole, 64–65
Vanity Fair (Thackeray), 56
Vaughan, Meghan: *Curing their Ills*, 17
veils, 11, 12–13, 16, 213n7
Vera, Yvonne, 91–92, 100–112, 115; *Butterfly Burning*, 101–4, 107, 108, 124; *Without a Name*, 101–4, 107–8, 111, 124
victimhood, 60–61, 140, 191
victims, 15, 65, 140, 164, 191
viewers, 138–39, 149, 150–51, 153–54, 157–58, 158–65, 165–67, 168–71, 177–78
vigilance, 46, 56, 58, 59, 61, 190, 195
violence: of representation, 194–95; revolutionary, 99; sexual, 59, 61, 119–20; social, 14–15, 60, 172
visibility: aesthetic, 155; in the arts, 170; of black female subject, 148; invisible, 11, 95, 142, 146; metonymy causing, 56; politics of, 155–56; postcolonial, 9; representational, 155, 157
visor effect, 162–63
Volcaniques (Miano), 214n2
voyeurism, 56–57, 160, 162, 164–65, 171

Wade, Abdoulaye, 42–43, 44
Walker, Alice, 52
Walker, Kara: *A Subtlety, or the Marvelous Sugar Baby*, 133–34, 138–39, 165, 166
war in the arts, 102–3, 118–21, 163–67, 176–77
Warner, Michael, 78

Weate, Jeremy, 77, 79, 209
West, influenced by Africa, 144, 146, 148
Western influence: on the arts, 45, 138, 142–44; on clothing issues, 36, 38; exerting power, 43, 60–61; on feminism, 44, 50–52, 54, 60, 84; modernity as, 40, 41; on sexuality, 29, 55, 57–58, 59–60, 83, 93, 96, 208; in social matters, 137, 173, 174; using war, 165–66
Wicomb, Zoë, 195–96, 201; *David's Story*, 190–97
widow immolation (sati), 11, 13, 16
wifehood, 45
Williams, Carla, 137; *The Black Female Body*, 136
Willis, Deborah, 137; *The Black Female Body*, 136
Wipper, Audrey, 39
Without a Name (Vera), 101–4, 107–8, 111, 124
Wolof language, 73, 95
women, African, *41*; anticolonialism and, 13, 53; clothing issues and, 9–10, 13, 15–16, 32–33, 39–41, 182, 186; colonialism and, 11–12, 45, 191, 208; feminism and, 61–64; postcolonialism and, 43, 45–47, 64, 191, 196–97, 208–9; in sphere outside home, 22; veiled, 11–12, 213n7. *See also* body, African female
women, black, 157, 165, 189, 203
women, white, 155, 157, 165
Women of the African Ark (Beckwith and Fisher), 181
The Wretched of the Earth (Fanon), 78–79

Xaba, Nelisiwe, 208; *Sakhozi Says Non to the Venus*, 1–3, 5, 189, 202; *They Look at Me and That's All They Think*, 202–3
xaxar (marriage ritual), 93

Yoko, Breeze: *Ode to Sarah Baartman*, 204–5
Yo Mama (Cox), 151

Zabus, Chantal, 123–25
Zara (fictional character), 197, 199–200, 201
Zeleza, Paul, 65, 80
Zero Hour (Olowu), 136, 137
Zulu Maidens, the Difference (postcard), 25, *27*

Index   245

IN THE EXPANDING FRONTIERS SERIES

Undesirable Practices: Women, Children, and the Politics of the Body in Northern Ghana, 1930–1972
by Jessica Cammaert

Intersectionality: Origins, Contestations, Horizons
by Anna Carastathis

Abuses of the Erotic: Militarizing Sexuality in the Post–Cold War United States
by Josh Cerretti

Queering Kansas City Jazz: Gender, Performance, and the History of a Scene
by Amber R. Clifford-Napoleone

Postcolonial Hauntologies: African Women's Discourses of the Female Body
by Ayo A. Coly

Terrorizing Gender: Transgender Visibility and the Surveillance Practices of the U.S. Security State
by Mia Fischer

Romance with Voluptuousness: Caribbean Women and Thick Bodies in the United States
by Kamille Gentles-Peart

Salvific Manhood: James Baldwin's Novelization of Male Intimacy
by Ernest L. Gibson III

Nepantla Squared: Transgender Mestiz@ Histories in Times of Global Shift
by Linda Heidenreich

The Camp Fire Girls: Gender, Race, and American Girlhood, 1910–1980
by Jennifer Helgren

Transmovimientos: Latinx Queer Migrations, Bodies, and Spaces
edited by Ellie D. Hernández, Eddy Francisco Alvarez Jr., and Magda García

Wrapped in the Flag of Israel: Mizrahi Single Mothers and Bureaucratic Torture
by Smadar Lavie

Queer Embodiment: Monstrosity, Medical Violence, and Intersex Experience
by Hilary Malatino

Staging Family: Domestic Deceptions of Mid-Nineteenth-Century American Actresses
by Nan Mullenneaux

*Hybrid Anxieties: Queering the
French-Algerian War and Its
Postcolonial Legacies*
by C. L. Quinan

*Place and Postcolonial Ecofeminism:
Pakistani Women's Literary and
Cinematic Fictions*
by Shazia Rahman

*Women, Empires, and Body Politics
at the United Nations, 1946–1975*
by Giusi Russo

*Gothic Queer Culture: Marginalized
Communities and the Ghosts of
Insidious Trauma*
by Laura Westengard

To order or obtain more information on these or other University of Nebraska Press titles, visit nebraskapress.unl.edu.

www.ingramcontent.com/pod-product-compliance
Lightning Source LLC
Chambersburg PA
CBHW030234240426
43663CB00036B/456